D
16.9
.W454
2002

❧ Western Historical Thinking ❧

MAKING SENSE OF HISTORY

Studies in Historical Culture and Intercultural Communication
General Editor: Jörn Rüsen, in Association with Christian Geulen

Western Historical Thinking: An Intercultural Debate
Edited by Jörn Rüsen

Identities: Time, Difference, and Boundaries
Edited by Heidrun Friese

Narration, Identity and Historical Consciousness
Edited by Jürgen Straub

The Meaning of History
Edited by Jörn Rüsen and Klaus E. Müller

BELL LIBRARY - TAMU-CC

WESTERN HISTORICAL THINKING

An Intercultural Debate

Edited by
Jörn Rüsen

Berghahn Books
New York • Oxford

Published in 2002 by

Berghahn Books

www.berghahnbooks.com

Copyright © 2002 Jörn Rüsen

All rights reserved. Except for the quotation of short passages for the purpose of criticism and review, no part of this book may be reproduced in any form or by any means, electronic or mechanical, including photocopying, recording, or any information storage and retrieval system now known or to be invented, without written permission of the publisher.

Library of Congress Cataloguing-in-Publication Data

Western historical thinking : an intercultural debate / edited by Jörn Rüsen.
p. cm. -- (Making sense of history)
Chiefly written by members of the Forschungsgruppe Historische Sinnbildung, Universität Bielefeld.
Based in part on Westliches Geschichtsdenken (1999).
Includes bibliographical references and index.
ISBN 1-57181-781-6 (alk. paper) -- ISBN 1-57181-454-X (pbk. : alk. paper)
1. History--Philosophy. 2. Civilization, Western. 3. Civilization, Asian. 4. Africa--Civilization--Historiography. 5. History--Methodology. 6. Historiographu. I. Rüsen, Jörn. II. Universität Bielefeld. Forschungsgruppe Historische Sinnbildung. III. Westliches Geschichtsdenken. IV. Series.

D16.9 .W454 2001
901--dc21   2001037830

British Library Cataloguing in Publication Data

A catalogue record for this book is available from the British Library.

Printed in the United States on acid-free paper.

Contents

III: Afterword

Preface to the Series

JÖRN RÜSEN

At the turn of the twenty-first century the very term "history" brings extremely ambivalent associations to mind. On the one hand, the last 10–15 years have witnessed numerous declarations of history's end. In referring to the fundamental change of the global political situation around 1989/90, or to postmodernism or to the challenge of Western dominance by decolonization and multiculturalism, "history"—as we know it—has been declared to be dead, outdated, overcome, and at its end. On the other hand, there has been a global wave of intellectual explorations into fields that are "historical" in their very nature: the building of personal and collective identity through "memory", the cultural, social and political use and function of "narrating the past", and the psychological structures of remembering, repressing and recalling. Even the subjects that seemed to call for an "end of history" (globalization, postmodernism, multiculturalism) quickly turned out to be intrinsically "historical" phenomena. Moreover, "history" and "historical memory" have also entered the sphere of popular culture (from history-channels to Hollywood movies). They also have become an ever important ingredient of public debates and political negotiations (e.g., to take the discussions about the aftermath of the wars in the former Yugoslavia, about the European unification or about the various heritages of totalitarian systems). In other words, ever since "history" has been declared to be at its end, "historical matters" seem to have come back with a vengeance.

This paradox calls for a new orientation or at least a new theoretical reflection. Indeed, it calls for a new theory of history. Such a theory should serve neither as a subdiscipline reserved for historians, nor as a systematic collection of definitions, "laws" and rules claiming universal validity. What is needed, is an interdisciplinary and intercultural field of study. For, in the very moment when history was declared to be "over", what in fact did abruptly come to an end was—historical theory. Hayden White's deconstruction of the narrative strategies of the nineteenth century historicist paradigm somehow became regarded as historical theory's final word; as if the critique of the discipline's claim for

---

Notes for this section can be found on page xiii.

rationality could set an end to the rational self-reflection of that discipline; as if this very critique was not a rational self-reflection in itself. Nevertheless, since the late 1980s the "critical study of historical memory" began to substitute historical theory. However, what has been overlooked in this substitution is the fact that any exploration into the ways of historical memory in different cultural contexts is not only a field of critical studies, but also contains the keystones for a more general theory of history. Each analysis of even a simple instance of historical memory cannot avoid questions of the theory and philosophy of history. And vice versa: the most abstract thoughts of philosophers of history have an intrinsic counterpart in the most profane procedures of memory (for example, when parents narrate past experiences to their children, or when an African community remembers its own colonial subordination and its liberation from it). As long as we fail to acknowledge this intrinsic connection between the most sophisticated historical theory and the procedures of historical memory most deeply imbedded in the culture and the everyday life of people, we remain caught in an ideology of linear progress, which considers cultural forms of memory simply as interesting objects of study instead of recognizing them as examples of "how to make sense of history."

The book-series "Making Sense of History", the first volume of which is at hand, aims at bridging this gap between historical theory and the study of historical memory. It contains contributions from virtually all fields of cultural and social studies, which explore a wide range of phenomena of what can be labeled "making historical sense" (*Historische Sinnbildung*). The series crosses not only the boundaries between academic disciplines but also those between cultural, social, political and historical contexts. Instead of reducing historical memory to just another form of the social or cultural "construction of reality", its contributions deal with concrete phenomena of historical memory: it seeks to interpret them as case studies in the emerging empirical and theoretical field of "making historical sense." Along the same line, the rather theoretical essays intend not only to establish new methods and theories for historical research, but also to provide perspectives for a comparative, interdisciplinary and intercultural understanding of what could be called the "global work of historical memory." This does not mean the exclusion of critical evaluations of the ideological functions of historical memory. But it is not the major aim of the series to find an ideal, politically correct and ideology-free mode or method of how to make sense of history. It rather intends to explore the cultural practices involved in generating historical sense as an extremely important realm of human thought and action, the study of which may contribute to new forms of mutual understanding. In an age of rapid globalization primarily manifesting itself on an economic and political—and, much less so, on a cultural level—finding such forms is an urgent task.

This is why—in contrast to the German version of this series—the English edition, addressing a much broader international audience, sets out with a volume documenting an intercultural debate. This volume questions whether or not the academic discipline of "history"—as developed at Western universities over the course of the last two hundred years—represents a specific mode or type of historical thinking that can be defined and differentiated from other forms and practices of historical consciousness. One of the most notable representatives of the modern historical profession, Peter Burke, delivers an essay outlining ten aspects of the specifically Western way of "making sense of history" that allow us to speak of "Western Historical Thinking" as a discernable type of historical thinking, differing from other ways of dealing with the past practiced in other parts of the globe. The editor then invites scholars from all over the world—from Western countries as well as from Asia, India, and Africa—to critically comment on these theses, to evaluate them in the light of their respective ideas of the sense and meaning of historical thinking, and to reflect on the possibilities of an intercultural communication on these issues. Peter Burke afterwards has the chance to reply to the different comments and criticism, to rethink some of his theses, and to further identify the possible common grounds on which an ongoing debate could be based. Thus this first volume of the series "Making Sense of History" goes to the heart of the matter, and, at the same time, highlights the major conflicts involved in any attempt to reflect forms and functions of historical memory and historical thinking on a global level.

The first volume, therefore, introduces the intercultural dimension of historical theory. The following volumes will represent it as a genuinely interdisciplinary field of research. Historians, anthropologists, philosophers, sociologists, psychologists, literary theorists, as well as specialists in fields such as media and cultural studies, will explore questions such as: What constitutes a specifically historical "sense" and meaning? What are the concepts of "time" underlying different historical cultures? Which specific forms of "perception" inform these concepts and which general problems are connected with them? What are the dominating strategies used to represent historical meaning? Ranging from general overviews and theoretical reflections to case-studies, the essays will cover a wide range of contexts related to the question of "historical sense," including topics such as collective identity, the psychology and psychoanalysis of historical memory, or the intercultural dimension of historical thinking. In general they will indicate that historical memory is not an arbitrary function of the cultural practices used by human beings to orient themselves in the world in which they are born, but that such memory covers special domains in the temporal orientation of human life. These domains demand precisely those mental procedures of connecting past, present and future which became generalized and institutionalized in the West as that specific field of culture we call "history." Among those special areas of human thought, action and suffering that call for a specifically "historical thinking," are (1) the construction and perpetuation of collective identity, (2) the reconstruction of patterns of orientation after catastrophes and events of massive destruction, (3) the challenge of given patterns of orientation presented by and through the confrontation with radical otherness, and (4) the general experience of change and contingency.

In accordance with the general aim of the book-series "Making Sense of History" to outline a new field of interdisciplinary research (and to not offer a single theory), the volumes are not designed to establish those general domains and functions of historical remembrance as keystones for a new historiographical approach. Instead they explore them further as subfields of the study of "historical cultures." One focus, for instance, will be on the notion of collective identity. General theoretical aspects and problems of this field will be considered, most importantly the interrelationship between identity, otherness and representation. But case studies on the construction of gender identities (especially of women), on ethnic identities and on different forms and politics of national identity will also be included. The essays on this subject will try to point out that any concept of "identity" as being disconnected from historical change does not only lead to theoretical problems, but also eclipses the fact that most modern forms of collective identity take into account the possibility of their own historical transformation. Thus the essays will suggest to consider identity not as a function of difference, but as a concrete cultural and ongoing "practice" of difference. Therefore they will try to prove the production of "sense" to be both an epistemological starting-point as well as a theoretical and empirical research-field in and of itself.

Another volume will focus on the psychological construction of "time" and "history" analyzing the interrelation between memory, morality, and authenticity, in different forms of historical or biographical narrations. The findings of empirical psychological studies (on the development of temporal and historical consciousness in children, or on the psychological mechanisms of reconstructing past experiences) will be discussed in the light of attempts to outline a psychological concept of historical consciousness around the notions of "narration" and the "narrative structure of historical time." A special volume will be dedicated to specifically psychoanalytical approaches to the study of historical memory. It will reconsider older debates on the relation between psychoanalysis and history as well as introduce more recent research projects. Instead of simply pointing out some psychoanalytical insights that can be adopted and applied in certain areas of historical studies, this volume will aim at combining psychoanalytical and historical perspectives, thus exploring the history of psychoanalysis, itself, as well as the "unconscious" dimensions underlying and informing academic and nonacademic forms of historical memory. Moreover, it will put special emphasis on transgenerational forms of remembrance, on the notion of trauma as a key-concept in this field, and on case-studies that may indicate directions for further research.

Apart from the first volume at hand, there will be another collection of essays dealing explicitly with the intercultural dimension of historical thinking, offering a systematic overview of historical cultures ranging from ancient Egypt to modern Japan. With a view to encouraging comparative research, it will consist of general essays and case-studies written with the intention to provide comparative interpretations of concrete material, as well as possible paradigmatic research-questions for further comparisons. In the light of the ongoing success of ethnocentric world-views, the volume will focus on the question of how cultural and social studies could react to this challenge. It will aim at counteracting ethnocentrism by bridging the current gap between a rapid globalization, manifesting itself in ever increasing economic and political interdependencies of states and continents, and the almost similarly increasing lack of mutual understanding in the realm of culture. The essays will try to point out the necessity of an intercultural communication about the common grounds of the various historical cultures as well as about the differences between them. Such a communication seems not only possible but indeed to be a necessary presupposition for any attempt to negotiate cultural differences on a political level, whether between states, or within the increasingly multicultural societies in which we live.

The special emphasis the series puts on the problem of cultural differences and intercultural communication shows the editors' intentions to aim beyond the realm of only academic interest. For the question of intercultural communication represents a great challenge, as well as a great hope, to a project committed to the general theoretical reflection on the universal phenomenon of "remembering the past." Despite the fact that "cultural difference" has become something like a master phrase of the 1990s, this topic is characterized by a paradox quite similar to that underlying the current fate of the notion of "history."

There has been an intensified political intervention and economic interest of the industrialized states into the political and economic affairs of the rest of the world, as well as an increased (if sometimes peculiar) appropriation of modern economic and political structures in the developing countries, and in the formerly or still officially "communist" states. But this process of mutual rapprochement on the political and economic level is characterized by a remarkable lack of knowledge of, or even interest in, the cultural and historical backgrounds of the respective nations. Thus, the existing official forms of intercultural communication, so often demanded in the public discourse, lack precisely what is "cultural" about them, leaving the themes and problems analyzed in this book-series (identity, memory, cultural practices, history, religion, philosophy, literature) outside of what is explicitly communicated: as if such matters would not strongly affect political as well as economic agendas.

On the other hand, however, the currently dominant approaches of cultural theorists and critical thinkers in the West either claim the general impossibility of an intercultural communication about the common grounds of "cultural identities"—based on the assumption that there are no common grounds (the hypostatization of "difference")—or they politicize cultural differences in such a way that they are relegated to mere material for the construction of cultural

subject-positions. Despite their self-understanding as "critique", these intellectual approaches appear to correspond to the exclusion of "culture" on the level
of state politics and economic exchange alike. Thus, cultural theory seems to
react to the marginalization of culture by way of its own self-marginalization.

The book-series "Making Sense of History" intends to challenge this marginalization by introducing a form of cultural studies that takes the very term
"culture" seriously again without dissolving it into either identity-politics, or a
hypostatized concept of unbridgeable "difference." At the same time it wants to
reintroduce a notion of "historical theory" that no longer disconnects itself from
historical memory and remembrance as concrete cultural practices, but seeks to
explore those practices, interpreting them as different articulations of the universal (if heterogeneous) effort to "make sense of history." Thus, the book-series
"Making Sense of History" relies on the idea that an academic contribution to
the problem of intercultural communication should assume the form of a new
opening of the academic discourse to its own historicity and cultural background, as well as a new acknowledgement of other cultural, but non-academic,
practices of "sense-formation" as being equally important forms of human orientation and self-understanding (in their general function not much different
from the efforts of academic thought itself). Such a reinscription of the universal claims of modern academic discourses into the variety of cultural contexts,
with the intention to provide new starting-points for an intercultural communication, is an enterprise that cannot be entirely fulfilled or even outlined in a
series of a few books. Therefore, the book-series "Making Sense of History"
should be regarded as something like a first attempt to circumscribe one possible research-field that might prove to suit those general intentions: the field of
"historical cultures."

Most of the contributions to the book-series are based on papers delivered
at a series of conferences organized by the research-project "Making Sense of
History: Interdisciplinary Studies in the Structure, Logic and Function of Historical Consciousness—An Intercultural Comparison" established at the "Center for Interdisciplinary Studies" (ZiF) in Bielefeld, Germany, in 1994/95. This
project was partly supported by the *Kulturwissenschaftliches Institut Essen* (KWI)
im Wissenschaftszentrum Nordrhein-Westfalen (Institute for Advanced Studies in the
Humanities at Essen in the Scientific Center of Northrhine-Westfalia).[1]

As editor I would like to express my deepest gratitude to the staff of the
ZiF and the KWI for providing a stimulating atmosphere for the scholars and
excellent assistance for their work. I also want to thank the editors and co-edi-
tors of the single volumes of this series for their cooperation. My special thanks
go to Christian Geulen, my assistant editor, for his engaged management of this
series and to my wife Inge for her intensive support in editing my texts.

Notes

1. In German the following books represent the project: Bodo von Borries, *Imaginierte Geschichte. Die biografische Bedeutung historischer Fiktionen und Phantasien*, Köln, 1996; Klaus E. Müller, Jörn Rüsen eds, *Historische Sinnbildung. Problemstellungen, Zeitkonzepte, Wahrnehmungshorizonte, Darstellungsstrategien*, Reinbek, 1997; Jocelyn Létourneau ed., *Le lieu identitaire de la jeunesse d'aujourd'hui. Études de cas*, Paris/Montreal, 1997; Jörn Stückrath, Jürg Zbinden eds, *Metageschichte. Hayden White und Paul Ricoeur. Dargestellte Wirklichkeit in der europäischen Kultur im Kontext von Husserl, Weber, Auerbach und Gombrich*, Baden-Baden, 1997; Hans G. Kippenberg, *Die Entdeckung der Religionsgeschichte. Religionswissenschaft und die Moderne*, München, 1997; Jürgen Straub ed., *Erzählung, Identität und historisches Bewußtsein. Die psychologische Konstruktion von Zeit und Geschichte. Erinnerung, Geschichte, Identität Bd. 1*, Frankfurt am Main, 1998; Jörn Rüsen, Jürgen Straub eds, *Die dunkle Spur der Vergangenheit. Psychoanalytische Zugänge zur Geschichte. Erinnerung, Geschichte, Identität Bd. 2*, Frankfurt am Main, 1998; Aleida Assmann, Heidrun Friese eds, *Identitäten. Erinnerung, Geschichte, Identität Bd. 3*, Frankfurt am Main, 1998; Jörn Rüsen, Michael Gottlob, Achim Mittag eds, *Die Vielfalt der Kulturen. Erinnerung, Geschichte, Identität Bd. 4*, Frankfurt am Main, 1998; Jörn Rüsen ed., *Westliches Geschichtsdenken. Eine interkulturelle Debatte*, Göttingen, 1999; Jörn Rüsen ed., *Geschichtsbewußtsein. Psychologische Grundlagen, Entwicklungskonzepte, empirische Befunde*, Köln 2000.

Introduction

Historical Thinking as Intercultural Discourse

Jörn Rüsen

Why historical thinking has to become intercultural

Historical memory and historical consciousness have an important cultural function: they form identity. They delimit the realm of one's own life—the familiar and comforting aspects of one's own life-world—from the world of others, which usually is an "other world", a strange world as well. Historical memory and historical thinking carry out this function of forming identity in a temporal perspective; for it is the temporal change of humans and their world—their frequent experience of things turning out different from what has been expected or planned—that endangers the identity and familiarity of one's own world and self. The change calls for a mental effort to keep the world and self familiar or—in cases of extraordinarily disturbing experiences of change— to reacquire this familiarity.

Identity is located at the threshold between origin and future, a passage that cannot be left alone to the natural chain of events but has to be intellectually comprehended and achieved. This achievement is produced—by historical consciousness—through individual and collective memory and through recalling the past into the present. This process can be described as a very specific procedure of creating sense.[1] This procedure welds experiences of the past and expectations of the future into the comprehensive image of temporal progression. This temporal concept shapes the human life-world and provides the self (the "we" and "I" of its subjects) with continuity and consistency, with an inner coherence, with a guarantee against the loss of its essential core or with similar images of duration within the changes of subjects. The location of the self, in terms of the territorial reality of living as well as in terms of the mental situation of the self within the cosmos of things and beings, has a temporal dimension. It is only through this dimension of time that the location of the self becomes fixed as the cultural habitat of groups and individuals. In situating themselves, subjects draw borderlines to others and their otherness within the locality and temporality of a common world, in which they meet and differentiate from each other in order to be subjects themselves.

Such boundaries are normatively determined and always value-laden. In that peculiar synthesis of experiences, which determines action and purposes of what one historically knows and wishes for oneself, can be defined remembered experience and intended goal at the same time; it is fact and norm, credit and debit, almost undistinguished. This is especially important for the differentiation between self and other, sameness and otherness. In order to survive in one's own world and with one's own self, and to find living here and now meaningful and livable, each one's own way of life is provided with positive perspectives, values and normative preferences. Negative, menacing, disturbing aspects are repressed and pushed away towards the "other," where they are exterritorialized and liquidated. It is part of the utility of historical memory, and of historical thinking's intentional approach to the past that whatever counts as belonging to one's own time and world order, and legitimizes one's self-understanding, is subject to a positive evaluation; thus it is generally accepted as good. In this way, negative aspects of the experience of time in relation to the world and to oneself, are eclipsed from one's own world and from the inner space of one's own self; they are pushed away to the periphery and kept in that distance. The identity-building difference between self and other is working in each memory, and any effort to remember is, in itself an asymmetrical normative relation. Ethnocentrism (in all its different forms) is quasi-naturally inherent in human identity.

This asymmetrical relationship between self and other, between sameness and otherness, makes historical memory controversial and open for conflicts. Just as the stressing of one's own group identity will be met with consent by its members, it will be denied by those beyond the border lines who do not recognize themselves in these time-tableaus, let alone consent to them. Degree and manner of such an asymmetry vary enormously; their general quality is that of tension, that is, they are always on the brink of a *bellum omnia contra omnes* among those who exclude each other in constituting their own selves. Of course, all parties usually have a common interest in preventing an outbreak of this tension. Therefore they seek and develop ways of intra- and intercultural communication in order to tame, civilize or even overcome the ethnocentric asymmetry.

"Historical consciousness" is a specific form of historical memory. It is rooted in it, to a great extent, even identical with it, but it is also distinguished in some important aspects. The specificity of "historical consciousness" lies in the fact that the temporal perspective, in which the past is related to the present and—through the present—to the future, is designed in a more complex way. Especially in its modern forms "historical consciousness" pushes the past away from the present thus giving it the appearance of being something else. This is not done to make the past meaningless for the present, but—on the contrary—

as a means of ascribing to the past the special importance of a historical relationship. A historical relationship is determined by a temporal tension between past and present, by a qualitative difference and its dialectics and argumentative-narrative progress in time.

The vital power of memory lies in its keeping alive the past which those who remember have really experienced. The past becomes historical when the mental procedure of going back into time reaches beyond the biographical lifespan, back into the chain of generations. Accordingly, the future prospects of historical thinking reach far beyond the life expectancy of individuals into the future of coming generations. Thus, the historical relation to the past is enriched by an enormous amount of experience. Only in this specifically historical kind of memory does the weight and the meaning of historical experience come into view and evaluation. It also changes the ways of meaningfully appropriating the treasures of past experiences. These ways of appropriation become much more complex, since they can employ a big range of narrative strategies. Nevertheless, the general patterns of creating sense in the formation of historical identity are still the same: as the past is interpretatively transformed into history, "being self" and "being other" remain strongly separated and evaluated as opposites.

Even when the interpretative achievements of "historical consciousness" are being brought about in the academic form of historical studies, the formative power of the normative factors of historical identity remain prevalent. Even a historiography based on methodologically controlled research is determined by the political and social life of its time and by the expectations and dispositions of its audiences. Academic historiography is ascribed to a historical culture, in which the self and the others are treated differently and evaluated as normative points of view. Thus, in this context as well, the questions remain if and how the difference between—and the differentiation of—forms of belonging, which generally determine and socially organize human life, can be approached; and how the conflictory dimension of ethnocentric sense-making can be tamed and overcome. The answers to these questions may be very diverse: academically historical studies are obliged to enforce an intersubjective validity of their interpretative transformation of the past, into a historical construction of belonging and difference. Here, "intersubjective" validity also includes the principle that others can agree as much as the members of one's own group. However, such an agreement would not abolish the difference between the respective forms of belonging, or the particular identity of those affected by the respective histories. Differences and identities, which on the contrary, are to be articulated and coined by this appeal to the past. So academic claims of truth ultimately depend upon the very ways in which the procedures of "creating sense" in the framework of methodologically controlled research are regulated.

Today, the quest for such a regulation is becoming increasingly important. For today not only mere historical differences within a common culture are at stake as they were, for example in a historiography committed to the national perspective and orientation of European standards of historical professionality. By now processes of migration and globalization have produced new constellations of intercultural communication. The European countries, nations, societies and states find themselves questioned and challenged in a new way by non-European nations and cultures. They criticize the cultural hegemony of the West and forcefully intend to liberate themselves from the historical interpretations that the West has imputed to them. Western historical thinking has to reflect the critique of ideology, which holds that behind the universalist claims of validity, and behind the standards of reason, there are claims for power and domination that endanger, if not destroy, the sovereignty of other cultures. This confrontation has already caused a habit of self-criticism within Western interpretations of historical thinking. Yet this does not mean that the established institutions and methods of historical culture have already found new ways of relating themselves to the others or of coming to terms with them about their cultural differences. A similar problem evolves within Western societies, themselves, in the way of treating minorities whose cultures are thought of as not only different, but definitely uncommon and strange. How can this otherness find a place in the ways of life of the majority?

How should history become a source of intercultural orientation?

There are two traditions of (not only) European historical thinking, in which a possible way of overcoming ethnocentric perspectives is embedded. One of these traditions goes back to the classical, ancient mode of historical interpretation coined in Cicero's phrase "*historia magistra vitae*", which can be described typologically as an exemplary mode of creating sense.[2] Within this way of historical thinking, the space of past experiences widens beyond the boundaries of the historian's own culture. Thus it opens up the limits of a historical perspective that traditionally focuses on the given cultural context. The exemplary mode of memory regards the past as a gigantic reservoir of experiences from which general rules of, and for, human behavior can be drawn. This experiential quality is ascribed to the past of the human world in general, no matter what valuations and adaptations the rules drawn from it might serve in respect to the self-esteem and self-approval of the present. However, the past becomes subordinated to those self-interests in the course of interpretation. The exemplary way of creating sense opens up the historical horizon and the possibility of generalizing historical judgements. It is thus—at least in a strictly logical sense—in a position of neutrality regarding the different agendas of fitting the past into the asymmetrical dichotomy between self and other. Therefore the perception of the Other becomes more open to the influence of actual experience, but it is not yet completely protected from ethnocentric narrowness. Experience-based rules of open-minded behavior that are drawn from historical experience strengthen the competence of acting and orientation, but they do not break the power of normative forms of belonging and differentiation.

Eighteenth-century "Enlightenment" and its concept of universal history widened the historical perspective to a global aspect. At the same time humanity became the universalistic norm to which the reconstruction, foundation and explanation of identity-building particularities had to be related in order to gain intellectual plausibility. This empirical and normative universalization opened up new horizons for historical thinking, in which the others were taken notice of to an extent hitherto unknown.[3] In principle the universalistic view pierced the perspective limits of selfness so that it could be reflected by the other.

Within the category of humanity, historical thinking gained new possibilities of critique, liberating itself from its restriction to particular interests and power-claims. At the same time, however, those interests and political power claims became charged with the legitimatory power of universalization, themselves gaining an extremely ideological power of veiling the processes of privileging the self and of devaluating everything strange to it. The generalized self-esteem embedded in the "spirit of modernity" destroyed the self-esteem of those subordinated to it.

"Historicism" opposed this generalization of a sense-creating concept of humanity along with its ongoing teleology of progress by enforcing the principle of individuality and general legitimacy of difference and particularity. Ranke's famous statement: "Every age relates immediately to God, and its value does not at all depend on what comes from it, but on its existence as such, on its own self"[4] expresses a historico-philosophical paradigm in which identity-building sense is created under the condition that the particularity of the self is not to be regarded as the only one fit for generalization, but has to be understood as a difference to another particularity, and therefore to be enforced in and as that difference.

Yet even in this historicist paradigm, the determination of the relationship to the Other remained precarious. That "God" who honors the particular with the quality of the singular has proved silent when the diverse historical subjects of nations, states, and cultures struggled for power and supremacy. In the long run, this God continued to be a god of the respective selves, in whose face the others could be called strangers and thus be marginalized under the aspect of development and evolution; they were degraded to mere representatives of a preliminary stage of one's own development or pushed to the margins of the historical universe, where they had geographically belonged all along. The representation of China in the universal and world-histories of historicism is a particularly revealing example.[5]

Also the concepts of history that transcended the realm of historicism to global aspects of world-interpretation and self-understanding could deny neither their eurocentric origin nor the perspectives and perceptions even if they considered realms hitherto thought of as natural and timeless. Europe and the West remained the measure of all things even when historical comparisons became analytically more precise and the global perspective was based on social-scientific methodologies.

The eurocentrism of historical perception becomes especially obvious when history and historical thinking themselves are the subjects. The Others may be regarded as historically meaningful and hermeneutically rewarding for human diversity, yet what counts as specifically "historical" in respect to the way of "dealing with the past" has usually—and without question—been determined by our own way of thinking. Even, today books that bear "historiography" as their subject or title, but in fact exclusively consider the Western-European tradition, can receive academic approval.[6] Occasional remarks that there is an important historiography outside one's own tradition[7] do not undermine the claim for monopoly of the European as being the essential, since those other traditions are acknowledged only insofar as they reveal traces or equivalent aspects of European historical thinking without offering alternative or oppositional views. From such views we could, in fact, learn what (apart from the tendency to generalize the specific and to transform it into the essential) makes "our" history a special one in the first place.[8]

That is not to say that sheer eurocentrism actually dominates the history of historiography or contemporary historical theory. In fact, historicism has strengthened the sensibility for cultural difference so that with the help of hermeneutics our knowledge of the historical thinking of non-European nations and cultures has steadily increased. Historical didactics, in particular, propagated polyvocal strategies of interpretation and representation and enforced them, at least partly, in the field of history textbooks.[9] Applying research methods of social science has provided historical thinking with systematic methods for interculturally comparative studies. Yet multiperspectivity has not become a representational principle of a historiography dealing with non-European history or with subjects and problems of global history. Nor has the history of historiography, focusing on non-European ways of historical thinking and the intercultural comparison, led to a critical rethinking of general assumptions about what actually comes into view as historical thinking in such comparisons.

Of course, the assumed metahistorical role of one's own historical thinking has not gone unnoticed. At least, the postmodern critique of the categorical application and ideological use of a variety of modernization models has undermined the hermeneutic tone of utter conviction that used to be heard when researchers in the field of humanities declared their patterns of interpretation to be intersubjectively valid—that is, across all cultural differences. However, this critique threw out the baby of cognitive validity in historical reasoning with the bath of eurocentrism. The result is an epistemological and political culturalism, which confines its insight into the specific character of cultures temporally and regionally to the innate scope of different cultures. In so doing, it has become dependent on the horizon of those cultures' own self-understandings. Besides the immense epistemological and hermeneutical problems of such an interpretation, there is the irritation for the next generation when freeing the value and self-esteem of Others from eurocentric models of otherness. They find themselves compelled to relate the liberated other self to its own culture so that it may indeed recognize the other. This kind of culturalism transforms cultural difference into a hermeneutic monadology, preventing intercultural communication at all or enabling it only at the expense of any generally accepted rules.

A first attempt—problems and results

Thus historical thinking is not well prepared to solve the questions rising objectively from the context of international and intranational constellations. In the context of a predicted "clash of civilizations"[10] the task is to bring about a new communication in which the subjects involved may be able to learn how and why they differ from each other, and accordingly have built up a feeling of tension. Such a mutual understanding is necessary at least in order to ease or perhaps even to overcome conflicts. Those conflicts are struggles for identity, reaching the self-understanding, the innermost cores of the self. Here history is a necessary medium for articulating and actively approaching questions of identity, so cultural and historical studies can't but be involved. They are epistemologically rooted in these very problems of contemporary cultural orientation. They form a cultural organ of and for modern societies, producing essential knowledge as input for the discussions, manifestations and practices in which identity, belonging, self-determination and the boundaries to others are at stake.

Therefore we have to answer the question of how the production of cultural and historical knowledge, which is always the production of cultural competence as well, can be aligned with the goal of providing to future generations the means of intercultural communication? This calls for a variety of efforts. They range from simply fulfilling the requirements for information and understanding to critically rethinking the foundations and habits of one's own intellectual work in research, teaching and public representation. Here growing participation of non-Western experts would be of extraordinary importance. Notwithstanding their own efforts to overcome the asymmetry of valuations in historically determining contemporary situations, and to recognize the self-understanding of others—this question can only be answered by the practice of direct communication. The objective task of cultural orientation can be regarded as subjectively achieved and solved only when the others and we ourselves agree, when we historically relate ourselves to them and vice versa. Then the mutual consensus of selfness and otherness in historical self-realization has been achieved. (Of course, this is not conceivable as a once and for all accomplished task but only as an open and ongoing process. The ever recurring experiences rising from everyday life, struggles for power, collisions of interest, and the unintended side effects of our own actions and of the reactions of others, call for a continuous effort to historically position oneself and to understand the self-understanding of others.)

The essays collected in this volume represent such an attempt: They do not seek to reason *about* the Others from one's own angle of historical thinking, but they rather discuss and analyze the common grounds and differences in the mental space of historical culture *with* them. It is not surprising that the starting-point of this attempt is the tradition of historical European thinking; since it has dominated the international discourse up to our time. Yet, as a paradigm determining the ways in which human beings relate historically with the world and with themselves, this tradition is no longer taken for granted. But this is much less the case in the discourse of historians in non-Western countries than it is in the place of its own origin. Postmodern criticism of the cultural strategies of modernization has made us fully aware of the ideological bias of such strategies and their inherent will to power. What actually counts as being specifically Western—even in the definition and perception of its opposite—has become an open question.

The relevant reflections in this book provide an interesting answer: the specificity of Western historical thinking certainly cannot be tracked down in any easy and clear-cut manner. It is represented in this book in multiperspective[11]—and this is not due to the book's form independent from its content. The idea that there is an ontologically fixed "essence" of different cultures no longer plays any significant role. Thus seen from the angle of theory of history, the Spenglerian monadology of cultural differences has lost its argumentative power. (Whether it has also lost its grip on politics is quite a different question. The enthusiasm with which the argument of Samuel P. Huntington's "Clash of Civilizations" was taken up in the popular media makes one hesitate to answer in the affirmative.)

In this respect, Peter Burke's argument sets the tone: "Western" is not one single principle of cultural orientation and self-interpretation, but it represents a combination of elements creating historical sense, each of which can be found in other cultures as well. Moreover, the debate about Burke's configuration of ten typical characteristics of Western historical thought unmistakably points out that even this constellation is open to dissolution and restructuring. In non-Western comments, however, we find a recurring distinctive approach, which is only indirectly addressed in respect to one's own historical culture; here some sort of traumatic resistance to Western claims for dominance is being articulated. This resistance may have different forms either by juxtaposing historical thinking as equally valid or even superior alternatives to the Western mode, or by detecting typical characteristics that are usually ascribed to Western thinking in one's own tradition as well. One contributor generalizes this as a principal problem and—quite typically—laments the general lack of acknowledgment of originality and importance in African culture.

This debate has brought about a wide range of alternative typologies and helped to determine the logic of such typologies: they are based upon elementary and fundamental criteria of sense. These are of categorical importance when in differentiated process averse systems of culture are in the making. They cannot be applied only to the sphere of historical consciousness and culture in a strict sense. This wide range of aspects, however, is limited as well. We can detect that typologies lack the dynamic temporal category of the developmental logic of historical thinking with its long-term mode of existence as continuity or change. Yet occasionally it is pointed out that Burke's typology does not cover the whole sphere of experiences of Western historical self-understanding. And, quite astonishingly there is a lack of intensive discussion of a fact Karl Löwith[12] pointed out: Western historical thinking has its own dynamics of development, which go beyond the temporal limits of the modernization process. This applies as well to the presentations of non-Western traditions. It is especially their immense duration and long-term power that reveal a temporal depth calling for a diachronic typology.

The typological approach breaks the power of Western dominance in historical thinking in various ways, especially by differentiating the perception of other forms of historical thinking: what is defined as specifically Western or European can also be detected as an important factor within the various typological constellations of other cultures. Indirectly, however, a trace of Western dominance yet to be overcome remains visible. Too often the contrasting presentations of other cultural traditions (especially of the Chinese and African) emphasize the lack of one or the other European element; cannot be found in one's own tradition; and the functional equivalents are not pointed out.

The character of the debate documented in this book prohibits a final and systematic conclusion. On the contrary, further discussions seem to be necessary so that further distinctions of the intercultural perception may provide a higher degree of reflection in the comparisons and communication. Nevertheless, this insight rests upon a stimulating result of the debate: the fact that sharp borderlines between the different traditions of historical culture can no longer be drawn and that there is no such thing as cultural essentialism. Despite all brevity and provisionality of the documented discussion, it did bring to light the fact that some characteristics of Western historical thinking previously regarded as culturally specific are not: they can be shown in other traditions of historical thinking as well. The pressure of ideological self-determination in dealing with difference in historical thinking should thereby be lessened. Relieved of this pressure, the chances for an unbiased perception of the common grounds and differences in the intercultural constellation of historical thinking are thus increased.

Further steps

The many voices contributing to this debate easily combine into a general tenor regarding further progress in conceptualizing historical thinking as a medium of identity-building, determining the otherness of others, and relating this otherness to the self: The "decomposition of Western historical thought" already in progress, its deconstruction to elements and factors to be further differentiated diachronically, should be continued. With the deconstruction of the special Western character of historical thinking into a complex constellation of factors, each of which are not culturally specific, the significance of cultural difference is decreasing. But it does not mean the Western character is dissolving into a potpourri of historical sense-creations lacking the contours of an identity-building self-esteem.[13] On the contrary: the self-esteem wins greater clarity with the complexity of the constellation in which it appears. At the same time the mutual perception focuses on the fact that what is different about the other is composed of elements that also belong to oneself.

Together with the decomposition of the Western peculiarity, the special characteristics of non-Western forms of historical thinking and historical culture should be outlined; they should be made visible as peculiar constellations of general factors in the creation of historical sense. Such a task calls for an immense effort in research. However, such research should be fundamentally guided by the goal of creating the means for an intercultural comparison of its results. Naturally this also applies to the history of Western historiography as well. Without the perception of the others the narrow-mindedness of historical attitudes is strengthened: In the past and in the light of fundamental differences to others, this narrow-mindedness could have been regarded as a naive trust in our own exceptionality. So what used to addressed as a simple-minded carelessness of an unconscious ethnocentrism, today must be critically reflected.

Systematic cultural comparisons ought to enforce questions of the common grounds as well as of different tendencies in respect to future developments. So-called *microhistoire* has not rendered obsolete macrohistorical temporalizations. But, far from it, the cultural effects of globalization have become increasingly visible on the micro-historical level. In whatever way this necessary research is being carried out, its results would be weakened without a critical rethinking of the decisive questions and interpretations that make other traditions and interpretations comparable. At the very point where they can objectify and intellectually support intercultural communication, they would hamper it without theoretical reconsiderations. Considering the urgent problems of cultural conflict in an age of globalization and increased migration, such a use of theoretical reflections and empirical data should take place in direct discussion of our own as well as of other traditions and contemporary forms of historical thinking. The current features and forms of academic discourse do not yet correspond to these imperatives: Too often, the respective experts have still been talking without giving them a voice in this discourse. But that can be changed.

Translated from the German by Inge Rüsen

Notes

1. See Klaus E. Müller and Jörn Rüsen, eds, *Historische Sinnbildung. Problemstellungen, Zeitkonzepte, Wahrnehmungshorizonte, Darstellungsstrategien*, Reinbek, 1997.
2. See Jörn Rüsen, *Zeit und Sinn. Strategien historischen Denkens*, Frankfurt am Main, 1990, 181ff.; Reinhart Koselleck, *Vergangene Zukunft. Zur Semantik geschichtlicher Zeiten*, Frankfurt am Main, 1979, 38-66.
3. A remarkable example is the *Universal History from the Earliest Account of Time* that appeared 1736–1766 in 66 volumes and was translated into German beginning in 1744.
4. Leopold von Ranke, *Über die Epochen der neueren Geschichte. Historisch-kritische Ausgabe. Aus Werk und Nachlaß*, vol. 2, eds Theodor Schieder and Helmut Berding, München, 1971, 59f.
5. See Andreas Pigulla, *China in der deutschen Weltgeschichtsschreibung vom 18. bis zum 20. Jahrhundert*, Wiesbaden, 1996.
6. Christian Simon, *Historiographie. Eine Einführung*, Stuttgart, 1996.
7. Rüdiger vom Bruch and Rainer A. Müller, eds, *Historikerlexikon. Von der Antike bis zum 20. Jahrhundert*, München, 1991.
8. See for example Donald E. Brown, *Hierarchy, History and Human Nature. The Social Origins of Historical Consciousness*, Tuscon, 1988, whose valuable culturally comparative study of historical consciousness is based upon a strictly European paradigm of historical thinking.
9. See Jörn Rüsen, 'Das ideale Schulbuch. Überlegungen zum Leitmedium des Geschichtsunterrichts', in id., *Historisches Lernen. Grundlagen und Paradigmen*, Köln, 1994, 156-170.
10. Samuel P. Huntington, *Der Kampf der Kulturen. The Clash of Civilizations. Die Neugestaltung der Weltpolitik im 21. Jahrhundert*, München, 1996.
11. I note that there is only one female voice among the authors of this book. In the Bielefeld conference, upon which this book is based, many female scholars participated and many were explicitly invited to bring in the gender perspective, which for the understanding of the history of historiography and historical theory is of immense importance. That there was, in the end, little response from feminist scholars is partly due to accidental circumstances. However, it has probably also something to do with the fact that the feminist discourse in cultural studies has recently become increasingly fixed as a subsystem shutting itself off from the rest of the academic discussion.
12. Karl Löwith, *Weltgeschichte und Heilsgeschehen. Die theologischen Voraussetzungen der Heilsgeschichte*, Stuttgart, 1953.
13. See Jörn Rüsen, 'Some Theoretical Approaches to Intercultural Comparative Historiography', *History and Theory*, 35 (1996), Special Issue 'Chinese Historiography in Comparative Perspective', 5-22.

I: THESES

Western Historical Thinking in a Global Perspective – 10 Theses

PETER BURKE

The "historical thought" to be examined in this paper is concentrated on the assumptions of working historians and the implications of their practices. However, it also refers from time to time to philosophers of history. Indeed, given more space, time and knowledge, I would have liked to have extended the topic even further, to include everyone's perceptions of the past, or in the useful phrase of Bernard Guénée, the "historical culture" of the West.[1] Unlike some earlier historians, Hans Baron for example, I shall not be referring to the "awakening" of historical thought at a particular moment (in his case, the early Renaissance).[2] Nor will I be assuming or arguing, like Hegel, that historical thought or historical consciousness is a monopoly of the West. On the contrary, interest in the past appears to have existed everywhere and in all periods.

All the same, since people from different cultures have different conceptions of time and space, and since European cultural and social movements such as the Renaissance, the Reformation, the Enlightenment, Romanticism and positivism all had important consequences for historical thought and writing, it is only to be expected that European historical writing is distinctive. The problem lies in specifying that distinctiveness. Consider how many historical works have been written over the centuries, from Herodotus to the present, in how many European languages. Consider that to discuss what is distinctive in European historical thought it is also necessary to have a good knowledge of other historiographical traditions, such as the Chinese, Japanese, Islamic, African, indigenous American, and so on. No wonder that virtually no one has tried to study historiography in a comparative way (it is a pity that one of the few explicitly comparative studies is vitiated by the author's assumption that the Western style of historical writing is superior in every way to the alternatives).[3] It is obviously foolhardy for a single individual to offer conclusions on this huge subject.

Notes for this section begin on page 28.

Hence what follows is a list not so much of "conclusions" as of the reverse, of openings, in other words of provisional assertions that are intended to encourage debate and research. Let me make it clear at the start that I see the distinctiveness of Western historical thought not as a series of unique characteristics but rather as a unique combination of elements each of which is to be found elsewhere, a pattern of emphases, which themselves vary by period, region, social group and individual historian.

Another point to clarify at the outset is the problematic nature of the concept "Western," or indeed of the obvious alternative, "European." The examples which follow run from Herodotos to the present. Since the rise of the idea of Europe, from the Renaissance onwards, the intellectuals of that continent have claimed the ancient Greeks and Romans as ancestors. However, it is far from clear whether Herodotus or Ammianus Marcellinus (say) would have agreed. It is more likely that they saw themselves as part of a Mediterranean world in which they looked east rather than west. In any case, Greek intellectual traditions were influential in the Muslim world as well as (indeed earlier than) in Western Europe, thus undermining any contrast between an "us" which includes the Greeks and a "them" which includes Islam. The West is itself a historical construct.[4]

The paper is presented in the form of ten points in order to emphasize its schematic nature, not the nature of the subject, as well as to facilitate reference and discussion. For the same reasons, the sections have been numbered, without any pretensions to scientific accuracy or philosophical rigor. The points will be illustrated with reference to the historical classics of the Western tradition without assuming that these classics sum up Western historical thought in an exhaustive manner. The comparisons, explicit and implicit, will refer to a few classics from other traditions, for example to Ssu-ma Ch'ien and Ibn Khaldun, and also to a small cluster of secondary works in Western languages that are cited in the bibliography. It is because this work concentrates on China and Islam that I shall take most of my non-Western examples from those parts of the world. Every attempt will be made to avoid the misleading binary opposition between "the West" and "the rest."

The ten points which follow are not isolated but linked. The links are sometimes historical and sometimes logical (despite tensions or even contradictions between some of them). In this sense the points add up to a "system," "model" or "ideal type" of Western historical thought. Like other models, this one necessarily exaggerates the differences between Western and non-Western historians and minimizes intellectual conflict within the Western historical tradition. It should be considered as no more than a schematic description of a pattern of emphases.

It is of course tempting to try to relate Western historical thought to other characteristics of Western culture, indeed to present it as the product of Western history. From time to time I shall indeed be pointing to possible connections between Western historiography, Western science, Western law, Western individualism, Western capitalism and Western imperialism. The emphasis falls on description simply because it is logically prior to explanation. Only after we have made the inventory of differences between historical thought in the West and in other parts of the globe will it be possible to make a systematic investigation of the reasons for these differences.

The model presented in the following pages is intended to be a dynamic one. Change over time will be discussed in each section. My general conclusion is that although differences between Western and other historiographies have always been visible, they have been more important at certain times than at others. For example, there was an increasing divergence between Western and other historiographies from the Renaissance onwards because Western historical writing developed in a more and more distinctive way.

The phase of divergence was followed by a phase of convergence in the nineteenth and twentieth centuries, the result of a worldwide interest in the Western paradigm, or as Masayuki Sato puts it in his study of Japan, an "encounter" between that paradigm and indigenous traditions.[5] In some places, colonial Peru for instance, the meeting took place much earlier, in the age of Garcilaso de la Vega "El Inca" and of Guaman Poma del Ayala.[6] The result of this process has been to weaken, if not to dissolve, the specific qualities of Western historiography and to produce a global community of professional historians, with similar if not identical standards of practice. There are of course a number of different styles of history practiced today, but these styles (intellectual history, microhistory, quantitative history and so on), are available to historians more or less anywhere in the world.

Whether the general historical culture of different parts of the world today is equally unified I rather doubt. My impression is that the situation in historiography is rather like the situation in painting. Visual cultures differ from region to region, but superimposed is the global culture of professional artists, whose international exhibitions correspond to the international congresses of historians. This global professional culture is not uniform, but the major options available (op art, pop art, minimal art, and so on) are internationally available like the major options in history.

The following ten propositions concerning the "peculiarities of the West" are presented in approximate order of importance.

1. The most important, or at least the most obvious characteristic of Western historical thought is its stress on development or progress, in other words its "linear" view of the past.

1. 1.

The term "progress" is used here in a broad sense, to refer to the idea that change is cumulative (one generation standing on the shoulders of another), or that it is irreversible (summed up in the popular phrase, "you can't put back the clock"). Hegel's *Philosophy of History* and Macaulay's *History of England* may be cited as famous expressions of this cluster of ideas. However, the assumption of irreversibility does not imply that historical change is necessarily or usually for the better. Many of the practitioners of a new branch of history, the history of the environment or "eco-history," assert or imply that change is usually for the worse.

The assumption of progress or development has not been a constant feature of Western historical thought. On the contrary, it has its own history.[7] That "history" is going somewhere, that it is guided by destiny or Providence (or even that its subject is the action of God rather than of men, for example *Gesta Dei per Francos*), is an old as well as a widespread assumption in the West. So is the idea that the process is irreversible and will come to an end. These ideas are deeply embedded in the Jewish and the Christian traditions, where they were elaborated in terms of "fulfillment," "consummation," "messiah" and "millennium." The philosophy of history of Joachim of Fiore and his followers, including the ideas of the three ages, the angelic pope and the last world-emperor, is only one of the variations on this theme.

As Karl Löwith has argued, modern concepts of historical development may be viewed as secular forms of these religious ideas.[8] The idea of modernity itself is one example of this process.[9] The idea of "revolution," at least as it has been used since 1789, is another expression of this idea of cumulation and irreversibility.[10] So is the alternative concept of "evolution," a term that was adopted by late nineteenth-century historians (as it was by sociologists and lawyers), not only to give scientific, Darwinian respectability to their craft but to sum up what they already believed or assumed.[11] There was also the more precise and limited idea of "development" in a particular area of culture (religious doctrine for instance), an idea which itself developed in the course of the seventeenth, eighteenth and nineteenth centuries.[12] From the end of the eighteenth century, biographies of individuals came to be organized around the idea of development.[13]

1. 2.

These different ideas of progress have long coexisted with the opposite, cyclical theory of historical change, which was dominant in ancient Greece and Rome but can also be found in the Old Testament.[14] In the Renaissance, for instance, political theorists often asserted that change in regimes followed a cyclical pattern from monarchy to aristocracy to democracy and back again. It was this assumption of a cyclical movement that underlay the traditional idea of revolution, a word which was coined on the model of "revolve." The same assumption underlies the ideas of Re-naissance and Re-formation.[15] The idea of equilibrium, a balance that may be tilted but is always redressed, was a fundamental organizing concept in Western historical thought from Giovanni Villani to Edward Gibbon.[16] For example, in the sixteenth and seventeenth centuries, the discovery of America was sometimes interpreted as a compensation to the West for the loss of Constantinople thirty-nine years earlier.

In the eighteenth century, Vico reformulated the idea of historical cycles with his view of *corsi* and *ricorsi*. Voltaire and Gibbon may seem to assume that history progresses, since they often refer to recent centuries as a period of increasing civilization in contrast to the more remote past. However, both historians believed that this progress was fragile, that a new age of barbarism might sweep all these gains away. In this sense their fundamental schema was cyclical.[17] In our own century, speculative philosophers of history and sociologists such as Spengler, Sorokin, Pareto and Toynbee returned to the cyclical view of history, elaborated in various forms such as the alternate dominance of entrepreneurs and *rentiers*.

1. 3.

Needless to say, linear views of history can be found outside the West. Messianic and millenarian expectations form part of Muslim as well as Jewish and Christian traditions. They can also be found in many parts of the world in the nineteenth and twentieth centuries (in China, in Africa, in the "cargo cults" of Polynesia) the result not only of the spread of Christianity but also of its interaction with indigenous traditions.[18]

All the same, I shall risk the assertion that the idea of cycles is normal and that of progress exceptional in non-Western historical cultures. One might illustrate these cycles from the traditional presentation of Chinese dynasties by Chinese historians, or from the famous theory of the alternate dominance of nomads and settlers in the pages of the *Muqaddimah*.[19]

2. Linked to the idea of progress but distinct from it is the Western concern with historical perspective.

2. 1.

By "concern with historical perspective" or the "sense of anachronism," I mean the idea that the past is not uniform, more and more of the same thing, but on the contrary extremely variable, each historical period having its own cultural style, its own personality. One might describe this idea as a sense of "cultural distance," a view of the past as "a foreign country."[20]

This idea too has its own history. It can be found in ancient Rome but its continuous history in the West goes back to the Renaissance to the time of the discovery of visual perspective (an analogy stressed by the art historian Erwin Panofsky).[21] This increasingly acute sense of the past may be illustrated not only from philology (Valla's interest in changes in Latin and Greek), and from law (the increasing awareness of the relation between Roman law and ancient Roman culture), but also from art (Mantegna's concern with accurate representations of ancient Roman costume and buildings).[22] An awareness of the history of costume is at once a superficial and a revealing expression of a sense of the "otherness" of the past. This sense of otherness is evident in the work of both forgers and their critics, each stimulating the other to new heights of sophistication in their attempts either to avoid or to recognize "anachronism" (a term which was coined in the seventeenth century).[23]

The concern with period style, like the concern for "local color," became even more acute in the early nineteenth century, linked to the concern with the individuality of each epoch commonly associated with Romanticism. It is exemplified not only in historiography and in the increasingly popular genre of history painting, but also in the rise of the historical novel in the age of Scott and Mansion.

2. 2.

This sense of the past was not universal even among elites after the year 1500. On the eighteenth-century English stage, for example, it was common for actors in plays by Shakespeare to wear eighteenth-century clothes, including wigs. From the Renaissance to the nineteenth century, it was customary for sculptors in particular to represent heroes past and present in Roman costume, whether armor or toga irrespective of their actual costume.

2. 3.

The awareness of changes in cultural style is not uniquely Western. In China, for example, there is a long tradition of interest in period styles in the arts, leading to forgery and to the elaboration of techniques for discovering forgery.[24] Renaissance philologists also had their Chinese counterparts, at least by late imperial times.[25] The term "historicism" is sometimes used by Sinologists to refer to these practices and attitudes.[26] There were similar trends in Japan, where scholars were very much aware of Chinese cultural precedents and paradigms. All the same, I propose that a concern with anachronism has been more central to Western historical thought, and for a longer time, than has been the case in other cultures.

3. The sense of anachronism may be seen as part of a larger cluster of Western ideas and assumptions, often described by the word "historicism" (Historismus), defined by Friedrich Meinecke as a concern with individuality and development.[27] Development having been discussed above, let us turn to individuality.

3. 1.

I am using the term "individuality," to refer to an awareness of, or an interest in the specific in, what makes one person, or group, or culture different from others: the "idiographic," in contrast to the "nomothetic" approach of scientists, including social scientists.[28]

The European tradition of biography from Plutarch and Suetonius onwards (a continuous tradition from the late Middle Ages), suggests that the concern with the specific or the unique goes back a long way. That events were seen as unique by some early modern thinkers may be shown by referring to two famous controversies, between Machiavelli and Guicciardini, and between Hobbes and Hyde (later Lord Clarendon). Guicciardini and Hyde criticized Machiavelli and Hobbes respectively for their lack of awareness of the specificity of events. The concern with individuality and specificity was much more intense in the romantic era. That it was a characteristic of Western historical thought in the late nineteenth and early twentieth centuries may be illustrated from the writings of philosophers of history such as Dilthey, Croce and Collingwood.

3. 2.

The examples of Machiavelli and Hobbes as well as those of many other Western thinkers who have searched for "laws" of human behavior, are a reminder that—when it can be found at all—the concern with specificity has coexisted with the opposite concern for generality.

In any case, the long tradition of biography is not such good evidence for a sense of individuality as it may appear. We must be careful not to project modern notions of biography or the individual on to writers of (say) the Renaissance, who often presented their heroes as exemplars, in other words as concrete examples of traditional ideals that readers should attempt to follow.

A similar problem to that of the meaning of biography arises in the case of the painted portrait. The rise of this genre has often been cited as evidence of a concern with individuality (or individualism) from the Renaissance onwards. However many portraits represented types rather than specific people. Sixteenth-century collections of engraved portraits might use the same image to represent more than one person.[29]

3. 3.

The tradition of portrait painting in China, in Japan, and also (despite religious prohibitions) in parts of the Islamic world, including the courts of Ottoman sultans and Mughal emperors, is a warning not to underestimate the interest in individuality outside the West. The same point might be made about biographies. Ruler-centered historiography is of course common in many cultures, while the lives of Chinese artists by Chang Yeng-Yuan precedes the *Vite* by Vasari.

It might be better to frame the question about individuality not so much in terms of its presence or absence, as in terms of the particular "category of the person" implicit in a given historiographical tradition.[30] All the same, it has proved difficult to find examples of historians in other parts of the world (and uninfluenced by Western paradigms), who demonstrate the acute interest in the individuality of epochs, regions or persons characteristic of Western historical writing from the beginning of the nineteenth century onwards. Given Hindu and Buddhist views of the unreality of the person, one would not expect an emphasis on individuals in cultures where these religions are dominant.

4. Collective agency, or at least certain collective agents, are given unusual stress in Western historiography.

4. 1.

This trend goes back at least as far as the Roman history by Cato (now lost) in which the author refused to name any individual (with the exception of an elephant which distinguished itself by its bravery in battle).

In the course of time, importance has been imputed not only to peoples or nations, but also to such agents as families, cities, churches, religious orders, armies, commercial companies, political assemblies, crowds, political parties, and social classes. I mention these groups in particular because each has given rise to a particular historical genre, as well as occupying a place in more general histories. This stress on the collective is not a recent one. Civic histories have been a common genre since the Renaissance. In the seventeenth century, Clarendon's history of the English Civil War placed considerable emphasis on the agency of the court, the parliament and the army.[31]

The stress on collective agency has been a particularly strong one since the nineteenth century, and not only among Marxists. Comte, who wrote of *"histoire sans noms"* and Durkheim and the historians who followed them moved in the same direction. There was even a Comtean project by Heinrich Wölfflin to write art history as Cato wrote Roman history, "without names."[32] In short, the so-called decentering of the subject is not an invention of the postmodern age, but a long Western tradition.

4. 2.

The concern with the individual, discussed in thesis 3, runs counter to the stress on collective agency. As in the case of linear and cyclical history, we are dealing with the coexistence and interaction of opposed trends.

4. 3.

Histories of states or empires or dynasties are common in various parts of the world. It may therefore be prudent as well as useful to refine the argument, and to suggest that the most distinctive collective agents in Western historiography are groups smaller than the state, people or nation. Of these smaller groups one might single out social classes and voluntary associations, which appear to have played unusually important roles in Western history, with consequences that Montesquieu and Tocqueville have analyzed in detail.

Among the most obvious counterexamples to cite at this point are Buddhist monasteries and Muslim brotherhoods—but have they ever enjoyed a place in historiography similar to that of their counterparts in the West?

5. Western historiography is distinctive in its preoccupation with epistemology, with the problem of historical knowledge.

5. 1.

Historians in most if not all places and times have been concerned with practical criticism in the sense of the evaluation of, and discrimination between, the particular stories about the past that they hear or read, in order to choose what appears to be the most reliable version of events. What appears to be distinctive in the Western tradition is the concern with this problem at a general as well as a specific level. Thus Greek and Renaissance skeptics denied the possibility of historical knowledge, and Descartes elaborated their criticisms. In response to the challenge of historical Pyrrhonism, as it was called, historians of the late seventeenth and early eighteenth centuries elaborated a defense, distinguishing various degrees of probability among statements about the past, thus initiating a tradition that has lasted till our own time.[33]

5. 2.

In his concern with the foundations of knowledge, Descartes was himself reacting to the challenge of the scientific revolution, which undermined traditional views of nature. The relation between Western historiography and Western science, especially from that time onwards, has been both a close and a difficult one. Some historians have tried to imitate natural scientists and apply mathematics to the past. Thus in the seventeenth century, John Craig imitated Newton by producing a list of historical principles and axioms. The Cambridge historian J. B. Bury once declared that "history is a science, no less and no more." Other historians from Vico to Collingwood, have defined themselves by contrast to the "scientists." In both cases, the debate with modern science has given Western historiography a distinctive stamp.

5. 3.

Even at the level of practical criticism, it may be possible to distinguish a particularly Western approach to problems of "sources," "evidence," and "testimony." The last two terms were of course borrowed by historians from the discourse of lawyers. In the Western tradition of historiography, legal metaphors are commonplace—references to the "laws" of history, to the "tribunal" of history, to "witnesses" and "testimony," to analogies between historians, detectives and judges. The law in question may be Roman law or common law, but it is always a distinctively Western legal system to which the historiographical system is compared. Thomas Sherlock's *The Trial of the Witnesses of the Resurrection of Jesus* (1729) was organized in the form of a trial.

I know of no study of this problem, let alone a comparative study, but it may be worth following the lead of this key metaphor and considering the possibility that distinctively Western ideas and assumptions about historical "evidence" have developed out of ideas and assumptions embedded in Western law. Muslim, Chinese and other courts have traditionally operated in other ways and with different assumptions from those in the West.[34] Have historians in these traditions taken over assumptions from indigenous legal systems, or have they been less concerned with the law than their Western counterparts?

6. Attempts at historical explanation are universal, but the couching of these explanations in terms of "causes" is a distinctively Western characteristic.

6. 1.

This historiographical tradition goes back to ancient Greece, as the examples of Thucydides and Polybius demonstrate. Their idea of cause (*aition*) and its distinction from a mere "symptom" suggests that the paradigm they were following was that of Hippocratic medicine, from which historians have also borrowed the term "crisis," originally applied to fevers. In other words, the Western ideal of a historiography modeled on the natural sciences is an old one. It is often associated with the idea of laws of history in the sense of laws of human behavior, as in the case of Thucydides, for instance, or Machiavelli.

6. 2.

There has of course been a countertrend, the "historicist" or "historist" trend that rejected the comparison between historians and natural scientists, as well as emphasizing the uniqueness of historical events (cf. 3. 1 and 5. 2). At the level of historical explanation, this reaction has taken the form of hermeneutics, of a stress on meaning rather than cause, or on what R.G. Collingwood called the "inside" rather than the "outside" of a historical event.[35] For the last hundred years, at least, Western historiography has been marked by the uneasy coexistence, if not open conflict, between hermeneutic and causal approaches.

7. Western historians have long prided themselves on their so-called objectivity.

It may be useful to distinguish two stages in a Western tradition of historical detachment. In the first stage, the ideal is best expressed with the term "impartiality." It was considered important to write *sine ira et studio*, in other words without emotional involvement and without self-interest. The ideal was most discussed at the time when it was most difficult to follow, in the hundred and fifty years of religious conflict that followed the Protestant Reformation. For example, the German Protestant Johann Sleidan claimed that his history of the Reformation told the story of those events "as they happened," *prout res quaeque acta fuit*. The similarity to Ranke's famous formula will be clear, as it is in the case of the French Protestant La Popelinière, who tried, he said, to tell the story of the French religious wars as it happened (*réciter la chose comme elle est advenue*). Both Sleidan and La Popelinière, incidentally, had an unusually acute sense of history as a profession.[36] A third famous example of the attempt to write the history in a detached manner was Gottfried Arnold's *Unparteiische Kirchen- und Ketzerhistorie*, from the end of the seventeenth century. A common metaphor used especially in England from the seventeenth century onwards was taken from the game of bowls. The historian's ideal was to avoid "bias," whether religious or political.

In the second stage, under the influence of the model of natural science, the traditional ideal of impartiality or freedom from bias was reformulated as the ideal of "objectivity," a detached presentation of the "facts." Ranke was frequently cited as a shining example of a historian who tried to "extinguish himself" and extract from the documents "the pure facts." The idea that the historian's task is to present all the facts and nothing but the facts has been reiterated many times since Ranke's day. Despite challenges, this view of the historian's task may still be dominant in the empiricist English-speaking world.[37]

8. The quantitative approach to history is distinctively Western.

The development of more and more sophisticated quantitative methods by "serial historians" in France, historical demographers in France and England, and "new economic historians" in the U.S.A., especially in the 1950s and 1960s, is well known. However, these movements grew out of a much older tradition. The study of price history was already taken seriously in the later nineteenth century, especially in the German-speaking world. The history of population was taken seriously in the eighteenth century. As early as the fourteenth century, Giovanni Villani stuffed his chronicle with figures, including the numbers of children attending different kinds of school in Florence, a spectacular example of what has been called the "arithmetical mentality."[38] It is surely no accident that one of the kinds of school mentioned by Villani was the "abacus school," which taught elementary numeracy. In Florence, with its numerous banks and merchant houses, this knowledge was particularly useful. In short, we may argue that Western historiography has been shaped by Western capitalism as well as by Western law and science. Can a similar interest in statistics be found in any other historical tradition?

9. The literary forms of Western historiography are distinctive as its content.

9. 1.

Polybius referred to some historians of his own day as "tragedians" because of their striving for pathos. A famous study of Thucydides has underlined the analogy between his history and the Greek drama of his time, notably the concern with peripeteia.[39] Sixteenth- and seventeenth-century studies of the art of history compared historians to composers of epic, and emphasized the importance of such literary set pieces as the battle, the character, and the speech. They made more explicit the classical idea of the "dignity" of history, that is, the idea that only some events and some individuals are of sufficient status to be worth recording or remembering.[40] Some recent studies have followed and developed these points.[41] Other scholars have noted analogies between historical narratives and the narratives of novelists, and the influence of each group on the other.[42]

However, it is above all Hayden White who (following Norbert Frye) has forced historians to be aware of the literary forms they follow (often as unconsciously as Monsieur Jourdain). White has described "emplotments" of history in the form of comedy, tragedy, romance and satire. [43]

It might be useful to discuss other prefabricated plots. The battle, for example, whether literal or allegorical.[44] Ernst Cassirer's study of Neoplatonism in England in the seventeenth century is an extreme example of an intellectual history presented in the form of a battle, a *psychomachia* full of personifications.[45]

Another mytheme, obviously linked to the idea of progress, is that of the forerunner, St. John the Baptist. In Protestant ecclesiastical history, for instance, Jan Hus, Girolamo Savonarola and other critics of the papacy are presented as forerunners of Martin Luther. Again, this is the role that Cimabue plays in Vasari's story of the rebirth of the arts in Italy, the true protagonist being Giotto.[46] In the historiography of Latin American independence, Francisco de Miranda has been formally labeled "El Precursor," in other words the man who plays St. John the Baptist to Simon Bolívar's Christ. More recently, in the history of psychoanalysis, Charcot has been allotted the role of the precursor of Freud.

The comparison of great men with Christ is usually considered too daring to be explicit, but it does occur from time to time. For example, a medieval account of the life of Thomas Becket refers to his "passion." There is an underlying assumption here that deserves to be analyzed in more detail: the assumption that historical events are (at least sometimes) conscious or unconscious reenactments of models, so that the written histories that recount these later events are in a sense allegories.[47]

9. 2.

What is distinctively Western here? White's point is, I take it, intended to be a universal one about what he calls "the historical text as a literary artifact." However, his examples of emplotment all come from traditional Western literary genres.[48] The classical epic, to which Renaissance writers compared the history is a Western genre (or a variation on a genre that also includes the *Mahabharata*).[49] A similar point might be made about tragedy. Do Japanese historians emphasize the "nobility of failure" that is such a favorite theme in Japanese literature?[50] Does the Ottoman history of the Ottoman Empire reveal the influence of the Turkish epic?

The novel too, at least in the relatively precise sense of the term "novel" that refers to certain kinds of narrative developed from the eighteenth century onwards, is a Western invention, even if it is one that has been adapted with considerable success to local conditions in Egypt, India, Japan and elsewhere. My question, therefore, to historians of non-Western historical writing, is whether indigenous literary genres play the same role of conscious or unconscious models in the work of historians as White suggests they do in the cases of Ranke, Burckhardt and Tocqueville. The famous study of the representation of reality in Western literature by Erich Auerbach (which devotes a chapter to classical historical writing) suggests a still broader question.[51] To what extent do the mimetic conventions of historical writing vary from one culture to another?

10. Western historians have characteristic views of space no less than of time.

10. 1.

Braudel's *Méditerranée* is a famous example of a study in which the problem of distance is absolutely central. Some of Braudel's followers shared this preoccupation, notably Pierre Chaunu, who studied the Atlantic in a broadly similar way. However, Braudel's *géohistoire*, as he called it, is not completely without precedent. Gibbon's *Decline and Fall* pays as much attention to the communication problems of the Roman Empire as Braudel did in the case of the empire of Philip II. In the sixteenth century, Jean Bodin wrote, much like Braudel, of geo-historians (*geographistorici*).

10. 2.

I have no intention of claiming that Western historians are alone in their interest in historical geography, or in what Renaissance historians called "chorography." In China, the tradition of local histories is a long one.[52] Ibn Khaldun's famous discussion of differences between nomads and settlers was mentioned in section 1.3. However, there is a cluster of Western historical studies organized around the relation between human groups and the land. It does not seem coin-

Peter Burke

cidence that these studies are Western but not European. They are the work of
Neo-Europeans. The best known of these studies is doubtless Frederick Jackson
Turner's essay on the frontier in American history, but it is easy to add other
examples, including the work of Capistrano de Abreu and Sergio Buarque de
Holanda on the importance of routes and frontiers in the colonization of Brazil,
or Geoffrey Blainey's *The Tyranny of Distance*, which analyzes the consequences
of Australia's geographical position for the development of its economy and
society. These books express a sense of space and a sense of being on the world's
periphery, far from the centers of power and civilization. Like Western law, capitalism and science, the colonizing process—whether we call it "discovery,"
"encounter" or "imperialism"—has helped to shape the characteristic features
of Western historical writing.

I have tried to summarize what might be called a "system" of historiographical
assumptions and principles. A system not in the strong sense of deductions from
axioms but in the weaker sense that some at least of the characteristics imputed
to Western historical writing are linked to one another. However, as we have
seen, the system is not free from conflict and countertrends. For better or worse,
there has not been any consensus (for centuries, at least) on major issues such as
uniqueness versus the illustration of historical laws, progress versus cycles, or
causes versus meanings. It is ultimately this conflict of systems—or system of
conflicts—the particular shifting balances between different "forces," which has
characterized historical thought and historical writing in the West.

Notes

1. Bernard Guénée, *Histoire et culture historique dans l'occident médiéval,* Paris, 1981.
2. Hans Baron, 'Das Erwachen des historischen Denkens', *Historische Zeitschrift* 147 (1932-3), 5-
    20.
3. Donald E. Brown, *Hierarchy, History and Human Nature. The Social Origins of Historical Con-
    sciousness,* Tucson, 1988.
4. Carlo Sigonio, *De occidentali imperio* (1577) is an important contribution to this construct.
5. Masayuki Sato, 'Historiographical Encounters. The Chinese and Western Traditions in Turn-
    of-the-Century Japan', *Storia della Storiografia* 19 (1991), 13-21.
6. Margaret Zamora, *Language, Authority and Indigenous History in the Comentarios reales,* Cam-
    bridge, 1988; Rolena Adorno, *Guaman Poma. Writing and Resistance in Colonial Peru,* Austin,
    1986.
7. John B. Bury, *The Idea of Progress,* London, 1920.
8. Karl Löwith, *Weltgeschichte und Heilgeschehen,* 2nd edn, Stuttgart 1953.
9. Hans Blumenberg, *Die Legitimität der Neuzeit,* Frankfurt, 1966, Engl. transl.: *The Legitimacy of
    the Modern Age,* Cambridge, Mass., 1983.

10. Karl Griewank, *Der Neuzeitliche Revolutionsbegriff,* Weimar, 1955; Felix Gilbert, 'Revolution', in *Dictionary of the History of Ideas,* ed. Philip P. Wiener, vol. 4, New York, 1973, 157–167; Karl-Heinz Benda, *Revolutionen,* Munich, 1977.

11. John Burrow, *Evolution and Society,* Cambridge, 1966.

12. Owen Chadwick, *From Bossuet to Newman,* Cambridge, 1957.

13. Bruce Mazlish, 'Autobiography and Psychoanalysis', *Encounter,* October 1970, 28–45.

14. G. W. Trompf, *The Idea of Historical Recurrence in Western Thought from Antiquity to the Reformation,* Berkeley 1979.

15. Peter Burke, 'Renaissance, Reformation, Revolution', in *Niedergang,* ed. Reinhart Koselleck, Stuttgart, 1980, 137–47.

16. Louis Green, *Chronicle into History,* Cambridge 1972, 17ff, 27; Gerald J. Gruman, 'Balance and Excess as Gibbon's Explanation of the Decline and Fall', *History and Theory* 1 (1960), 75–85.

17. Hans Vyverberg, *Historical Pessimism in the French Enlightenment,* Cambridge, Mass., 1958.

18. Vittorio Lanternari, *The Religions of the Oppressed,* London 1963.

19. Arthur F. Wright, 'Chinese Historiography', in *International Encyclopaedia of the Social Sciences,* ed. D. Sills, New York 1968, 400–7; Mushin Mahdi, *Ibn Khaldun's Philosophy of History,* London, 1957; Aziz Al-Azmeh, *Ibn Khaldun,* London, 1982; Tarif Khalidi, *Arabic Historical Thought in the Classical Period,* Cambridge, 1994.

20. Leslie P. Hartley, *The Go-Between,* London, 1953; David Lowenthal, *The Past is a Foreign Country,* Cambridge, 1985.

21. Erwin Panofsky, 'The First Page of Vasari's Libro' (1939), in *Meaning in the Visual Arts,* New York, 1957, 169–225.

22. Peter Burke, *The Renaissance Sense of the Past,* London, 1969; Roberto Weiss, *The Renaissance Discovery of Classical Antiquity,* Oxford, 1969; Donald Kelley, *Foundations of Modern Historical Scholarship,* Cambridge, Mass., 1970.

23. Anthony Grafton, *Forgers and Critics,* London, 1990.

24. Craig Clunas, *Superfluous Things. Material Culture and Social Status in Early Modern China,* Cambridge, 1991, 109–15.

25. Benjamin A. Elman, *From Philosophy to Philology. Intellectual and Social Aspects of Change in Late Imperial China,* Cambridge, Mass., 1984.

26. On-Cho Ng, 'Historicism in Chinese Thought', *Journal of the History of Ideas* 54 (1993), 561–84.

27. Friedrich Meinecke, *Die Entstehung des Historismus,* München 1936, Engl. transl.: *Historicism,* New York 1972.

28. Wilhelm Windelband, *Geschichte und Naturwissenschaft,* Berlin, 1894.

29. Gottfried Böhm, *Bildnis und Individuum,* Munich, 1985; Peter Burke, 'The Renaissance, Individualism and the Portrait', *History of European Ideas* 21 (1995), 393–400.

30. Michael Carrithers et al., eds, *The Category of the Person,* Cambridge, 1985.

31. Peter Burke, 'Structural History in the 16th and 17th Centuries', *Storia della Storiografia* 10 (1986), 71–6.

32. Arnold Hauser, *Philosophy of Art History,* Cleveland, 1963, 120, 124.

33. Carlo Borghero, *La certezza e la storia. Cartesianesimo, pirronismo e conoscenza storica,* Milan, 1983.

34. Lawrence Rosen, *The Anthropology of Justice. Law as Culture in Islamic Society,* Cambridge, 1989.

35. R. G. Collingwood, *The Idea of History,* Oxford, 1946.

36. D. R. Kelley, 'History as a Calling. the Case of La Popelinière', in *Renaissance. Studies in honor of Hans Baron,* eds A. Molho and J. Tedeschi, Florence 1971, 773–89; id., 'Johann Sleidan and the Origins of History as a Profession', *Journal of Modern History* 52 (1980), 577–98.

37. Peter Novick, *That Noble Dream. The 'Objectivity Question' and the American Historical Profession,* Cambridge, 1988.

38. Alexander Murray, *Reason and Society in the Middle Ages,* Oxford, 1978.

39. Francis Cornford, *Thucydides Mythistoricus*, Cambridge, 1907; cf. Frank Walbank, 'History and Tragedy', *Historia* 9 (1960), repr. in his *Selected Papers*, Cambridge 1985, 224-41.
40. Peter Burke, 'The Rhetoric and Anti-Rhetoric of History', in *Anamorphoren der Rhetorik*, ed. Gerhard Schroeder et al., Stuttgart, 1997, 71-79.
41. J. H. Brumfitt, *Voltaire Historian Oxford*, 1958; Roland Barthes, 'Historical Discourse' (1967), repr. in *Structuralism*, ed. M. Lane, London, 1970, 145-55; Burke, *The Renaissance Sense of the Past*, London, 1969.
42. Leo Braudy, *Narrative Form in History and Fiction*, Princeton, 1970.
43. Northrop Frye, 'New Directions for Old' (1960), repr. in his *Fables of Identity*, New York 1963, 52-66; Hayden V. White, *Metahistory. The Historical Imagination in Nineteenth-Century Europe*, Baltimore and London, 1973.
44. Angus Fletcher, *Allegory*, Ithaca, 1964.
45. Ernst Cassirer, *Die platonische Renaissance in England*, Hamburg, 1932, English translation: *The Platonic Renaissance in England*, Edinburgh 1953.
46. Michael Baxandall, *Giotto and the Orators*, Oxford, 1971.
47. Peter Burke, 'History as Allegory', unpublished.
48. Cf. Earl Miner, *Comparative Poetics*, Princeton, 1990.
49. But cf. Jaroslav Prusek, 'History and Epic in China and the West', *Diogenes* 42 (1963), 20-43.
50. Ivan Morris, *The Nobility of Failure. Tragic Heroes in the History of Japan*, London, 1975.
51. Erich Auerbach, *Mimesis*, Bern, 1946.
52. W. Franke, 'Historical Writing during the Ming', *Cambridge History of China* 7, ed. L. Mote and D. Twitchett, Cambridge, 1988, ch. 12.

II: COMMENTS

Perspectives in Historical Anthropology

Klaus E. Müller

As a rule, the gaze of the historian is directed back into his or her own history. But of late this gaze has been extending its field, roaming beyond its familiar landscape, seeking to comprehend not only its own but also the "foreign historical," and to draw the latter into the arena of comparative examination. The eurocentric perspective is beginning to falter and could ultimately erode.

Comparison has its roots in the age-old attempt by the human being to bring order into the diversity of the phenomena in his surroundings. It is based on ethnocentrism: traditional societies with an intact identity, that is, a largely unified conception of the world, order phenomena as part of their own culture insofar as they appear to be consistent with this culture, and exclude others that are inconsistent, often by way of deriding them. The Danish ethnologist Kaj Birket-Smith (1893-1977) conjures up the image of the "first Stone Age man who made the other members of his tribe laugh by telling of the comical and incredible customs of the neighboring horde."[1] The forms subsequently taken by this early, imagined amusement have been many and varied. It is based on the satisfying, inductively gained certainty that the correspondences and similarities which the gaze registers in its own limited surroundings—the constant recurrence of experiences—justifies the conclusion that they are linked by a commonality, an "essential invariance" as Konrad Lorenz put it[2], that is, the rule which accounts for their perpetuation in terms of form and sequential order. In the view of the participant, the culture thus corresponds to an iron system of rules, which finds expression in a consistent, unified conception of the world, establishes order and guarantees a reliable orientation. In the opinion of the philosopher Karl Raimund Popper, there exists a "tremendously powerful need" for such a system, a need which is so strong that it sometimes does not "allow for the perception of existing regularities at all."[3] However, all around, beyond the borders of one's own world, the forms become indistinct, mis-shapen; ever new, exotic experiences follow one another, and, in proportion to the distance from the observer, an increasing chaos seems to prevail that does not adhere to any rule at all. In order to make this at least comprehensible as an expression of "anti-order," it is defined as rudimentary, deviant or as degenera-tion, as a distorted image or caricature of the well-proportioned form of one's own world; worthy of contempt, perhaps of amusement, but ultimately hardly of attention, let alone of serious study—and if at all, then as a diffuse silhouette of the sublime formal clarity of one's own culture, which is positioned at the center of the world.

The Greeks, too, saw themselves as inhabiting this center, locating it at dif-ferent times in Olympia, in Delphi and in Ionia, depending on the origin of the author.[4] The Greeks, moreover, were themselves already practiced ethnogra-phers, as a result of their establishment of colonies and their trading and recon-naissance expeditions. This compelled them to make comparisons, in the process of which they consciously selected. What seemed to them above all notewor-thy was that which conspicuously deviated from the Greek way of life; for it was precisely here that they thought they were able to recognize what was charac-teristic of a foreign culture. Hippocrates (c. 460-370 B.C.), who not only acquired importance as a physician, but also as an ethnographer—undertaking research expeditions to, among other places, the territory of what is today Georgia—and ethnological theorist, reduced the principle to a formula: "I intend to depict only those peoples who differ from one another very consid-erably in terms of their nature and their customs, but to leave out of consider-ation those who exhibit a large degree of similarity."[5] This approach was extended to create a system that differentiated foreign cultural peculiarities: the Mediterranean core area of the archaic civilizations was surrounded by con-centric circles: with the first being constituted by the peripheral peasant cul-tures, the next by the nomadic societies of North Africa, Arabia and Scythia, for example, and the third, at the outermost edge of the world, by the hunting and gathering peoples of Africa, India and northern Eurasia. Corresponding to this horizontal differentiation was a vertical concept of stages, giving rise to a pic-ture that was "three-dimensional," and which was also conceived of as a devel-opmental pyramid—the axis of which was in Hellas.[6]

In itself, this was nothing new given the common identity-ideological self-awareness of traditional societies, according to which each ethnic group sees itself at the pinnacle of the developmental potential of all humanity, while the diverging forms of life of neighboring peoples are comprehended as merely rudimentary prototypes or imperfect products of processes of stagnation, faulty development or degeneration.[7] The Greeks were the first to develop a theory for this: the thesis—already intimated in the work of Herodotus (c. 490-430 B.C.)[8], and then reformulated conclusively by Hippocrates—that there existed a determinative interrelation between geographical environment and cultural development.[9] The systematic framework for this was provided by a corresponding theory of climatic zones, according to which the world was for the most part divided into three typical major spheres: a cold damp one in the north, a dry hot one in the south, and a temperate changeable one in the Mediterranean central area. While the extreme conditions in the north and the south , as it were, paralyzed the people there, so that they persisted in stages close to that of animals, it was only in the central sphere, with its benevolent but at the same time fluctuating and to that extent intellectually stimulating climate, that all the conditions of a constant and progressive development pertained.[10]

Beyond the boundaries of Greek culture lived "barbarians"—literally "babblers," human beings who do not have a command of a "proper" language— who were variously categorized and seen as enslaved by the adverse conditions of their environment. They were measured in Hellenic terms. Extreme cases were constituted by the genuine "primitive peoples." The Mossynoics in the inaccessible mountainous northeast of Asia Minor, for example, appeared to Xenophon and his like to be "particularly raw and barbaric"—for "their customs deviated the most from those of the Greeks" (*Anabasis* V 4). Hellenes who went among the barbarians, even settling among them, could only degenerate; whoever had direct contact with them or went so far as to grant them incorporation into his own homeland threatened the continued existence of the culture, or at least his personal ability to participate in it. Between barbarians and Greeks, as Plato (427-347 B.C.) found, there existed a natural (*physei*) antagonism (*Politeia* 470 C). Athens, which, on the basis of its position, was preferred and loved by the gods above all other regions of the earth, owed its greatness to the very circumstance that its inhabitants always remained "purely Hellenic and separate from the barbarians." For that reason, they had grown—"so strong and healthy of nature"—into a race of people which "surpassed all others in intellect" (*Menexenos* 237 B - 238 B, 245 C-D); any lasting contact would have necessarily weakened their noble breed and led to bastardization. Aristotle (384-322 B.C.) was of exactly the same view. On the basis of the central position of Greece, he argued conclusively that its population united in itself only the merits of the barbarians living around it: the courage and the yearning for independence of the Europeans (in the north) and the technical skill and intellectual prowess of the Asians (in the east). For this reason, according to Aristotle, the Hellenes remained "merely continually free, but also most importantly within a state order and would be able to establish rule over all other peoples, if they were united in a single state" (Politics VII 7. 1327 b, 20ff.). Occidental erudition began to reveal its Janus face.

The end of the nineteenth century was marked by the triumphal march of Darwinian thought. It had been preceded by pioneering successes in the natural sciences, which seemed all the more striking when their practical application proved capable of producing perceptible improvements in the quality of life. The concept of development, promoted above all by discoveries in geology and biology, increasingly asserted itself, finding its heightened expression in the linear-evolutionary perspective. This in turn raised the question as to whether not only natural history, but also cultural development was not necessarily to be compre-hended as evolution, of whether cultural history was not to be grasped as a part of natural history, and thus as governed by iron, universally valid laws.[11] Elevated to the status of a dogma, the idea immediately assumed a dominant role in the ethnology of the time. Edward Burnett Tylor (1832-1917), one of the leading thinkers of ethnological "evolutionism," gave expression to this conviction:

> To many educated minds there seems something presumptuous and repulsive in the view that the history of mankind is part and parcel of the history of nature, that our thoughts, wills and actions accord with laws as definite as those which govern the motion of waves, the combination of acids and bases, and the growth of plants and animals.[12]

One consequence of this was that a range of invariant antecedent condi-tions could now also be presupposed within the cultural and historical sciences. One such condition had its roots in the Enlightenment: it was generally postu-lated that all human beings were of the same psychological and intellectual pre-disposition.[13] From this was derived the postulate that there existed everywhere in the world at least the tendency for the development of similar, if not corre-sponding ideas and institutions, that is, a tendency for unitary-evolutionary development. The history of human society, according to the Scottish ethnolo-gist John Ferguson McLennan (1827-1881),"is that of a development following very closely one general law."[14]

However, this appeared to run counter to the fact that all known cultures in part differed very considerably from one another. Here the second invariable came into play, supplemented by a range of variable additional conditions: for the evolutionists, the *instrumentum regium* for the explanation of cultural variance was constituted by the Darwinian principle of selection. James George Frazer (1854-1941), another leading representative of evolutionism, was certain "that in the competition between forces, whether in a physical or mental respect, the strongest on the whole asserts itself and the fittest survives ... when all is said and done it is the better ideas, which we describe as truth, which emerge vic-torious."[15] At a secondary level, factors seen as contributing to the divergence of courses of development were the necessity of adapting to different environ-ments, processes of diffusion and migration,[16] wars (as an instrument of selec-tion)[17]—even racial varieties. Indeed the latter view was one shared without exception by all evolutionists.[18] If the principle of selection itself already exhib-ited a certain lack of consistency with the postulate of equality, the latter was thoroughly violated by the addition of racialist explanations.

Both were based in eurocentrism, a phenomenon that Peter Burke rightly argues should be seen in relative terms. Added to this was another central the-sis of evolutionism, according to which all cultural development, in accordance with biological evolution, in principle progressed from simple to ever more differentiated and complex forms. The Euro-American nations were themselves regarded to be the obvious proof of this: they represented the historically highest degree of cultural complexity and consequently occupied the leading position among the peoples of the world—and deservedly so, since in the "competition between abilities" they had unmistakably emerged victorious as the "most capable" of all. The principle of selection—a naturally inherent "developmental constant" according to the biological model—provided them with the "scientific" confirmation of this. Since it was grounded in biology, this principle could not leave the body unaffected: the Europeans were necessarily also members of a superior "race." Lewis Henry Morgan (1818-1881), highly admired (and "parroted") by Karl Marx and Friedrich Engels, included in this category—albeit only partially—the "Semitic" as well as the "Aryan race." In both he celebrated the "main streams of human progress," referring to them as the "founders of [archaic] civilization."[19] Later, of course, leadership was "assumed by the Aryan family alone,"[20] which from then on constituted the "central stream of human progress, because it produced the highest type of mankind, and because it has proved its intrinsic superiority by gradually assuming control of the earth."[21] According to his American compatriot, the political scientist John William Burgess (1844-1931), only the Aryan race possessed "that genius which shapes civilization."[22] Its superior intelligence and gift for government predestined it, also in Tylor's opinion, to control of the world.[23] Others tended to express themselves even more bluntly; the claim merely changed according to the nationality of the author. "I maintain," declared Cecil Rhodes (1853-1902), who was president of Cape Colony from 1890 until 1896 and who expanded the British "colonial possession" in southeastern Africa to include Bechuanaland and the area later named after him as Rhodesia, "that we are the world's first race, and that the more of this world we rule, the better it is for the entire human race ... What a dream! And yet its realization is possible."[24]

The apparently elevated position of the Euro-Americans was seen as based on nature's gift of a superior genetic make-up, favored by their central position in temperate latitudes and hardened in the test of natural selection, and thus their claim to control of the world appeared to be predestined by the laws of nature, an act of providence. Naive ethnocentrism had effectively stylized itself into a scientifically legitimized, regally clad eurocentrism.

Little wonder then, that science was given credence—to an almost unlimited extent. Even social problems, it was thought, could with certainty be mastered with its help. Condorcet had already made a claim to this effect,[25] Malthus had envisaged a previously underrate-of refining of the human body and intellect, lasting peace and an endless life-expectancy.[26] And Trotsky saw in science the possibility of forming a human being who would be "incomparably stronger, cleverer and more refined" than the present one: "his body will become more harmonic, his movements more rhythmic and his voice more musical"; even average persons would "raise themselves to the level of Aristotle, Goethe and Marx."[27] Decades earlier, Herbert Spencer (1820-1903) had decreed even more apodictically: "the development of the ideal human being is logically certain—as certain as every logical conclusion to which we can give absolute credence."[28]

But what of other, non-European human beings, the "lower races"; were they to have a part in the paradisiacal future; or had they not been long since condemned by the pitiless court of "natural selection"? They, of course, were to be measured against the standard of the European type. "The educated world of Europe and America," according to Tylor, "practically settles a standard by simply placing its own nations at one end of the social series and savage tribes at the other."[29] "Deposited" and ingrained there by the logic of ethnocentrism—according to which one's own reality represents the summit and that which most differs from it the lowest point—they could only appear as "fossils" of earlier, "lower" developmental stages,[30] as "backward,"[31] poor in terms of culture and, in Darwinian terms, fated by dint of the mechanism of selection to be completely erased from the earth.[32]

But the heart of the world was ruled by an inexorable impetus. According to the eurocentric perspective, combined with the basic criteria of evolutionism, this had to appear as a single linear process of progression in order to satisfy the required postulate of continuity. It is this view of things which Peter Burke describes as "the most important, or at least the most obvious characteristic of Western historical thought" (Thesis 1). However, whether intentionally or not, this suggests that what we are addressing here is a specific quality of "Western peoples."[33] In fact, the above merely represents an extreme variant of the identity-ideological—in this case eurocentric—justification for prioritization.

Traditional agricultural village societies were as a rule based on kinship associations (lineages, clans), were of easily comprehensible sizes of between 80 and 200 members bound together by strict rules of reciprocity, were for the most part economically autarkic, politically autonomous and, due to their settled existence, could develop and hand down consistent theories of nature based on unchanging experience. This constituted the precondition for the systems of explaining and legitimizing their social order, institutions, and norms of behavior remaining as comprehensible as they were incontestable. Since such societies were, moreover, relatively isolated from one another, they became differentiated over time—in this sense, similar to "species" in biology—forming cultural individualities with fixed contours and an optimally unifying identity, kept stable by a range of integrative and supportive mechanisms (mutual confirmation and affirmation, demarcation from the outside world, rigorous traditionalism). One consequence of this was the fiction of an uninterrupted continuity stretching back to the beginning of time and the conviction that any serious infringement of a norm could at the same time endanger the functional capacity of the whole, that is, place the existence of all at risk.

In identity-theoretical terms, traditional agricultural societies to this extent constitute ideal-typical model groups, whose generally corresponding characteristics—i.e., those not environmentally or historically conditioned—seem open to generalization as a way of also gaining a better understanding of other societal forms insofar as they fulfill roughly comparable conditions—for instance, comprehensible size, a fixed location over at least three generations, cooperation, a common culture and tradition ("history"). These can then be understood in analytical terms as atrophied, mixed or hypertrophied forms of the identity-theoretical "standard groups."

A principle feature of the ideology of identity is the tendency to render one's own sense of self-worth absolute. Groups with an intact consciousness of identity tend to regard the way of life that has been handed down to them to be the best possible, the ultimate form of all conceivable human realizations of being. Such groups regard themselves as located at the center of the world, the only place where ideal climatic conditions prevail, and claim to descend in a direct line from the first human being, who received life (vitality and free spirit) at precisely this location, directly from the creator. Accordingly, ethnic designations in many cases mean nothing more than "human beings."[34] As the "chosen," one's own people enjoy the particular favor of God. The Bondo in the Indian State of Orissa understand themselves "as the first-born of the whole of humanity; the rest constitute parvenus."[35] A member of the Limbu people in eastern Nepal explained the Limbu view of the world to Rex and Shirley Jones as follows: "In the center are the Limbu, because this is our land and our home. We are number one."[36] According to Plato, as cited above, this role befitted only the Athenians. In the name of early Christendom, Justin "the Martyr" (second century) claimed: "We are a holy people ... not a barbarian tribe or an ethnic mass like the Carians or the Phrygians, but God's chosen."[37] In the prologue to the *Lex Salica* (*Recensio Pippina*) the Franks boast of themselves as an "illustrious people, founded by God the Creator,"[38] while the Byzantines understood themselves as the only ones endowed with God's blessing.[39]

The ideology of identity, that is, ethnocentrism, has a necessary complement, its dark side, so to speak. It follows from the absolutizing of self-worth that everything different found in the ethnically foreign external world, that is, everything that stands in contradiction to one's own order of being, can only appear as inferior, as a product of rudimentary or "abnormal" development, a quality logically proportional to the degree of deviation. A tendency exists to "belittle" the exotic—tools and technologies are dismissed as limited in their usefulness and "raw," customs and ideas as ridiculous, absurd or repulsive, and the people themselves are declared to be "primitives" or "savages." Existing on the periphery of the viewer's respective field of vision, they appear to occupy a position next to that of animals. The instances of such categorization are legion. When questioned by Hans Nevermann, a group in New Guinea declared that their name was *Uir* (men or human beings): for, as they added dismissively: "the other tribes, of course, do not consist of real human beings."[40] The Kurnai in southeastern Australia bluntly described their neighbors of foreign origin as "savage"(*brajerak*).[41] Others, such as the pygmies in the Congo,[42] the Isanzu in Tanzania,[43] or the Mundurukú in north-eastern Brazil categorized them even more uncompromisingly as "animals."[44] Europeans have also been grouped within the ethnic anti-world. To the Trobriand Islanders (New Guinea) they appeared to be mistakes of creation, to be "cripples"[45]; the Washo in Nevada describe them with an expression (*mushege*) usually used to refer to wild animals.[46] In China "the simple equating of barbarian and animal when referring to non-Chinese remained an established commonplace in the two millennia of the imperial period."[47] Aristotle proved the "fact" with the following syllogism: since the human being "is by nature a being which aspires to a state community," other forms of life which exist "external to all state community by nature and not due to accidental circumstances" can only be either more or "less than a human being"—spiritual beings or animals (Politics I 2. 1253 a, 1ff.)!

Societies with some degree of unity and stable identity have a conception of the world that is composed of two antagonistic spheres: the endosphere of one's own world, the only sphere in which human existence appears as ideally realized, is surrounded by an outer-worldly exosphere, which represents the former's negative counterimage and is accordingly ruled by pernicious, destructive forces.[48] This point of view allows for comparison only insofar as it serves the demonstration of one's own uniqueness; it thus tends to amount to "constructed dissimilarity."

In Europe, endospherical development merely took a very special, almost extreme course, one characterized by an exponential increase in the wealth of differentiation processes of all kinds. It follows from this that every transfer of information or goods has to pass through considerably more systems and system groups than in less differentiated cultures, i.e., is subjected to a correspondingly higher number of "diffraction" and "refraction effects." It is precisely this diversity, and therefore apparent "mobility" of events which, when transferred into a temporal perspective, gives the deceptive impression of an acceleration of events.[49] As a consequence, Europeans experience their history as imbued with a particular dynamism. Synthesized with the ideologemes of eurocentrism, this gives rise to the belief that "progressiveness" is a specifically European property, which legitimizes presumption and possibly entails the obligation to engage in a mission of enlightenment.

Diversity of development means "history." In the exospherical external world, where, measured against the central area, hardly anything seems to change or to "move," people are pinned down by stagnation. According to Leopold von Ranke, those living there were "the peoples of an eternal standstill" (*die Völker eines ewigen Stillstandes*). It would be absurd, he argued, to take them as a starting point "in order to grasp the internal movement [!] of world history [!]."[50] Such peoples, as analogously formulated by Kurt Breysig, were "peoples of an eternal primeval time."[51] The historian could consequently disregard them. As an expression of the eurocentric ideology of identity, Ranke and Breysig were certainly not the first to champion this conception. Otto von Freising (c. 1112-1158) provides an example. Comparing Christians and non-Christians ("Jews and Heathens"), he comes to the conclusion that the former make up "all the more significant states, while the latter are insignificant not only before God, but also before the world"; there were "hardly any of their deeds which would be worthy of mention and which would merit being passed on to posterity."[52]

Interest in the savage world was only aroused once profitable treasures began to beckon. This incursion took place without the slightest scruple. After all, the treasures were located—according to the linguistic usage of the time—on "empty" or "abandoned" land[53]—without people in the genuine sense. The English mathematician, biologist and socialist Karl Pearson (1857-1936) described those found there as follows: "The path of human progress is strewn with the decaying bones of old nations, everywhere we can see the traces left behind by inferior races, the victims of those who have not found the narrow path to perfection." They could nevertheless console themselves with the fact that they had formed "the steps upon which humanity has risen to the higher intellectual stage of contemporary life."[54] Yet it was to be expected that in the near future the further ascent of "those who had reached perfection" would leave them behind crushed underfoot.

However, there were still quite a few breathing; indeed, they appeared astoundingly vigorous. Given their numbers, the option of annihilation, although often considered and partially practiced, did not really offer itself as an operable solution. Thus, there remained the choice of training and enslavement or the civilizing process. The colonial powers had the authority to engage in both on the grounds of their being of a higher species. "We are," as an American senator of the time (Albert J. Beveridge) put it, "a conquering race, we must follow the command of our blood ... Our skill in the art of government is a gift from God so that we can govern savage and servile peoples." His compatriot, the historian James Kendall Hosmer (1834-1927), expanded on this: "Anglo-Saxon institutions, Anglo-Saxon thought and the English language will have to become principle features of the political, social and intellectual life of humanity."[55]

There was general agreement on the use of training; it accorded with the nature of the savages, which approximated to that of animals. The Indians, Chinese and Malays had already drawn a distinction between "wild" and "tamed" barbarians.[56] The great Islamic philosopher of history Ibn Khaldun (1332-1406) argued—like many others—that it was more reasonable to accustom the savages to meaningful labor, such as carrying loads, than to let them sit brooding impassively or to conduct costly wars of annihilation against them.[57] Slavery was a universal phenomenon.

The civilizing process appeared more problematic. Some gave it no chance at all. In the case of the Africans there were particular doubts. Voltaire estimated their intellect to be "considerably lower" than that of Europeans, and as simply "incapable of operating with ideas in any discriminating fashion, or of forming connections between them."[58] In their work, *Types of Mankind* (1854), the American physical anthropologists J.C. Nott and G.R. Gliddon expressed the conviction that Black Africa was populated by people "whose intellect is as dark as their skin and whose cranial structure makes every hope of future improvement appear to be a utopian daydream." The German cultural historian Friedrich von Hellwald (1842-1892) rounded off the assessment with the categorical declaration: "The negroes can be trained but not educated."[59]

Others had at least made the attempt; they had held out their hand to the savages and had success—in making them into human beings, a result which was of course exclusively due to the fact that the necessarily iron hand, as the British historian John Beattie Crozier (1849-1921) puts it, took hold "disguised and softened by the paternal glove."[60] This had already been practiced by the Romans in exemplary fashion when they Romanized large parts of the barbarian world. Later an even more elevated motive was added. The church father Clemens of Alexandria (second century) was able to promise the barbarians that as soon as they had "freed themselves from their existence as animals through transformation, through belief in the Lord," they would become "God's people" (*Stromateis* VI 50).

There was yet another motive, the culmination of all others, as it were: with the civilizing process the savages also received the gift of the capacity for history. In this sense Tacitus (c. 55-120 A.D.) is quite consistent in having the history of Britannia in *Agricola* (c. 13-17) first begin with the Roman occupation. In classical Islamic historiography, events among those of a different faith received attention only when they "came into direct contact with the Islamic world."[61] On the hand of their colonial masters, even the "underdeveloped" stepped out of the darkness that had cast a shadow on them into the circle of light of "world history"—initially into the peripheral area of "colonial history." There they have recently been tracked down by "historical ethnology," which only grants them history insofar as it is attested in written form—with means of documentation of "Western" provenance. That which precedes this in time had already been dismissed by the functionalists as "conjectural history."

Peter Burke compares the general "historical culture" of the present with the practice of painting, which, while regionally differing, is overlaid worldwide by the general criteria of the profession together with its possibilities of alternative options. I myself would suggest that a large studio be envisaged in which a master goes from easel to easel and guides the differently colored hands of his pupils—so adroitly that they believe themselves to be painting.

The drawing up of the "General Declaration of Human Rights" by the United Nations (1948) was influenced in no small part by American ethnologists—above all Melville Jean Herskovits (1895-1963), who exercised a decisive influence on the draft declaration presented by the American Anthropological

Association, which in turn had a fundamental influence on the formulation of the "declaration." The document was uncompromising in its adoption of the principles of "cultural relativism." The term was coined by Herskovits himself, who was also the most consistent representative of the concept associated with it. It implied that all cultures represent individual, unique and thus noncomparable units of self-worth that were to be comprehended exclusively in terms of their own conditions, i.e., which could be neither legitimately nor adequately judged by others.[62]

This represented a visible and hopeful step in the direction of the "de-barbarization" of the "primitive" and colonial peoples. Moreover, there were already models that it could refer to. The pioneering forerunner of cultural relativism, the American ethnologist Ruth Benedict (1887-1948) acknowledged the orientation of her work to German traditions. Her work drew in particular on that of Herder, who had emphatically championed the thesis that every culture possessed its own intrinsically valuable individuality and historical uniqueness and was therefore incommensurable with others. In Herder's view, the reason for this was to be found in the action of varying environmental conditions, which shaped cultures in different ways . Every people thus possessed a specific "national character" (or *Volksgeist*—the "spirit of the people"), which lent all its forms of cultural manifestation (social, moral, artistic, religious) their typical, unitary form-giving aspect. But Herder was also a European and thus could not resist taking this bold concept further. He integrated it into a universal "doctrine of development," according to which not only every people, but also humanity in general underwent (by divine will!) a quasi-biomorphemic process of growth that began with "childhood," passed through phases of "boyhood" and "youth," reached its apex in the phase "manhood" and then entered a phase of decay, the phase of "extreme old age." In this model, savages are located at the level of childhood, while Europeans occupy the highest point—"at the top of the tree" (*auf dem Wipfel des Baums*)—without showing any recognizable signs of the onset of senility.[63] The boldness of cultural relativism expired under the weight of eurocentrism, and the advent of evolutionism was heralded.

Nevertheless, the "*Volksgeist* idea" lived on in the shadow of evolutionism, with which it was incompatible. Scholars such as the legal historian Karl von Savigny (1779-1861), the ethnopsychologist Heymann Steinthal (1823-1899), the philosopher Wilhelm Dilthey (1833-1911), the ethnologist Adolf Bastian (1826-1905) and the sociologists Albert Eberhard von Schäffle (1831-1903), Paul von Lilienfeld (1829-1903), Ludwig Gumplovicz (1838-1909) among others remained committed to it, also in conceptual terms.[64] At the same time, it provided the legitimatory basis for the emergent nationalism of that era, entering into an ill-fated alliance with the evolutionism that constituted the driving force behind the inflation of this nationalism into the European conceit of supremacy.

Peter Burke's support for the concept of relativism is both decisive and welcome: "People from different cultures have different conceptions of time and space." Europe is only one case among others. The problem, according to Burke, is determining what is specific to its particular character. He sees consistent cultural comparison as a fundamental means to this end.

However, strictly speaking, relativism excludes comparison, which of course rests on the proposition of possible commonalities. Furthermore, the requirement that cultures be comprehended solely on the basis of their own conditions can only lead to circular explanations. The "liberal" dictum of postmodern authors that each culture has its own "truth" is thus consistent, but the question remains as to who can determine what this truth is.[65] It is precisely here that one finds a fundamental self-contradiction within cultural relativism in general—it formulates a thesis that claims general validity, something which does not accord with its own premises.[66] And it should not be forgotten that the entire construct is a product of Euro-American thought, and in this sense was "prescribed" to the United Nations. Once again, this is based on an—at least—crypto-eurocentric claim, one which Justin Stagl interprets more radically as constituting a type of power dictate.[67]

In physics relativism is based on the demand that there be no privileged observer with reference to both space and time,[68] given the known premise that the same laws of nature apply in all cases at all times. In the case of human societies, at least the first postulate is excluded, since these societies are always—and for good reason—hierarchically structured. Physicists are also members of societies; and some of them, quite contrary to the principles of relativism, understand themselves as being "privileged observers"—they are in this case victims of the "academocentric" viewpoint.[69]

A dilemma remains. Cultural relativism takes the sting out of ethnocentrism, but it is to be understood more as an appeal than as an explanatory theory; it is capable of explaining neither ethnocentrism nor itself. Even more questionable is the fact that it drives cultures into the isolation of "monadically organized individual systems,"[70] a form of overstatement that renders them as genuine singularities, which as such are neither comparable nor capable of explanation.

Singularities can be "facts" that can be played off against all too bold conceptional constructs. At the end of the nineteenth century, the critique of evolutionism began, drawing on the increasing wealth of material being brought to light by archeological finds, ethnographic field research and archival research.[71] There was a desire to know "how it actually was." Peter Burke has shown that such demands were already being expressed before Leopold von Ranke's time. Only now though did research present the possibility of providing a convincing response to the appeal. Dilthey, a student of Ranke, declared that the goal of science could only be that of aspiring to advancing knowledge of the real on the basis of experience. "All science," according to Dilthey's credo, "is experiential science" (*alle Wissenschaft ist Erfahrungswissenschaft*).[72] The Neo-Kantians Wilhelm Windelband (1848-1915) and Heinrich Rickert (1863-1936) provided the philosophical-systematic foundation for this claim. Historical knowledge, argued the latter, solely concerned the recording "of the unique event in terms of the individual course it takes,"[73] while, according to Windelband, natural science was concerned with "establishing, collecting and assimilating its facts only from the standpoint of and for the purpose of understanding the general laws to which these facts are subject."[74] Natural science considered "the always constant form," whereas the object of the historical sciences was "the unique internally defined content of the real event"—that "which once was." In the former case, he spoke, as is well known, of "nomothetic," in the latter of "idiographic" sciences.[75] Rickert's position, while analogous, more precisely addressed the cultural sciences: "The cultural significance of a reality is not based on that which it shares with other realities, but precisely on that which distinguishes it from them … Indeed, the cultural significance of an object commonly increases the more exclusively the cultural value concerned is tied to the distinctive form given to that object."[76]

This signaled a turning away from "nomothetic" evolutionism towards the individualizing, "idiographic" historicism orientated to facts that Friedrich Meinecke, for example, lauded as "one of the greatest intellectual revolutions which occidental thought has undergone."[77] Here too, Peter Burke rightly casts this in relative terms (Thesis 3). His reference to the fact that the nomothetic and idiographic traditions of thought proceeded parallel at least from antiquity onwards, that individualizing tendencies can thus be proved to have a long history, also in cultures outside Europe, somewhat blurs the contours defining why, when and under what concrete conditions one or the other assumed a dominant position. The implications and consequences flowing from this are also worthy of consideration.

In spite of the empirical character of this "factual research"—it was not free of irrationalities. Individualities are not open to explanation. This can be remedied, it is believed, by connecting certain of them with one another where they exhibit proximity to one another temporally or spatially, where they allow the recognition of a relationship, a causal connection on the grounds of similarities.[78] Taken in itself, such an assumption is anything but compelling; this would be the case only if the "event" referred back to a minimal amount of invariant antecedent conditions—only then would it occur repeatedly, thus standing in contradiction to the postulate of individuality. There are nevertheless reasons for positioning related or similar phenomena in relation to one another—reasons, that however, appear to precede historical considerations. David Hume defined them as universal "principles of conceptual combination": one of these employs the criterion of "resemblance," another that of spatial or temporal proximity, or "contiguity."[79] His Scottish compatriot, the previously cited ethnologist James George Frazer, was able to show that what is involved here are the two fundamental principles of magic: the—as he put it—"law of similarity" and the "law of contact or contagion."[80] Psychologists who have specifically looked into the principle of contiguity, and who have thereby been able to provide the clearest proof of its effectiveness in experimental terms, describe it as "a significant and deeply rooted characteristic of thought," which gives rise to "apparent dependence."[81]

If several events are linked in a sequence, a chain of dependence is formed, each link of which increasingly strengthens the others; the impression emerges of a serial, quasi-law-governed succession, an "apparent continuity." The longer the sequence, the more reliable the connection, and the more established the position of the governing link—uninterrupted continuities have a legitimizing function.

This function increases with the significance of the first link, which founded the sequence and lent it the "causal thrust" upon which legitimization is established. Divine ancestors, hegemonic genealogies, heroes as creators of important institutions, legendary city founders, founders of religions and "forerunners" all stand for this. European scholars have referred—as Peter Burke notes—to the scholars and intellectual traditions of antiquity (and not only since the Renaissance). In antiquity itself, traditions circulated according to which great minds such as Pythagoras, Thales of Miletus, Eudoxos of Cnidus and Plato traveled to the Orient to learn from the "sages" there (among them Zarathustra!).[82] The Copts claim to be the "racially pure successors" of the ancient Egyptians.[83] Islamic Somalis claim to be the oldest representatives of their faith on the basis that Adam, from whom they claim to be descended "in an uninterrupted line of succession," was the first Muslim to walk the earth[84]—here too, the evidence is legion.

The "question of the 'first'," says the scholar of Islam Albrecht Noth, is "quite legitimate and also fundamental for the modern historian." There are writings in Islamic literature from the middle of the ninth century "in which the exclusive focus is the question of the initial instance, applied to a wide range of areas"; the beginnings of such an approach can be found from the seventh century onwards. The concern here is with determining, for example, who first forced his way into a defeated city, who first killed a Persian, who the first commander was to advance into Syria, who first constructed a two-story building in Cairo, who first forbid the wearing of the burnous.[85]

The search for the *prima causa* holds a particular fascination—due to both its primary causal and its legitimatory functions; if the "origin" is named, it is believed that one is better able to understand, indeed explain the subsequent course of development, including the final result. The well-known French paleontologist and prehistorian André Leoi-Gourhan expresses the conviction that since "earliest times and at all levels of the development of civilisation" this search has numbered "among the fundamental occupations of human beings."[86] For Leibniz, as Werner Conze in particular points out, the question of the *origines* was an elemental concern of the historical sciences.[87]

This is certainly consistent with the ethnological experience—albeit not in the sense of a procedural postulate. There is no ethnic group that is not keen to name its ancestors and its place of origin. In most cases this point of origin is

identified with the territory inhabited by the group, the place where the fore-
bear was allegedly created by the hand of God as the first human being, the
place to which he descended on a rope from heaven or where he emerged from
the earth. The implicit assertion is that whoever seizes possession of something,
creates something, transforms wilderness into cultivated land is entitled to it, has
a "prior right" to it. The ancient, mythical founding figure retained a consistent
presence throughout the literature of antiquity. In the—more in-depth—consideration by both the Greeks and the Romans of peoples, cities and cults,
among other things, the "story of origin," *archaiología* or *origo*, formed a fixed
topos of ethnology and historiography, usually performing an introductory function; in part it continued to play a role up to and including the development of
the medieval "historiography of peoples" (Jordanes, Isidor of Seville, Gregory of
Tours, Paulus Diaconus, Widukind of Corvey).[88] As part of his declared
endeavor to define the specific character of the Euro-American understanding
of history, it is precisely in the purposeful research into causes that Peter Burke
claims to have identified "a distinctively Western characteristic" (Thesis 6). In
this connection he also refers to the ancients—establishing a continuity—and in
particular to the significance of the *aitia* for the Greeks. Ethnology, however,
recognizes a specific genre of transmission, which is represented by stories
whose subject is precisely this particular interest in causes—and which are
therefore not by chance described as "etiologies." Their themes can include, for
example, why certain birds have red beaks or why women are not skilled at
hunting, the origin of the sunset or why neighboring peoples build their huts
in another fashion. Here too, then, a relative approach is required.

Perhaps the question should rather be posed as to the cause of the historical interest in causes. Normally the identification of primary causal instances
involves the naming of one person (a founder, ruler, commander, inventor) or
one particular event (the birth of a future figure of greatness, a battle, the post-
ing of Luther's theses, the Hidshra,[89] a discovery, a catastrophe). The impression
emerges of a cone stood on its vertex—the "cause" contracts to a point, a
nucleus or a seed that holds the possibility of development into an open future;
if one reverses the cone, movement upwards converges to a point—towards a
foreseeable end, a prospect which is only reluctantly identified with. This would
constitute a possible identity-theoretical explanation.

And why precisely this ruler, that invention or that battle? A closer investigation reveals further "causes" underlying the one identified, which for their
part are interwoven with a wealth of vertical and horizontal branchings that
extend ad infinitum until ultimately reaching the "uncertain" world of particle
physics governed by the laws of probability. And there one likewise finds only
"endless layers of increasing subtlety." Every attempt, according to the physicist
David Peat "to reach the most fundamental level" leads into a veritable labyrinth
of "still deeper, unexplained processes."[90] De facto there is no "single cause" just
as there are no "causal chains ... which can be reduced to linear connections

between single events." Such causal chains are dissolved and cushioned by the general interconnectedness of events.[91]

And even given it were possible to define an isolatable point of origin, this would only represent a Pyrrhic victory; since what is involved here is a singularity, which as such is not only itself resistant to explanation, and thus not suitable as a conclusive explanatory tool, but which shares with others of its kind the quality of its dimensions being irrelevant to its definition. The smallest imaginable particle is just as much a singularity as the universe is. Contracting causation to a point would not achieve a result other than that of perhaps being thrown back into universal interconnectedness.

However, just as within social reality there are clearly "privileged observers," "single origins" can also be fixed there, by dint of decisionistic access. More or less conscious decisions based on more or less conscious criteria of choice play a role here (the "power interests" often referred to constitute only one, albeit an influential aspect). The "causes," "causal chains" and "continuities" which then become apparent constitute only one possible rough version of how the point of origin "actually" was.

Nevertheless, in such a version—whatever the "accompanying interests" involved—arbitrary choice plays only a limited role. Those who acted (and who act—as historians, for example) were always members of groups and thus followed, to a lesser or greater extent, the criteria of identity-specific behavior, also in the formation of ideas. Ethnology is capable of exactly identifying these with the aid of wide-ranging cultural comparison. They conform in terms of their essential features everywhere, being founded on a set of universal guiding principles. This, as it were, would constitute a nomothetic framework. Peter Burke seems to indicate something similar when he insists at the outset that "what is particular to Western historical thought" is to be understood "not as a series of unique characteristics, but rather as a unique combination of elements each of which is to be found elsewhere."[92]

Identity-theoretical precedents can also account for the emergence of historical consciousness: as comparative studies show (and by no means only in reference to traditional societies and archaic civilizations) it ignites or revives without fail in societal conflict situations—as a consequence of quarrels that cast doubt on inherited legal rights, in cases of ethnic overlap, in the wake of enforced acculturation or radical innovations that shake the edifice of tradition as a whole. The consequences are social, ethnic, religious processes of differentiation: splits, alliances, the formation and reformation of groupings result, with corresponding disassociations and breaks in the ideology of identity. Cracks appear in myth (the story of creation) as a generally binding basis of authentication. The separated clan, partially or newly formed groups, strata, classes necessarily modify this basis according to their particular needs, but in addition look for further secondary grounds for their identity-specific postulates of priority; the localization of such grounds is inevitably confined to the post-primeval phase, in which human beings increasingly gain influence over events. These are then disseminated by sagas and legends—and also by historical traditions, and, ultimately, by professional history.[93] They name founders, kings and innovators, pioneering migrations, miraculous events, victorious battles and reforms that have contributed to the ascent of one's own group to the apex, or at least provide grounds for its legitimate claim to this position. Individuals and events gain significance—singularities attract renewed interest. The need for grounds and the efforts to assemble individual proofs to, as it were, "smoothly pave" the "historical" avenue of claims increase in proportion to the dynamism and complexity of the differentiation processes involved. The science of history becomes indispensable; idiography comes into its own.[94] And the longer the historical tradition of one historically representative instance lasts, the more the impression is created of focused interconnections of events, that is, of linear, progressive development.

Nonetheless, in the medium-term, constant tendencies to "recycle," so to speak, are noticeable. The safeguarding of identity within the system, the preservation of its coherence, also requires the stabilization of institutions and norms. The periodization of the life and work processes, annual and commemorative festivals attached to specific dates, jubilee celebrations of foundation, electoral cycles and the demarcation of periods of political office fabricate the "eternal return," the preservation of that which is indisputably worthy of continued existence, safeguarding and consolidating the foundation that annuls the threatening aspect of dynamism and change.

Nomothetics and idiography by no means have to suppress one another. On the contrary, they necessarily form a complementary whole. In itself, each perspective leads into the "academocentric" if not fideistic cul-de-sac and distorts knowledge. "Historical anthropology" represents one possible means of a unitary interpretation—not because it is somewhat fashionable at the moment, but because of the optimal conditions it offers, precisely in its combining of ethnology and history—for a better and also operable understanding of human societies in both historical and present contexts.

Seen in the context of this task, historical anthropology can also be linked with a "founding father" worthy of the title. As Herodotus once put it: if required "to select the customs of highest quality from all those available, each people, after examining all of the different customs, would prefer its own above all others. So great is the pervasiveness among human beings of the opinion that the forms of life which they themselves have developed are the best" (III 38). Herodotus recognized the ethnological rule, and he is rightly celebrated as the "father of history."

Centuries later and still before our own epoch, Spinoza wrote down something which could be recommended to all, and not least eurocentrically deluded, human science: "*humanas actiones non ridere, non lugere, neque detestari, sed intelligere.*"[95]

Notes

1. Kaj Birket-Smith, *Geschichte der Kultur. Eine allgemeine Ethnologie,* Munich, 1948, 5.
2. Konrad Lorenz, *Die Rückseite des Spiegels. Versuch einer Naturgeschichte menschlichen Erkennens,* Munich, 1973, 162f.
3. Karl R. Popper, *Objektive Erkenntnis. Ein evolutionärer Entwurf,* Hamburg, 1973, 36.
4. Klaus E. Müller, *Geschichte der antiken Ethnographie und ethnologischen Theoriebildung. Von den Anfängen bis auf die byzantinischen Historiographen,* vol. 1, Wiesbaden, 1972, 55, 65, 75f., 126.
5. Ibid., 142.
6. Klaus E. Müller, 'Geschichte der Ethnologie', in *Ethnologie. Einführung und Überblick* ed. Hans Fischer, Berlin, 1992, 28f.
7. Müller, Klaus E., 'Grundzüge des menschlichen Gruppenverhaltens', in *Biologie von Sozialstrukturen bei Tier und Mensch,* Göttingen, 1983, 109.
8. Müller, *Geschichte der antiken Ethnographie,* (see note 4), 126.
9. Ibid. 137ff.
10. Klaus E. Müller, 'Geschichte der Ethnologie', (see note 6), 27f.
11. Reinhard Goll, *Der Evolutionismus. Analyse eines Grundbegriffs neuzeitlichen Denkens,* Munich, 1972, 23.
12. Edward B. Tylor, *Primitive Culture,* vol. 1, London 1871, 2.
13. Goll, *Evolutionismus* (see note 11), 83; cf. Theodor Waitz, *Anthropologie der Naturvölker,* vol 1, Leipzig 1877, 12; Edward B. Tylor, *Researches into the Early History of Mankind and the Development of Civilization,* London 1870, 90.
14. John F. McLennan, *Studies in Ancient History,* London 1896, 9.
15. James George Frazer, *Psyche's Task. A Discourse Concerning the Influence of Superstition on the Growth of Institutions,* London, 1913, 168.
16. Robert L. Carneiro, 'Classical Evolution', in *Main Currents in Cultural Anthropology* eds Raoul & Frada Naroll, Englewood Cliffs, 1973, 82ff.
17. Caneiro, 'Classical Evolution' (see note 16), 109f.
18. Ibid., 90ff.
19. Lewis H. Morgan, *Ancient Society,* Cambridge, Mass., 1964, 427, 40f.
20. Ibid., 41.
21. Ibid., 475.
22. Hansjoachim W. Koch, *Der Sozialdarwinismus. Seine Genese und sein Einfluß auf das imperialistische Denken,* Munich, 1973, 120f.
23. Edward B. Tylor, *Anthropology. An Introduction to the Study of Man and Civilization,* vol. 1, London, 1930, 58.
24. Koch, *Sozialdarwinismus* (see note 22), 91.
25. Goll, *Evolutionismus* (see note 11), 16.
26. Koch, *Sozialdarwinismus* (see note 22), 27f.
27. Leo Trotzkij, *Literatur und Revolution,* Berlin, 1968, 215.
28. Koch, *Sozialdarwinismus* (see note 22), 20.
29. Tylor, *Primitive Culture* (see note 12), 23.
30. Carneiro, 'Classical Evolution' (see note 16), 72ff.
31. James George Frazer, *Folk-Lore in the Old Testament. Studies in Comparative Religion, Legend, and Law,* vol. 1, London, 1919, p. vii.
32. Charles Darwin, *Die Abstammung des Menschen und die geschlechtliche Zuchtwahl,* vol. 1, Stuttgart 1871, 139.
33. This is in fact held by many to be the case. Rudolf Wendorff, for example, refers to "thinking in terms of progress as a new, dynamic attitude on the part of Western humanity [my emphasis] towards its history." See Rudolf Wendorff, *Zeit und Kultur. Geschichte des Zeitbewußtseins in Europa,* Opladen, 1980, 326.
34. Müller, 'Grundzüge' (see note 7), 102f.

35. Verrier Elwin, *Bondo Highlander*, Bombay, 1950, 266.
36. Rex L. and Shirley K. Jones, *The Himalayan Woman. A study of Limbu Women in Marriage and Divorce*, Palo Alto, 1976, 40.
37. Iustinus Martyr, 'Dialogus cum Tryphone Judaeo', c. 119, in *Patrologiae Cursus Completus. Series* ed. J.P. Migne Graeca, vol. 6, 212, col. 752. Cf. Clemens of Alexandria, *Protreptikos XII* 123, 1.
38. Cited in Walther Lammers, 'Vorwort', in *Geschichtsdenken und Geschichtsbild im Mittelalter*, ed. Walther Lammers, Darmstadt, 1965, xvl.
39. Müller, *Geschichte der antiken Ethnographie* (see note 4), vol. 2, Wiesbaden, 1980, 426.
40. Hans Nevermann, *Die Naturvölker und die Humanität*, Leipzig, 1948, 11f.
41. Alfred William Howitt, 'The Jeraeil, or Initiation Ceremonies of the Kurnai Tribe', *The Journal of the Anthropological Institute of Great Britain and Ireland* 14 (1885), 301, fn. 3, 311, fn. 8.
42. Peter Weidkuhn, 'Die Rechtfertigung des Mannes aus der Frau bei Ituri-Pygmäen', *Anthropos*, 68, no. 3-4 (1973), 447.
43. Ludwig Kohl-Larsen, *Wildbeuter in Ostafrika. Die Tindiga, ein Jäger- und Sammlervolk*, Berlin, 1958, 31.
44. Robert F. Murphy, 'Intergroup Hostility and Social Cohesion', *American Anthropologist*, 59 (1957), 1028.
45. Bronislaw Malinowski, *The Sexual Life of the Savages in North-Western Melanesia*, London, 1932, 258.
46. James F. Downs, *The Two Worlds of the Washo. An Indian Tribe of California and Nevada*, New York, 1966, 78.
47. Claudius Müller, 'Die Herausbildung der Gegensätze. Chinesen und Barbaren in der frühen Zeit (1. Jahrtausend v. Chr. bis 220 n. Chr.)', in *China und die Fremden. 3000 Jahre Auseinandersetzung in Krieg und Frieden*, ed. Wolfgang Bauer, Munich, 1980, 60.
48. Klaus E. Müller, 'Identität und Geschichte. Widerspruch oder Komplementarität?', *Paideuma*, 38 (1992), 25f..
49. Müller, 'Identität und Geschichte' (see note 48), 20.
50. Leopold von Ranke, *Weltgeschichte*, 4th edn., vol. 1, section 1, Leipzig 1886, viii.
51. This is the title he gave the first volume of his *Geschichte der Menschheit*, Berlin, 1907.
52. Otto von Freising, *Chronica sive Historia de duabus civitatibus*, V, Proömium.
53. Otto Köbner, *Einführung in die Kolonialpolitik*, Jena, 1908, 15, 196. Cf. Charles Dickens, *Martin Chuzzelwit*, Munich, 331.
54. Koch, *Sozialdarwinismus* (see note 22), 117f.
55. Ibid., 115, 120f.
56. Wilhelm E. Mühlmann, *Rassen, Ethnien, Kulturen. Moderne Ethnologie*, Neuwied, 1964, 191; Müller, 'Die Herausbildung der Gegensätze' (see note 47), 53.
57. Susanne Enderwitz, *Gesellschaftlicher Rang und ethische Legitimation*, Freiburg i. Br., 1979, 49, cf. 26ff.
58. Carlos Moore, *Were Marx and Engels White Racists? The Prolet-Aryan Outlook of Marx and Engels*, Chicago, 1972, 12.
59. Wilhelm Schneider, *Die Naturvölker. Mißverständnisse, Mißdeutungen und Mißhandlungen*, vol. 2, Paderborn 1885/6, 168.
60. Koch, *Sozialdarwinismus*, (see note 22), 93.
61. Bertold Spuler, 'Islamische und abendländische Geschichtsschreibung. Eine Grundsatz-Betrachtung', *Saeculum* 6, no. 2 (1955), 130.
62. Müller, 'Geschichte der Ethnologie', (see note 6), 45.
63. See above all his *Ideen zur Philosophie der Geschichte der Menschheit*, 4 vols., first published 1784-91. See also Eberhard Berg, 'Johann Gottfried Herder (1744-1803)', in *Klassiker der Kulturanthropologie*, ed. Wolfgang Marschall, Munich, 1990, 51-68; Müller, 'Geschichte der Ethnologie' (see note 6), 34.
64. Müller, 'Geschichte der Ethnologie' (see note 6), 43f.

65. Hans Georg Soeffner, 'Kultursoziologie zwischen Kulturwelten und Weltkultur. Zu Joachim Matthes (ed.), Zwischen den Kulturen? Die Sozialwissenschaften vor dem Problem des Kulturvergleichs', *Soziologische Revue*, 18 (1995), 12.

66. Müller, 'Geschichte der Ethnologie' (see note 6), 46.

67. Justin Stagl, 'Über die Stellung der Ethnologie zur Entwicklungspolitik', in *Soziokulturelle Faktoren der Entwicklungszusammenarbeit und der Beitrag der Ethnologie*, ed. Frank Bliss, Bonn, 1986, 57.

68. Timothy Ferris, *Die rote Grenze. Auf der Suche nach dem Rand des Universums*, Basel, 1982, 126.

69. Magoroh Maruyama, 'Endogenous Research vs. Delusions of Relevance and Expertise among Exogenous Academics', *Human Organization*, 33 (1974), 318ff.

70. Soeffner, 'Kultursoziologie' (see note 65), 12.

71. Klaus E. Müller, 'Grundzüge des ethnologischen Historismus', in *Grundfragen der Ethnologie. Beiträge zur gegenwärtigen Theorie-Diskussion*, eds Wolfdietrich Schmied-Kowarzik, Justin Stagl, Berlin, 1993, 199.

72. Wilhelm Dilthey, *Einleitung in die Geisteswissenschaften. Versuch einer Grundlegung für das Studium der Gesellschaft und der Geschichte*, Leipzig, 1923, xvl.

73. Heinrich Rickert, *Kulturwissenschaft und Naturwissenschaft*, Freiburg i. Br. 1899, 39, cf. 37ff., 52.

74. Wilhelm Windelband, *Präludien. Aufsätze und Reden zur Philosophie und ihrer Geschichte*, vol. 2, Tübingen, 1924, 143.

75. Ibid. 145ff.

76. Rickert, *Kulturwissenschaft* (see note 73), 45, cf. 37.

77. Friedrich Meinecke, *Die Entstehung des Historismus*. Werke, vol. 3, Stuttgart, 1959, 1.

78. Edward Hallet Carr, *Was ist Geschichte?*, Stuttgart, 1972, 8f.

79. David Hume, *Essays and Treatises on Several Subjects*, vol. 2, Edinburgh 1809, 24.

80. James George Frazer, *The Magic Art and the Evolution of Kings*, vol. 1, London, 1963, 52ff. See Klaus E. Müller, *Das magische Universum der Identität. Elementarformen sozialen Verhaltens*, Frankfurt a.M., 1987, 207ff.

81. John Cohen, Mark Hansel, *Glück und Risiko. Die Lehre von der subjektiven Wahrscheinlichkeit*, Frankfurt a.M., 1961, 38.

82. Müller, *Das magische Universum* (see note 80), 210.

83. Muna Nabhan, 'Kopten und Muslime in Ägypten. Eigenverständnis und Vorurteil', MA–Thesis, Frankfurt a. M., 1988, 57ff.

84. Günther Schlee, *Das Glaubens- und Sozialsystem der Rendille, Kamelnomaden Nord-Kenias*, Berlin, 1979, 277.

85. Albrecht Noth, *Quellenkritische Studien zu Themen, Formen und Tendenzen frühislamischer Geschichtsüberlieferung*, Bonn, 1973, 97f.

86. André Leroi-Gourhan, *Hand und Wort. Die Evolution von Technik, Sprache und Kunst*, Frankfurt a. M., 1980, 13.

87. Werber Conze, *Leibniz als Historiker*, Berlin, 1951, 58f.

88. See Klaus E. Müller, *Geschichte der antiken Ethnographie* (see note 39), 340ff.

89. See Julius T. Fraser, *Die Zeit. Auf den Spuren eines vertrauten und doch fremden Phänomens*, Munich, 1992, 118f.

90. F. David Peat, *Synchronizität. Die verborgene Ordnung*, Munich, 1992, 210.

91. Ibid., 53, 56ff.

92. Cf. Soeffner, 'Kultursoziologie' (see note 65), 13.

93. Müller, 'Identität und Geschichte' (see note 48), 26; Klaus E. Müller, '"Prähistorisches" Geschichtsbewußtsein. Versuch einer ethnologischen Strukturbestimmung', *ZiF: Mitteilungen*, 1995 (no.3), 13ff.

94. Müller, 'Identität und Geschichte' (see note 48), 28.

95. Spinoza, *Tractatus politicus*, I 4.

Searching for Common Principles
A Plea and Some Remarks on the Islamic Tradition

TARIF KHALIDI

Peter Burke's paper is an elegant and finely nuanced defense of a thesis, which, when stripped of elegance and nuance, argues that since the Renaissance Western historical thought has developed a number of characteristics that appear to distinguish it from other, non-Western historical thought. What is the purpose of this thesis? The answer is: "Only after we have made the inventory of differences between historical thought in the West and in other parts of the globe will it be possible to make a systematic investigation of the reasons for these differences." Implicit in this particular formulation of the problem is a challenge: This is what we think, or have thought, about history. What is your response?

There are various strategies of commentary that one can adopt by way of an answer. One such strategy would be to consider the following scenario. Let us suppose that UNESCO (United Nations Educational, Scientific, and Cultural Organizations) has delegated a committee to put together an anthology of world historiography. Let us further assume that the members of this committee divided into two groups as regards the table of contents of that anthology. One group argued for a geographical division into, for example "Western," "Western Asian," "African," and "Eastern Asian" historical texts. The other group argued for a thematic division into, for example "Argument," "Cause," "Preface," "Evidence" and "Style." What might the arguments be on either side of this divide? I can think of at least one overriding advantage of the thematic division: it would rid us of the illusion that texts can be considered simply or solely as "examples" of their civilization or nation. In other words, one might argue that the broad principles of historical writing and thought emanate from a common human environment where the investigation of the diversity of stimuli to historical writing would be our primary concern.

What these "broad principles" of historiography might be can, I think, be briefly set forth as follows. Historiography everywhere and in all ages has been a borrowing and sheltering activity. It borrows its purpose from ethics and politics. It borrows its method from philosophy and natural science. It borrows its style from literature. And it seeks shelter under the umbrellas of reason or revelation. If one were to posit this or a similar image, one might then be tempted to emulate Thomas S. Kuhn's *Structure of Scientific Revolutions* and to seek for a structure of historiographic revolutions. It would seem to me that this sort of pursuit would be not only more intellectually exciting but also truer to the way things have been.

As regards the "diversity of stimuli," one might cite the following areas of investigation. First is the way in which a particular culture or people learn a new historiography when they acquire a new religion or ideology, and how this affects their perception of things like time, causation, origins and ends. Second is the way in which new formulations of the power or legitimacy of states affect historical writing and thought, in such areas as identity formation or the struggle between natural and supernatural sources of law. Third is the way in which bureaucratic elites have defined the agenda of history and dictated its standards of veracity. It would seem to me that the search for these or similar stimuli across cultures is ultimately more rewarding than to cordon historiographic traditions off from one another in pursuit of Burke's "inventory of differences."

I suspect that Peter Burke would not necessarily object to the reformulation of the problem set forth above. After all, his own very pronounced interests in comparative historiography would lead one to this conclusion. But perhaps something more is required than the suggestion of alternative strategies to the inventory-of-differences-approach. I have in mind a number of special difficulties that beset Burke's approach and that I would like to enumerate, in no particular order of importance, as follows:

1. Linear vs. cyclical (thesis 1)

I have always felt rather uneasy about this contrast, particularly when it is used to distinguish between two quite different approaches to the tempo and the end of history. When posited as an either/or alternative, it tends to oversimplify. Let us, for the sake of argument consider the spiral view of history. Would it not be possible to maintain that a historian can indeed believe in cycles but also believe that history is moving towards a definite end? It would seem to me that many working historians are impressed by both recurrent patterns as well as linear evolution or progress. Perhaps one should speak not in terms of linear and cyclical but rather of teleological and nonteleological conceptions of history. Where Ibn Khaldun's *Muqaddimah* is concerned, it is not at all clear that the overall pattern of historical development can simply be described as cyclical. Thus, the arts and sciences of a particular era may well survive and continue to develop *sine fine*. Khaldun was himself acutely aware of the fact that his own science of human culture was entirely original.

2. The Idea of Progress

This idea is linked by Burke to the idea of cyclical and linear historical thought. But it too needs to be anatomized a little further. In the same historian, different conceptions of progress may coexist, for example moral and intellectual. It is possible, for instance, to hold that mankind is declining on the moral level but advancing on the intellectual. I suspect that the belief in intellectual progress in all cultures is intimately linked to intellectual climates that are deeply impressed by the achievements of natural science. These climates of historiography seem to me to offer the most challenging avenues of exploration.

3. "Distinctive" means "central" and "for a longer time" (thesis 2)

That this or that pattern of historiographic emphasis is "distinctively Western" is said by Burke to be so because of its centrality and continuity. But neither quality, it seems to me, is particularly easy to substantiate when historiographic traditions are being investigated. To begin with, historical thought as such is by no means confined to historians. Indeed one might be tempted to argue that in all cultural traditions theoretical reflections on history are most frequently to be found in works of belles-lettres, philosophy and political science, rather than among bread-and-butter historians. At such levels of generality, the establishment of centrality and continuity within any one particular historiographic tradition becomes acutely difficult. Burke asks: has the problem of historical "evidence" been as tightly "embedded" in law in other historiographic traditions as it has been in Western tradition? The answer, for the Islamic historiographic tradition at least, is a very extensive and pervasive tradition of interaction: not yet fully investigated, it is true, but clearly both central and continuous. One might cite the legal literature, on questions such as witness (*shahada*), the chain of transmitters (*isnad*) and single versus multiple transmission (*ahad, tawatur*) and the impact that all these legal discussions had on historiography.

4. The "emplotment of history" (thesis 9)

Here too, I have often felt uneasy about the usefulness of literary tropes for historical analysis. Quite apart from the arbitrariness of the tropes themselves and their capacity for almost infinite multiplication and variety, the more general question as to how literary conventions have affected historical styles resembles the question of law and historical evidence discussed above. It seems to me axiomatic that if historiography is indeed a borrowing activity, it would be only natural for it to borrow its style too from the literary conventions available to it at any one period of time. This is particularly so when history itself is regarded, as it has so often been, as an adjunct to the complete education of a courtier, say, or "gentleman." Where the Islamic tradition is concerned, one can point to the tradition of *Ahab* (belles-lettres or, better still, *Paidea*) as formative in the genesis and evolution of Islamic historiography.

5. How European are such movements as the "Renaissance" and the "Reformation"?

I suspect that no extensive historiographic tradition can ever be free of these major landmarks of historical periodization. In any history of culture or ideas, one can hardly do without them. The fact that these particular terms were applied, beginning in the nineteenth century, by European Orientalists to the history of non-European cultures seems to me to be a reflection of the great accumulation in knowledge of the non-European world by modern Europe. But there is nothing inherently or distinctively European about them or about their use as descriptions of what Burke calls "cultural and social movements."

But then what might happen if we reverse the course of argument so far and attempt to answer Burke's challenge while accepting his basic assumptions of European distinctiveness? Let us assume, in other words, that the inventory of differences is a legitimate way to proceed. I would almost certainly begin with a sense of unease as I try to record the distinctiveness in certain features of, say, Islamic historiography when I do not know the other historiographic traditions as well as I should. But let us for the sake of argument attempt a very brief Burkean counter-inventory for Islamic historiography. I will speak of only two:

1. A sustained and distinctive interest in the history and ethnography of non-Muslim nations

It may be argued that the Islamic historiographic tradition displays, from its inception and right until the eighteenth century at least, a distinct, extensive and very decided interest in the history and culture of the non-Muslim world. The *India* of Biruni (c. 1050) is one of the finest monuments of this anthropological-historical tradition. But long before Biruni, Muslim historians had decided that as Islam was the last religion of mankind, so it also was the heir of world civilizations. From this emanated a concern, clearly "distinctive," for civilization as a concept accompanying the history of various nations.

2. A sustained and distinctive interest in biography

Biographical dictionaries constitute an immense and distinctive part of Islamic historiography right until the present day. These dictionaries contain the biographies, long as well as short, of hundreds of thousands of men and women of almost all walks of life and in almost all periods of Islamic history. They have hardly been used as sources for the reconstruction of the faces and characters of premodern and modern Islam. Accepting Burke's caveat about the danger of imposing modern notions of the personality on premodern biography, one can nevertheless assert that these biographies endow Islamic historiography with a vividness, a variety and an individuality unique, or so one might argue.

Clearly one can add to this counterinventory. But if we now follow Burke's advice and proceed to a "systematic investigation of the reasons for these differences" what sort of results will we obtain? Would we conclude, for instance, that Islam's chronological position among world religions is responsible for its thinking of itself as heir to world civilizations? Was Islam's emphasis on moral challenge and individual salvation the reason for its excessive interest in the details of individual biographies? I do not think that these or similar answers lead us very far. By their very nature, such explanations are arbitrary, unstable, ambiguous.

The object of detailed studies of specific historiographical traditions is not to leave us marooned on little islands of unique particularities but rather to try to formulate these detailed studies so as to encourage an inventory of resemblances. I have suggested above that the comparative investigation of what may be called the stimuli of historical thought and writing across cultures could offer a more fruitful avenue of exploration for comparative historiography.

The Coherence of the West

AZIZ AL-AZMEH

Peter Burke's text is structured by two elements, uneasily juxtaposed, in the manner of the 1990s: these are the two tropes of modern historical conception, the vitalist and the positivist. The former supplies the notions of distinctiveness and continuity in combination, and is underwritten by the culturalist and relativist temptations and desires of the 1990s. The latter prompts self-reflection, reserve about the strong ideological and mythological implications of distinctiveness and continuity, and is sustained by scholarship. I will follow suit in radically questioning some assumptions upon which the vitalist trope stands.

1.

It is difficult to ground the "distinctiveness of the West" meaningfully without resort to the vitalist trope and to metaphors of the organism and of generic continuity. Professor Burke is clearly not in the business of constructing yet another version of "the uniqueness of the West" romance, recently in renewed ascendance in the shadow of impoverished readings of Weber; and it may indeed be fair to see Western distinctiveness as "a unique combination of elements each of which is to be found elsewhere, a pattern of emphases, which themselves vary by period, region, social group and individual historian." But do we thereby, in this combination of elements, have a structured pattern, that is, a combination of elements internally connected and consistent (without this necessarily implying consistency)?

I believe we do not. What we have, rather, is a register of various views and divergences without necessary connections, sequences, or taxonomic implications; views and divergences whose unity is seen to be a direct consequence of their putative Western genealogy, this being their implicit principle of generic continuity and organismic unity. The West is here understood both as a place which is associated with a fairly homogeneous (hence Western) conception of

Notes for this section can be found on page 54.

history, and as a continuous sequence of time. I should like empirically to contest both these elements, and, further, to suggest that endowing them with a
substantive presence, an ontological weight, requires extrahistorical assumptions
of durability and consistency. These assumptions can only derive from
metaphors of the organism.

I take the liberty of making this last assertion because I believe the modern age—like previous ages—makes available a limited repertoire of conceptual means by which people might formally state positions on the past, on the
social order, on political organizations, and on much else besides. Sentiments of
identity, inclusion, and exclusion, like other sentiments, are not concepts, and
need a conceptual articulation in order to be enunciated. The two conceptions
of history available are the vitalist (premised, *nolens volens*, on an organismic
conception of significant historical objects, such as the nation, the people, the
West, or Islam), and the positivist (which does not necessarily have to bear a
teleological evolutionism).

The former[1] is of course of great moment in European and indeed universal political and social thought in the last two centuries, animating most particularly the universal ideologies of nationalism and populism, and other forms
of romanticism. Though its moment appears somewhat indistinct in recent
textbooks and to the contemporary consciousness, this is rather a wishful exci-
sion and abridgement of historical reality by the liberal order that followed
World War II. Organismic romanticism in the conception of history derives its
conceptual profile ultimately from medieval natural-philosophical and medical
notions, such as temper and nature as states of balance and rest and as an ent-
elechy: this connection is explicit in Herder, who even deploys the conception
of the "great chain of being," in its medieval and explicitly nonevolutionist
understanding. As often happens when thinking in metaphorical terms, the
derivative term is made fully to be the metaphor incarnate; a complete con-
substantiation is assumed to relate the metaphor and the metaphorized in which
the rhetorical distance is lost and the last becomes the first. Thus are historical
subjects conceived in terms of living organisms, and thus is history narrated as
the romance of this Western, Islamic, or otherwise denominated subject.

That the discourse on cultures today, with its emphasis on individuality
(rather than particularity), on correlative notion of "meaning," of "incommensurability," of "hermeneutics," declares itself postmodern, does not convince me
that it is not in direct conceptual continuity with medieval vitalism. The sentiments and political and social wills to distinctiveness can only be consistently
articulated in terms of the vitalist trope.

Clearly, this is not a trope of which Peter Burke partakes. What I wish to
emphasize by bringing up the matter of vitalism is that it is needed to sustain
the imputation of unity to the West—and the Western historical tradition—as a
historical object homogeneous in time (continuity) and in space (essential
coherence). It subtends the integrity of time and of place attributed to the West.

2.

Peter Burke does declare that the West is a historical construct, and casts doubts on whether Herodotus would have regarded himself a European or a Westerner. I should like to take this further than comforting recognition, and use it to question one element in the presumption of Western continuity and to subvert the mythogenic proclivity of genealogy.

That the Roman republicanist model and certain Greek traditions were traditionalized and adopted as a European heritage in the Renaissance is very well known. It is also well-known that, in the eighteenth century, the Egyptian and other "orientalizing" genealogies adopted by the Greeks themselves, were displaced in favor of one or another version of the tale of the Greek miracle, which constituted the initial terminus in the normative and progressive course of civility and rationality. The notion of the somehow miraculous nature of the Greek phenomenon is not unnatural, given the requirement of all genealogies that beginnings be absolute.

The recognition of these matters should in itself have a salutary influence, and stem, by a historical deconstruction, the temptation to translate the typological construction of history underlying all genealogies (this is a matter I shall come back to below) into an evolutionist register, to seek praiseworthy ancestry, to see the present prefigured in the remote past.

Yet this Greek, or a more generally antique past, is not in a serious historical way the past of the West despite the use of Roman typologies by Machiavelli, Ingres, or Napoleon, or of the Greek alphabet in mathematical formulas, or indeed of Athenian democracy as the putative fount of just political order. This is so similar that the notion of Judeo-Christian continuity and affinity—a doctrine that had some fundamentalist Protestant incidence before World War II but which acquired particular political salience thereafter—is not historically meaningful despite the wide use of Old Testament typologies by Christians (and, very extensively and perhaps more consequentially, by Muslims), and despite claims to intertestamental unity.

I would submit instead the thesis that antiquity had a geographical context stretching from the Mediterranean littorals to Persia, and that the millennial ebb and flow of conquest and counterconquest across the Eurasian ecumene reflected a long-term trend towards ecumenical unity. Initially, this thrust had been sustained by the Achaemenians, who served as a salutary model of sound polity to a great many contemporary Greeks, including the court of Philip of Macedon. The Alexandrian conquests and the first unification of the oecumene by Alexander, in his capacity as the last of the Achaemenians, was the fulfillment of a long-term tendency that was far more consummately and durably accomplished by the Caliphate nearly a millennium later. The Caliphate had composed together the military and economic trends towards unity, with the cultural monotheistic universalism of Byzantium, which was itself the product of Augustan imperialism and Eusebian Christianism. Late antiquity thus had two termini: Constantinople, and Baghdad, which had more in common with each other than either had (except nominally, or typologically) with Aachen, Magdeburg, Paris, or Gregorian Rome. The latter places were the tail that, in the fullness of time, came to wag the dog, as a result of a very distinctive line of development, incubated in isolation and discontinuity, in the northern and Western margins and wastes of the ecumene.

This conception of later antiquity may not be popular, but neither is it new or idiosyncratic; it is often stated, but its consequences—not least for periodization—are rarely drawn consequentially. Arnold Toynbee saw it quite clearly, although this vision was somewhat clouded by concern with the response of the Syriac civilization. Of orientalists, C.H. Becker discerned it. One historian clearly sketched its wide economic and cultural bearing.[2] Recently, it has been systematically sustained by one study of cultural universalism[3], and by another on conceptions and metaphors of order and power in relation to sacrality.[4]

3.

The historical traditions—and by these I mean, as I presume Peter Burke to mean, formal traditions rather than folk conceptions—of the antique ecumene, in this perspective, are historically coherent in terms of their vast geography as well as of their cumulative, cross-linguistic traditions, and cannot be characterized as Western (or Eastern) in the sense of an exclusively continuous tradition. Were Origen, Tertullian, Philo, Eusebius, Plotinus, Proclus, Arius, or Zeno, "Westerners"? I would submit, moreover, that in searching for distinctiveness one cannot reduce non-Western historical traditions to cyclism, not least because linear *Heilsgeschichte* is, despite Bossuet, a Zoroastrian, Jewish, Manichaean and late antique notion of history, which predominated in medieval Muslim conceptions of universal history no less than in that of Orosius. Cycles in religious (and nationalist) readings of history constitute eddies within a grander linear flow of time to a meeting with destiny, this being the Eschaton or national sovereignty. Time in *Heilsgeschichte* is spiral and three-dimensional; in mainstream Muslim traditions, cycles repeat one another with the last, inaugurated by Muhammad, performing this repetition at a higher and more consummate level of accomplishment. That history is habitually recidivist does not necessarily give time a cyclical structure with no end, as in Brahminical Yugas, although it does produce cycles, normally at irregular intervals, within a large linear structure. Augustine of Hippo (a "Westerner"?), for one, signaled the differentia of paganism to consist of believing the downward trends in history to be final; in secular historiography and political ideology, the notion of *translatio imperii* catered to the sustenance of linearity. In any case, cyclism itself is rather more complex than we are usually led to believe, and far more interesting, not least for the display within it of an urbanity at once sentimentalist and knowing, that characterized cultivated elements of the antique ecumene.

What is crucial in late antique notions of the past, and indeed in all pre-modern notions, is typology: certain events of the past are identified as types, and these are read as prefigurations of subsequent figures and events. History is conceived in the mode of repetition, of reenactment, where the Beginning (Garden of Eden) is recapitulated in the End (Paradise), where crusaders con-ceive of themselves as Israelites, where Constantinople becomes the Second Jerusalem, where Moscow becomes the Third Rome, where the Iulii descend from Romulus and Venus, Muhammad from Abraham, where medieval Euro-pean kings are characterized as *typus Christi*, and where Noah's Ark prefigures the Church. Muslim histories of prophecy are conceived entirely in this mode, as are the Muslim histories of the future, those narratives about the apocalypse are composed according to the formal canons of historical writing. Ibn Khal-dun's cycles are not of history, but of kingship, the rhythms of the two do not correspond necessarily.[5]

In conceiving history as typology, time becomes a space of taxonomy, of genealogical differentiation. Historical discourse here concentrates on identify-ing what it regards as continuities, and thereby conceives as distinctiveness. It sketches the narrative of a continuous subject, and subsumes "causality" in this narrative, conceiving it as "origin" and "influence." This is of course a causality implicitly conceived in typology and repetition. It is this notion of time as a continuous register subsuming causality in linearity, which makes possible the imputation of integrity to large-scale historical masses, such as "cultures," "civ-ilizations," indeed, histories: the West and Islam.

The distinctive feature of modern historical conceptions is the elision of Providence (but this does not do away with cycles), and the crucial role given to historical criticism (which was never absent, albeit selectively: medieval Muslim biblical criticism, for instance, anticipated and quite possibly precipitated Spin-oza's Tractatus).[6] Karl Löwith's view might well be justified yet the crucial point remains that linearity is neither in contradiction with cyclism, nor with a devo-tional reading of the past as a register of antecedents, pre-figurations, beginnings. What is secularized is the identity of the types sought out to construct a geneal-ogy: the Athenian agora, for instance, rather than Roman catacombs or the Tem-ple Mount, though a secular, political salience has been attached to the latter. Genealogies are typological, against the spirit of modern times, always constitut-ing, necessarily, what I have elsewhere termed "chronophagous discourse."[7]

4.

The distinctiveness of "Western" notions of the past is further vitiated by other matters, such as the concern with anachronism, of the awareness of change, on

which there is much in medieval Arabic historical writing and wisdom literature (Ibn Khaldun, Biruni, Mas'udi,Ya'qubi, to mention but a few).The same
could be said of source criticism. Medieval Arabic astrological histories and
prophetic histories of the immediate future were, moreover, highly quantitative.
The relation between medieval Arabic historical writing and other genres was
strong: as in the narrative types identified by Northrop Frye, they go back to a
prior general stock of structural types out of which they develop. Local histories and the histories of specific categories of people (philosophers, judges,
grammarians, Shafi'is) are ubiquitous in medieval Arabic historical writing.[8]
Finally, the notion of causal explanation in history is a matter requiring more
than a celebratory statement.

All these belong to a repertoire of Late Antique ecumenical notions, canons,
and genres of the historical craft and of political wisdom, in the highly distinctive form acquired under the Caliphate or in its shadow.That they are of incidence in "Western" writing derives from a point in time when they were not yet
conceived as Western.The differentia of modern conceptions of history, signaled
above, is indeed of Western origin, but is not an exclusively Western tradition.

5.

That all the characteristics are combined, is undeniable if we specify a time:
beginning with the Renaissance, but far more consistently from the Enlightenment, most particularly when steeled with the notion of objectivity, formally
constituted in the nineteenth century as a corollary to scientism.This combination was achieved in Europe at the same time as history became an academic discipline in its own right, at roughly the same time that saw the rise of
correlative cultural phenomena: literary naturalism, the photographic (and later
the cinematic) notion of realism, no less than taxidermy and Mary Shelley's
Frankenstein. As Peter Burke indicates, this combination has become a universal patrimony: this was accomplished by the universal modules of modernity,
enracinated globally in institutions of cultural, and in tropes of political, social,
and historical thought. It is produced and re-produced everywhere, indeed in
many instances more successfully outside Europe, for modernity is a global
development going back to the early nineteenth century, a combined global
development, which was (and still is) uneven in the rhythms and incidence, and
in which the "West" has not always been the pioneering location for these
convergent movements, despite the Eurocentric narrative that predominates
globally.The most profound consideration on history, its philosophies, crafts,
and histories, that I have read in two decades was written in Arabic,[9] and I
doubt whether it would be translated, as publishers are likely to think it much
too exotic on account of its language, and not sufficiently exotic on account
of its content.

Yet it must not be assumed that we have here a homogeneous eternity of a rational historical culture, objective, wary of anachronism. The robust and reflective positivism espoused by Peter Burke, albeit professionally originating in the epistemological utopia encapsulated in von Ranke's celebrated but not very profound phrase "*wie es eigentlich gewesen*," is socially confined to the formal and professional writing of history. There are layers of historical culture in all societies, and Westerners are as irrational in the conception of history as any others: Romantic notions of the past, vitalist conceptions of time and of otherness, the cyclism of national greatness and decadence, the very notion of decline, are all part of a concept of history that, for half a century, had been relegated to the demotic, but is now resurfacing, under the guise of culturalism and of postmodernism, to subvert historical reason as it had when it predominated until the end of the Second World War. I think it important that the history of history be set out clearly, that history reaffirm the parting of ways with rhetoric and religion that inaugurated Ranke's utopia in the nineteenth century and led to the rise of professional history; after all, for what better task is there for the composer of historical narratives, but to be the remembrancer celebrated by Peter Burke, as the "guardian of awkward facts, the skeletons in the cupboard of the social memory"?[10]

Notes

1. One might most usefully refer to J.E. Schlanger, *Les métaphores de l'organisme*, Paris, 1971.
2. M. Lombard, *The Golden Age of Islam*, Amsterdam, 1975.
3. G. Fowden, *From Empire to Commonwealth*, Princeton, 1993.
4. A. Al-Azmeh, *Muslim Kingship*, London, 1996.
5. A. Al-Azmeh, *Al-Kitaba at-tarikhiyya wa'l ma'rifa at-tarikhiyya [Historical Writing and Historical Knowledge]*, Beirut, 1995.
6. H. Lazarus-Yafeh, *Intertwined Worlds. Medieval Muslim Bible Criticism*, Princeton, 1992.
7. Thus the title of my contribution to *Religion and Practical Reason*, ed. D. Tracy and F. Reynolds, Albany 1993, 163 ff.
8. Medieval Arabic historical writing has been poorly served by scholarship. But see now T. Khalidi, *Arabic Historical Thought in the Classical Period*, Cambridge, 1994.
9. A. al-'Arwi, *Mafhum al-tarikh [The Concept of History]*, 2 vols., Beirut and Casablanca, 1992.
10. Peter Burke, 'History as Social Memory', in *Memory. History, Culture, and the Mind*, ed. T. Butler, Oxford, 1989, 110.

Toward an Archaeology of
Historical Thinking

FRANÇOIS HARTOG

How to begin? With a commentary and a brief discussion of each point brought
up by Peter Burke? This approach possesses a certain disadvantage in that the
proposed framework must be taken as a given, and then conveniently, the ensu-
ing analysis will bring out the nuances and put the finishing touches on this or
that point for which Burke has already provided the basic outline. After an initial remark about these issues, about the way to pose such questions today, I shall
invite the reader to focus her gaze on the beginnings of this "historical thought."

Given the difficulty of practicing comparative analysis in a meaningful
way, we can at least use it as a framework for our present reflections. A potential if not actual comparativism! A history of historiography, inspired, opened up
and even thrown into question by this demand to compare would be able to
escape constant repetition or might also avoid so much revisionism done always
from the inside. By inscribing "historical thought" within this comparative
framework, we would be able to take a certain distance from these Western historiographical paradigms and would perhaps be able write a renewed history or
even better an archeology. An archeology that would appreciate the successive
and retrospective teleologies that have organized and made "history" meaningful. To this we can add a further elaboration: historiography can be understood
as a kind of, or part of, intellectual history. To understand the books of historians, you must read books other than those by historians—otherwise you sound
the death knell of a profession! Burke is thus correct to speak more largely of
"historical thought."

This text which wants to be and is an opening onto a wider world, is without any doubt written from the heart of old Europe. Imagine that the same
question was asked from a Californian university, for instance: the answer would

most certainly be different. This said, we should thank Burke for taking the risk of beginning such a debate since as soon as these questions are uttered there is a strong chance of being criticized if not repudiated!

If he starts by recalling that the West is itself a historical construction, Burke refers only to the contemporary situation of professional historians who today make up a "global community" that shares the same professional standards (But who codified and transmitted them?). Only stylistic differences, which is to say different types of history, exist (quantitative, social, cultural and so forth). The historical interrogations and debates of the last thirty years are not directly invoked. Are they not just so much froth on the *"longue durée"* of "historical thought" that Burke rightly wants to make more visible (Would this be an attempt to avoid the idea that historical thought can be reduced or summed up by Hegel's philosophy of history?).

Does not the proclaimed universalism of Western social sciences, inscribed in the very heart of this historical (Who's the *leur?*) project, translate into the surest evidence of its eurocentrism? Is it not itself in need of "decolonizing"? Was not the universal once parochial? To translate the Arab word *târîkh* as "history" (this is undoubtedly the case since the sixteenth century) caused the specificity of Muslim historiography to be overlooked. The *târîkh*, as a recent translator felt that it was necessary to underline, "is also and especially a field of knowledge that is inscribed within a non-Western cultural system ... giving to itself objects, putting certain concepts in practice, assuming functions in society and in a general field of knowledge very far removed from what existed in the West."[1] Without this preliminary conversion, comparativism can only be myopic.

The diverse interrogations directed at the West concerning its historiographical practices in the last few years have all touched on the problem of the objectivity of this discourse and its attendant presuppositions. Whether it is a question of the linguistic turn that inquired into the relationship of history and fiction, or of investigations that introduced concerns about gender and later cultural studies, these approaches must all address the following questions: who speaks to whom, when, how and why? To this remark we can add a second. As long as Europe made history, the practice of writing history seemed self-evident: today when such is no longer the case, it is hardly surprising that the interrogation would turn back to how the making of this history had been written.

According to Burke, the specificity of Western historical thought, or to use the phrase of Bernard Guende, of its historical culture, is to be found less in the elements of which it is composed than in the combination of these parts. The ingredients can be found elsewhere, only its preparation is unique. Moreover, this "thought" is itself a composite: it is formed by an ensemble of propositions, each with its own history, its own chronology, without any necessary coherence but nevertheless coexisting, one with the others, more or less well. There is room for play and conflict with this consequence among others: the distance between—the historical "culture" and other historiographies—far from having been constant, has varied following the course of centuries, clearly rising with the Renaissance and diminishing in the nineteenth century.

Beginning with Herodotus, Burke wants to show the long trajectory of "historical thought," how earlier propositions contributed to the making and transforming, the reformulation and criticism of this "thought." By so clearly historicizing this Western model, such an approach deserves the credit for relativizing it.[2] This approach, which straightaway challenges the idea of the Great Divide, aims only to furnish a certain number of entry points for a "descriptive inventory of differences"; ten points are located, each one incited disputes or caused a tension to take hold at the heart of the Western tradition that formed it. These points make up a system or at least refer to one another, elaborating throughout the centuries the terms of a debate comprised of agreements, disagreements and even contradictions. Burke even suggests that it might be possible to see a "system of conflicts" here (perhaps in the image of democracy). The formulation is seductive but is it convincing?

Burke proposes a kind of mapping to prepare for a future stage that would address the "why" of differences in earnest. Nevertheless, this Western "model" still remains, a bit like a painting where one points to and measures absences and presences, that which "understands" other experiences however rapidly evoked by China, Japan or the Islamic world. If I must attempt an archeology of Western "historical thought," I would prefer rather to "take the measure of the possibilities that, in becoming Western, we have closed off." Maurice Merleau-Ponty made this statement in regard to the arts of India and China, but it seems to me equally valid for history.

In the following pages, I will restrict myself to a few general remarks on the "prehistory" of "historical thought": not out of a preference for origins but because here we can set up an experimental situation. We can grasp the configurations from which choices and bifurcations, which did not have to be or could have been different, were made. And later, they were forgotten or became so self-evident that no one any longer dreamed of questioning them. We can also measure the distance between "an interest in the past" and the emergence of "historical thought," which is above all concerned with present.

Let's go back for a moment to Mesopotamia where, at the end of the third millennium, the monarchy of *Akkade*, which was the first to unify the country under its authority, called in scribes to write "its" history, in other words, to legitimate its power in the present. Without pausing over this first model of monumental and royal historiography whose methods are as incontestable as they are simple, I would like to focus on the exchange that eems to have tied divination and history. In ancient Mesopotamia, as we know, divination played an important role in decision making.[3] How did the soothsayers work? They accumulated, classified events, made lists, compiled, constituted real libraries. They were guided by an ideal of exhaustivity, itself ruled by a logic of precedent that brings us close to the knowledge of a judge and juridical practices. In other words, divination is first of all a science of the past. A series of oracles were found at Mari (dating from the beginning of the second millennium) that modern researchers dubbed "historical oracles." Instead of employing a canonical modality: "If the liver of the animal (sacrificed) is thus, it is a sign that the king *will take* the town in such a way," they say "If the liver of the animal is thus, it is a sign that the king *took* the town in such a way." This passage from the future to a completed past is truly surprising even more so since the events to which they refer are thought by us moderns to actually have taken place. In addition, some have wanted to see here the very beginnings of Mesopotamian historiography: first divination then history. Sinologists such as Leon Vandermeersch held the same point of view in regard to Chinese historiography.

My incompetence keeps me from taking sides but what interests me is that these two methods, divination and historiography, seem to belong to the same intellectual space. From the point of view of the consultant, the king—he comes in search of assistance in making a decision; from the point of view of the specialists consulted, the scribes, who take note of the "historical" oracle, transcribe it and study it—they add the oracular configuration to their lists and thereby increase their stock of precedence. We might also imagine the work done in reverse: by beginning with the "event" (the news of the taking of the town) to decipher (verify) the signs inscribed on the liver. Another possibility would be that the scribes might recopy actual royal inscriptions relating this or that act by the king, and from the list of royal oracles, make it "correspond" to the state of the liver that these events implied or would imply.

We could extend this investigation to Rome through an examination of the famous *Pontifical Annals*, which are all the more famous for having disappeared. Each year the sovereign pontiff wrote a chronicle *(tabula)* that he hung on the front of "his" house. Cicero understands this transcription as the beginnings, albeit clumsy and unrefined, of Roman historiography. In recently reexamining this question, John Scheid demonstrated that this document, delivered at the end of each year, must have functioned as a kind of report on the state of the relations between the city and the gods. It was left to the *pontifex maximus* to compile it as the power to "retain on his *tabula* the memory of events" that had devolved to him.[4] What *events?* Victories, calamities and portents all were collected and treated only as signs that allowed for the keeping of accounts of piety. Especially important in this regard was how to decipher bad omens and eventually how to "expiate" for them.

An "official" history of Rome, if we like, or a "religious" history but this compilation, divided according to the rhythms of the city's calendar, responds to the following questions: Where are we in relation to the gods? Have we done what was necessary? What should we do? The pontiff was also a man of the archives guided by research into precedent (particularly concerning omens) but concerned with the present. Each year he furnished to the new consuls a report on the city's religious state.

The choices of the Greek city-state were different. Divination was certainly present and collections of oracles do exist. But what was historiography for the Greeks—and later to become "history" for the moderns—took a different path. This historiography presupposes the epic. Herodotus wanted to rival Homer, and he finally became Herodotus. He undertook to do for the Medic wars what Homer had done for the Trojan War. From this point on to write history would be to begin with a conflict and tell the story of a great war by fixing the "origin" (the determination of the *aitia* for Herodotus or the "truest cause" for Thucydides). In contrast to the Bible which tells a continuous story from the beginning of time, the first Greek historians fixed a point of departure and limited themselves to recounting a specific set of events.

The bard of the epic, who sang the exploits of heros, had to deal with memory, forgetting and death. Likewise, Herodotus wanted to prevent the signs of human activity from being erased if no longer told. But he limits himself to what "men made" happen, telling only what he "knows" in a delimited time period, the "time of men." Whereas the bard owed his knowledge to the Muse who was omnipresent and all-seeing, the historian will call upon *historia. He* means to procure for himself, via this substitute, a vision analogous to the one henceforth inaccessible that the Muse provided.[5] This first historiographical "operation" encounters and reinforces the primacy granted by the Greeks to the eye as an instrument of knowledge. Beginning here, the history of Western historiography could be written in counterpoint as a history of the eye and of vision!

If in relation to eastern historiography, the Greeks are late-comers, it is with them—precisely with Herodotus—that the historian emerges as a subjective figure. Without being directly commissioned by any political power, Herodotus marks and claims the story that begins with the inscription of his name as his own. From the outset, this place of knowledge is claimed and yet must nevertheless be entirely constructed: this construction will of course be the work itself. Additionally, the Greeks are less the inventors of history than the historians of the writing subject. Such a mode of self-affirmation and the production of a discourse were not at all only historiographical phenomena. To the contrary, they are sign, the true signature of a period of Greek intellectual history (between the sixth and tenth century B.C.) which witnessed at the same time the rise of "egotism" among artists, philosophers of nature and doctors.

A new figure on the stage of knowledge but one who did not emerge from nowhere, yet the historian will not take long to bow down in front of the philosopher, who, from the fourth century, will become the major reference and symbol, so to speak, of the intellectual. The philosopher will be a man of schools (not so with the historian), but his place, his relationship to institutions will from now on be posed without cease. As soon as history can no longer claim to be political science as Thucydides would have wanted it to be, the historian was left with the task of convincing his audience that history was also philosophy, that it was pleasing and useful. This will finally result in the presentation of history as a *magistra vitae*, and philosophy preaching by example: less a science of action than one of self-actualization. But from the choices of Thucydides, this point, often brought up by Momigliano, still holds that true history is first of all (and will be for a long time to come) political history, leaving aside the field of antiquities and erudition. It is only in the modern era that research on the ancient world will rejoin history.

Aristotle's formulation in the *Poetics* (ch. 9) leveled a blow of great consequence at the ambitions of Thucydidian history. Thucydides had the ambition of creating a work along the lines of the famous formula, *ktêma* (acquired) forever. His goal was no longer about saving threatened, valued actions from being forgotten, but about transmitting an instrument of intelligibility concerning the present to the men of the future. In going from the present (not the past) toward the future, the aim was not that of prevision but rather of deciphering the presents to come: because given what men are, other analogous crises would surely break out in the future. It is the permanence of human nature that establishes the exemplarity (ideal type) of this conflict, named (forever) by its historian, the Peloponnesian War.

When opposing history to poetry, Aristotle, as is well known, limited history to the "particular," to what Alieibiades did or what happened to him. The "general" is by definition outside of history's purview. It follows that poetry is more "philosophical" than history. Somewhat later Polybius tried to redirect Aristotle's argument by showing that history was more philosophical than poetry because its tragedies were real. His efforts met with little success. Even if the Italian humanists rediscovered the various arguments of this debate, posterity has not shown much interested in it. On the other hand, the Aristotelian division will remain one of the important themes and one of the recurrent interrogations (under diverse modalities: individual or collective, idiographical or nomothetic history, etc.), of Western historiography. We have here a configuration of a *longue durée*.

I will stop here with these rapid remarks, which do not attempt in any way to demonstrate that everything can be found in the beginning, or that all the important questions were already put into play a long time ago. Rather, I view these examples as an experimental space where the divergent experiences of history are communicated, divisions start emerging, positive choices are formulated, ruptures take shape, a "Western" tradition begins to be made.

Notes

1. Ibn Khaldûn, *Peuples et nations du monde*, translated and presented by A. Cheddadi, Paris, 1986, 25.

2. In this sense, he responds at least in part to the objections communicated from India by Ashis Nandy, 'History's Forgotten Doubles', *History and Theory*, 42 (1995), 65, where he criticizes Western historians for having historicized everything but history itself.

3. J. Bottero, 'Symptômes, signes, écriture', in *Divination et rationalité*, Editions du Seuil: Paris, 1974, 70-86; J.J. Glassner, *Chroniques mesopotamiennes*, Paris, 1993.

4. J. Scheid, 'Les temps de la cité et l'histoire des prêtres', in *Transcrire les mythologies*, under the direction of M. Detienne, Paris, 1994, 149-158.

5. F. Hartog, *Le Miroir d'Hérodote*, Paris, 1991, iii-xvi.

Trauma and Suffering
A Forgotten Source of Western Historical Consciousness

FRANK R. ANKERSMIT

1. Methodological problems

Comparison always requires some more or less neutral background, a *genus proximum*, in terms of which a description can be given of the items that one wishes to compare. This poses a difficult problem when we try to deal with the question that Professor Burke has put on the agenda: for what description of historical consciousness could one think of as actually possessing the required neutrality with regard to both Western and non-Western conceptions of the past? It is, arguably, precisely their "incommensurability" that has awakened our interest in the relationship of Western and non-Western historical consciousness and that has invited the comparison.

Hence, our initial problem will be how to start our investigation into this relationship and, more specifically, how to make sure that the right thing is compared to the right thing. To put it dramatically, it might well be that the closest analogue to the Western conception of the past is not to be found in non-Western historiography, as we might have thought as a matter of course, but, rather, for example, in the theological systems, conceptions of the self or in the works of art that we may find in non-Western cultures. Moreover, even Western historical consciousness itself may provide us with further examples of this kind of complication.

For instance, if one wishes to understand the evolution of Western historical consciousness from 1800 to 1830, one cannot leave literature, and more specifically, the historical novel, out of one's account. One would fail to identify one of the strongest determinants of this evolution if one were to restrict one's gaze to historical writing itself and to ignore the tremendous influence of Scott's historical novels, in particular, on the development of Western historical consciousness, during this absolutely crucial period in the evolution of Western

Notes for this section can be found on page 84.

historical thought. In this period, the history of historical consciousness temporarily abandoned historical writing itself and preferred to follow the paths of literature. Moreover, it could be argued that the nineteenth-century realist and naturalist novel was the result of a "contemporanization" of the historical novel:[1] the accuracy in the representation of the life and times of the characters of this historical novel (an accuracy that was the strictest requirement of the genre), was now transposed to the present as well. After this transposition had been achieved, the realistic novelist could be required to present to his readers *"une copie exacte et minutieuse de la vie humaine"* as Zola put it in the foreword to his *Thérèse Raquin*. And, to put the crown on all this, one may agree with Hayden White when he writes that historical writing, from the nineteenth century down to the present day, has carefully cultivated the style and the prose of the realistic novel, whereas in the novel itself, since the beginning of the twentieth century, many new and exciting experiments were made in the representation of human experience in language.

Thus, we may observe in the nineteenth century, from the perspective of the development of Western historical consciousness, a most complex intermingling of the genres of the novel and of historical writing. No exposition of the development of Western historical consciousness can claim validity if it does not properly account for these most complex interrelationships. And if such crossings can already be observed within one and the same culture, it is quite likely that they will similarly confound the far more ambitious and adventurous attempt to compare Western and non-Western historical consciousness.

A related and additional complication is that Western historical consciousness, in particular, has undergone so many and such profound metamorphoses since the days of Hecataeus, that it may well be that in several phases of its evolution it has been closer to variants of non-Western historical consciousness than to several earlier or later variants of Western historical consciousness itself (I shall return to this concept later on). Needless to say, were this actually the case, it would make nonsense of the whole question whether there are any categorical differences between Western and non-Western historical consciousness. All we would then have are different ways of experiencing the past, and the attempt to find any systematic difference(s) between Western and non-Western conceptions of the past would be just as vain as the attempt to discover systematic differences between two slabs of marble coming from exactly the same location of the same quarry. Differences there may, and even will be, but they will not allow us to make any inferences going beyond the nature of these differences themselves. In both cases differences would be nothing but the signs of themselves.

2. The "psychoanalysis" of historical consciousness

However, even though Professor Burke does not insist on this and similar methodological problems, this will not, in itself, be sufficient to put in doubt his exposition of the differences between Western and non-Western conceptions of history. For we should realize that each such comparison always has to begin somewhere. There will always be an initial phase where we cannot yet be sure about what exactly we are comparing with what, and in terms of what we are making this comparison: only after some initial, and probably, or even inevitably, abortive attempts are made in this direction, will it gradually become clear what we have been talking about all along. Inevitably, cross-cultural comparisons like these can only get started in such a trial and error manner; and we have at this early phase no foolproof methodological rules at our disposal that we can blindly follow. Nevertheless, we ought to be aware of the problem and try, as much as possible, to avoid the projection or "transference," in the Freudian sense of that word, of our own unconscious assumptions or "historical neuroses" onto other cultures.

I have deliberately been using Freudian terminology here: for the language of psychoanalysis might be helpful in making clear where I would differ with Professor Burke. Once again, I do not object to his list of ten points of where Western and non-Western historical consciousness differ. Everything he says along these lines seems to me entirely plausible, convincing, if not outright true. My question is, rather, how can we know that this list is exhaustive and, more specifically, not merely a random sample that could be enlarged at will, but one that really gravitates towards the center of our issue?

It is here that I should like to introduce one extra phase into the investigation. My suggestion is that we should not start with intuitions about the formal features of how the past is remembered by the West or in non-Western cultures, as is Professor Burke's strategy, but rather ask the quasi-transcendental question: what made historical consciousness possible in either the West or in non-Western civilizations? Similarly—and this is why I took psychoanalysis as my model a moment ago—if we are well acquainted with two persons A and B, we may enumerate any number of differences in how each of them relates to his or her past, but it is only from a psychoanalytical point of view that we may guess the importance and the relevance of these differences. Only the "depth" of a (quasi-) psychoanalytical assessment of the personalities of A and B may yield a hierarchization of these differences and give us an idea of their relationships and relative importance. And the explanation is that it is the psychology of A and B in which these observed differences have their ultimate ground, that has made these differences possible and therefore may enable us to really comprehend them. Hence, what I would like to suggest is that we should apply such a kind of "cultural psychoanalysis" to the Western and the non-Western attitude towards the past; and not be content merely to compile lists of agreements and differences in the absence of any reliable guide for how these might be connected, however useful and enlightening such lists may be at the start of an investigation like this one.

Now, I am aware that trying to do something like this is an ambitious enterprise that would require both a whole library for adequately working it out, and a perhaps even larger library on which the effort would have to be based. So what I shall be saying about this only suggests the kinds of topics that one might think of in this connection rather than what might be the right and most adequate thing to say about the issue.

3. Trauma as the origin of Western historical consciousness

If, then, we look at Western and non-Western historical consciousness with the eyes of the "cultural psychoanalyst" I introduced a moment ago, it must strike us that Western historical consciousness was strongly stimulated by and perhaps even originated in the traumatic experience of certain historical events. We may think here of what 1494 meant to Machiavelli, Guicciardini and to so many other sixteenth-century Italian historians, or of what 1789 and all that followed the Revolution meant to the French and the German historians of the beginning of the nineteenth century. It may well be that the fact that the Anglo-Saxon world has had the fortune of never having to undergo such a traumatic experience, helps us to explain why historical consciousness is so much an "invention" of the European continent. An additional argument for this thesis might be that what is undoubtedly the most interesting phase in the development of British historical thought, took place in the wake of 1649—hence, of the event coming closest to such a traumatic experience in the course of British history.

Furthermore, the view that (the origins of) (Western) historical consciousness should be related to trauma can be clarified with the help of the following argument. It has often been argued that our sole contact with or experience of reality in which reality discloses to us its true nature, its radical strangeness and majestic indifference to us occurs in trauma—for in the nontraumatic experience of reality, reality has already been forced within the limits of the known, the familiar and the domesticated. Nontraumatically experienced reality is a reality that has already been processed by us, in much the same way that the Kantian categories of the understanding "process" the raw data of experience into what Kant defined as "phenomenal" reality. Here reality has been appropriated by us, is familiar to us and has been robbed of all the threatening connotations of the traumatic. It is here that we may also observe a link with the Kantian sublime, since the sublime, as defined by Kant, transcends the experience of reality as conditioned and processed by the categories of the understanding, and thus presents us with reality in its quasi-noumenal quality, and therefore with a reality that has still retained all of its radical alienness. The trauma is the sublime and vice versa and at the bottom of both is an experience of reality that shatters to pieces all our certainties, beliefs, categories and expectations.

Continuing this line of argument, we might argue next that history as a reality of its own can only come into being as a result of the kind of traumatic collective experience I suggested a moment ago; and the implication would be that there is an indissoluble link between history and the miseries and the horrors of the past. Happiness, on the other hand, would, within this view, not significantly contribute to the substance of history. Reality "as such," noumenal reality—and this would be true of historical reality as well—is essentially a painful reality—fundamentally an encounter with death, as this reality "as such," in this century, most paradigmatically manifested itself in the traumatic sublime of the Holocaust. Of course, here we are in agreement with Hegel's well-known observation that the happy days of mankind are *eo ipso* the empty pages in the book of history.

Moreover, this line of argument would also elicit our agreement with Huizinga's view that history is tragedy, and that the belief in progress and our more euphoric views of the past are merely our attempts to hide this unpleasant reality from view. Thus, what Kant in his *Der Streit der Fakultäten* (1798) referred to as the "moral terrorist" and the "eudemonist" conceptions of the past, should not be placed next to each other at an equal level: (psycho-)logically the former really precedes the latter. Once again, the past is essentially and primarily a painful past; and histories rejoicing in, for example, the triumphs of monarchs, soldiers and heroes will never be able to give us that eudemonic essence. The great deeds of a nation, of a social class, or a civilization give it much less of a historically defined coherence and identity than trauma and suffering—at least if certain circumstances are satisfied—can achieve; this is probably an explanation why the victims of history may—once again, under certain and surely not all circumstances—discover in history a far more powerful ally than their victors will ever be able to do. Shared traumatic pain provides the collectivity with a common basis, in a far deeper layer of reality than happiness and joy ever could. Here Thierry and the Marxists were right, with regard to the bourgeoisie and the industrial proletariat respectively, when they showed that their past sufferings had been the condition of the so prominent role they would later play in the history of mankind.

Now, I believe that this will enable us to discern a fundamental difference between Western and non-Western historical consciousness. Though non-Western history has had more than its own share of tragedy, of war, murder and devastation; though 1494 and 1789 may even be considered mere ripples on the surface of history if compared to the abject fate of the Aztecs, the American Indians or of the unspeakable horrors that Mongol rule inflicted on Central Asia, it seems that only Western man was capable of a traumatic experience of history. Strangely enough there seems to be no proportion between the amount of suffering that a civilization has had to go through and its propensity to a traumatic experience of these horrors. Apparently experience also has its varieties—as interpretation does. Relatively minor collective disasters may, under certain circumstances, prove to be a stronger stimulus of historical consciousness than the worst that humanity has had to undergo in the course of its history.

I would even be prepared to defend the view that this insight may illuminate where Western civilization since the Renaissance differs essentially from the medieval West preceding it (and from the relationship to the past that we may find in non-Western cultures). For what were 1494 and 1789 if compared to the disintegration of the Roman Empire and the confusions that followed it, or to the Black Death of 1348 that killed one third of the European population and instilled an intense feeling of fear, despair and desolation in the mind of the West for almost two centuries—as Delumeau so brilliantly showed in his *La peur en Occident*? Once again, arguably, mere ripples on history's surface. Yet not even these frightful events of the early and the late Middle Ages, nor the tragedies and horrors of the Hundred Years' War,[2] effected anything even remotely resembling the coherence and the intensity of Guicciardini's experience of the past in the minds of the Gregory of Tours and the Froissarts, who so extensively and exhaustively (and with such curious dispassion) described these horrors.

One may wonder how to explain that tragedy, horror and human suffering at an unprecedented scale so often faded quietly away in the mists of time, whereas in the West relatively minor historical disasters could suddenly be experienced as the kind of trauma from which Western historical consciousness originated. Why and how did this unique capacity for collective trauma come into being in the West? Asking this question is to invite once again a number of unpleasant methodological problems. For, surely, at this highly abstract level we will typically be unable to distinguish *explanantia* from *explananda*, and it may even be that what we mention as the cause of this sudden Western susceptibility to historical trauma is the consequence of this susceptibility rather than its cause.

4. The traumatic past is an abstract past

But allowing for this and similar uncertainties, I would nevertheless venture the following explanation. As will be clear from the above, this susceptibility to collective trauma should not be explained by considering the quantity of "collective pain" that was inflicted on a civilization, nor even by the intensity of this pain, for even outright unendurable collective pain only rarely results in the creation of historical consciousness. I believe that the explanation is, rather, that in the West a shift may be observed from collective pain to an awareness of this pain and that this is how this peculiar Western capacity for suffering collective trauma originated. I hasten to add the following in order to avoid misunder-

standing. When thus emphasizing the significance of the awareness of pain, I
certainly do not intend to attack the commonsensical and unexceptionable
view that one cannot be in pain without an awareness of this pain: certainly, one
cannot be in pain without knowing that one is in pain. Certainly, I do not want
to argue that the Aztecs, or, for that matter, fifteenth-century Europeans, were
singularly unaware of their sufferings and stolidly underwent their historical fate
in the way that a rock may tumble down from a mountain.

What I wish to say is rather the reverse: that is, what is typical of trauma is
precisely an incapacity to suffer or to assimilate the traumatic experience into
one's life history. What comes into being with trauma is not so much an openness to suffering, but a certain numbness; a certain insensitivity as if the recep-
tacles for suffering have become inadequate to the true nature and the
proportions of suffering. It is in this way that a dissociation has come into existence between suffering itself and the awareness of this suffering; although the
two always and inevitably go together, it is here as if, when being in pain, I
experience my pain as being a mere, though absolutely reliable sign that someone (i.e., myself) is in pain, while not actually feeling the pain itself. While being
in pain myself I now feel tempted, so to speak, to look at myself from a point of
view that no longer, or at least no longer automatically, coincides with myself
as the person who is in pain.

Similarly, trauma effects a dissociation of a traumatically experienced reality and the subject of the traumatic experience. When Charcot and Janet were,
in the 1880s, the first to seriously investigate the phenomenon of traumatic
shock, especially Janet strongly insisted on the dissociation that trauma seemed
to effect in one and the same person between a normal self, with normal memories, and a traumatically disturbed self, to which this normal self and these normal memories are no longer accessible. Much of this original conception of
trauma is retained in what is presently known as the so-called Post-Traumatic
Stress Disorder and which is clinically defined as follows:

> In Post-Traumatic Stress Disorder (PTSD) ... the overwhelming events of the past
> repeatedly posses, in intrusive images and thoughts, the one who has lived through
> them. ... Yet what is particularly striking in this singular experience is that its insis-
> tent reenactments of the past do not simply serve as testimony to an event, but may
> also, paradoxically enough, bear witness to a past that was never fully experienced
> as it occurred. Trauma, that is, does not simply serve as record of the past but it pre-
> cisely registers the force of an experience that is not yet fully owned.[3]

The paradox of trauma thus is that it gives us a past that is neither forgotten nor
remembered; it gives us a past continuing to exist in us as a reality that we
remember precisely because we cannot remember it and because we have no
actual access to it. Trauma occurs because of the subject's incapacity to absorb
the traumatic experience within the whole of his life story, and that makes him
traumatically aware of a reality hiding itself from him as soon as it reveals itself

and makes itself felt to him. Or, to rephrase all this in the terms that were proposed by Janet: whereas "normal" history is the result of association, of a narrative integration or concatenation of experiences so that they can be "appropriated" or "owned" by us, "traumatic" history is the result of a process of dissociation, of presenting our faculty of historical and narrative association with a challenge that it is, as yet, unable to meet.

I would suggest that something closely resembling the foregoing description of trauma took place when Western historical consciousness came into being somewhere in the sixteenth and the seventeenth centuries. History became something that was remembered precisely because of this paradox of a remembering that one cannot remember, because of an awareness that memories did not enable us to "appropriate" or to properly "own" the objects of memory. Collective suffering now took on the features of a reality that is continuously most painfully present to us, but that we are, at the same time, unable to assimilate in ourselves: suffering now became strangely and unnaturally abstract, something to be explained (historically), but that is not experienced primarily, or, at least, not completely exhausted in or by the experience of suffering itself. It became an occasion for thought, much in the same way that both Hegel and Freud argued that what distinguishes human beings from animals is that thought places itself between desire and the satisfaction of desire in the case of human beings, whereas animals always look for an immediate satisfaction of their desires. Collective suffering now became a part of culture, something that could be expressed in the idiom of that culture, something that one could talk and write about. And in this "hollow" between suffering and the language used for speaking about it, a new kind of discourse gradually and gropingly came into being—that is, historical writing—having as its goal to relate this talking, and writing about suffering, to suffering itself. Historical writing, discourse and historical consciousness mediate between trauma and suffering themselves, on the one hand, and the objectification of trauma and suffering, on the other, that is so characteristic of Western civilization. The historian's language originates in the "logical space" between traumatic experience and a language that still had a primordial immediacy and directness in its relationship to the world—and then pushes this language aside. Historical language pulls language and reality apart and thus destroys the directness in the relationship of language to reality that the former still possessed in the pre-historicist phase of civilization—that is, in the Middle Ages or in non-Western civilizations—while at the same time attempting to bridge the gap it had thus inadvertently opened up.

This may also explain why Western historical consciousness is so intimately and so closely related to an awareness of the unintended consequences of intentional human action. We may intend to do one thing, but while trying to realize our purposes, actually achieve quite another thing. Thus Guicciardini sincerely believed that he had given the best possible advice to Clement VII, but at the same time, he was painfully aware that with his advice he had, in fact, achieved the Sack of Rome and therewith the destruction of the beauties and the glories of the Eternal City. It was his realization that, unwittingly, he had been no less disastrous to the history of the country that he loved more than himself, than Ludovico il Moro had been when he invited Charles VIII to invade Italy in 1494: a realization that made him aware of the unintended consequences of our actions with an almost existentialist intensity. This is what history essentially meant to him and would mean to later, postmedieval Western civilization. For it is when wondering about the torment of this frightful discrepancy between our intentions and actions, on the one hand, and their actual consequences, on the other, that we are forced to step back from—or outside—ourselves in order to be able to observe this discrepancy, and by doing so, to start thinking historically. The pain we feel under such circumstances is, peculiarly enough, a pain that alienates us from the painful event itself—as is typically the case in trauma as discussed above. And, lastly, it is a pain that, not only Guicciardini, but almost all of the sixteenth-century Florentine historians seemed to cultivate with an almost sadomasochistic pleasure: for one cannot read their histories without being struck by their strange propensity to attribute to their own country, to Florence, a far greater responsibility for Italy's disasters than is warranted by actual historical fact. Perhaps self-accusation is also an art that a civilization learns to practice properly only in the course of time (and from that perspective it would not be surprising that the discovery of the art of self-accusation began with such a strong overdose of it).

Obviously, one might now go back one step further and ask what the explanation is for Guicciardini's unprecedented susceptibility to the unintended consequences of his actions. Why did his awareness of what he had done to his country fill his mind with an unbearable and traumatic pain, whereas, for example, Philip the Good of Burgundy looked with complete equanimity at the destruction wrought on France because of his self-serving alliance with England? Once again, when considering this question it will be hard to distinguish causes from their effects and to establish exactly what preceded what. But now that we have already entered onto the path of reckless speculation, I may be forgiven for venturing the following view.

It might well be that for Philip the Good socio-political reality would remain fundamentally the God-willed order that it had always been, regardless of the nature of his actions. That is to say, he considered his actions to touch merely upon the surface of socio-political reality and to be incapable of stirring its depth—supposing that the distinction between its surface and depth would have made any sense to him at all. He did not yet have the notion of political action in the real, modern sense of that word, that is, of the kind of public action that truly "makes a difference" to what the world is, or will be like. Certainly, that does not in the least imply that he would be incapable of feeling any responsibility for what he did or did not do; but the crucial datum is here that this responsibility regarded only his own person and how that person might be seen by the eyes of God. And this was different for Guicciardini; for the responsibility that Guicciardini felt was a responsibility to the world (or to Italy) rather than to God.

But perhaps this is an unilluminating way of putting it. It might be more enlightening to rephrase the contrast into the terms of Ruth Benedict's well-known opposition between "shame cultures" and "guilt cultures." Following this lead one might say that in a certain sense Philip the Good could only feel ashamed of himself because and when he had, somehow, messed up his own life; but even if he had done so, in his own eyes, the consequences of his actions could, within his conception of the world, never have any real impact on the order that had been willed by God. He could only feel responsible towards himself and his own salvation. Precisely because he was so much part of reality, so completely submerged in it, so much surrounded by reality on all sides, precisely because of the complete osmosis between himself and reality, a responsibility towards himself was the maximum he could possibly be expected to feel. To feel guilty, to feel responsible towards the world would have been to him a presumptuous and preposterous blasphemy. That would have been as if an ant had thought of itself as having been the cause of the death of a whole civilization. And in that sense he could not properly be said to be "guilty" of his actions: for shame is a private feeling, whereas guilt always has to do with a debt that we owe the world. So what happened, sometime between Philip the Good and Guicciardini, is that the individual withdrew from the world (in which Philip the Good still felt immersed to such an extent that he could never detach his own actions from it), and now became enthralled by the idea that from this vantage-point outside reality, he could do things to reality that might make "a difference to it," or even fundamentally alter it. And the paradox is, therefore, that it was a withdrawal and not a further immersion in it that made Western man exchange shame for guilt, and transformed a fixation on the responsibility for one's own salvation into that for the (historical) world.

I would not have hazarded this risky contention if it did not find some additional support in what happened in our relationship to natural reality and in the origins that the sciences have in the same period that witnessed, in the writings of Guicciardini and his Italian contemporaries, the birth of modern historical consciousness. For from this vantage point we cannot fail to be struck by what the historical and the scientific revolution have in common. As we all know, the scientific revolution was only possible thanks to the creation of the scientistic, transcendental ego whose philosophical properties have been so eagerly investigated by Descartes, Kant and so many others down to the present day. And, as we all know, this transcendental ego was, just like historical consciousness, the product and result of a movement of *anachoresis*,[4] of a withdrawal of the self from the world itself within an inner, cognitive sanctuary that decides about the reliability of the data of experience. Quite revealing here is the *bene vixit, bene qui latuit* (he has lived well who knew how to hide himself well) that

Descartes took as his device: scientific truth will never be given to man as long as he fully participates in all the complexities of daily life. Science requires distance, not immersion and participation. The mastery of both the historical and the physical world is, therefore, the miracle wrought by a *reculer pour mieux sauter*: only after having left (historical and physical reality) itself and after having situated itself at an Archimedian vantage point outside reality itself—only after having adopted this paradoxical strategy—could the Western mind gain an ascendancy over historical and natural reality that it had never possessed before. And it is only in this way that what we have come to see as "history" and "science" in the West became possible.

But a price had to be paid. For the same numbness that we observed a moment ago when discussing historical consciousness, the same falling apart of the directness and immediacy of (historical) experience that gave us (Western) historical consciousness also gave us modern science but at the expense of the experience of nature. Instead of the experience of nature, we now have our scientific knowledge of how we can make nature subservient to our aims and purposes—and it is, perhaps, only in the arts that a faint reminiscence of the experience of nature has been retained. We can experience nature only by and through the artifacts that artists have of it in order to represent it.

Moreover, this is why we may well have our doubts about the tradition ordinarily associated with Vico suggesting an invincible epistemological barrier between historical writing, on the one hand, and (Cartesian) science, on the other. Certainly, there may be such a barrier between the direct and immediate experience of the past such as we find it in non-Western civilizations or in Western historical writing before the days of Guicciardini, but the historical writing of Vico's and of our own days is, like modern science, the result of the *anachoresis*, or modernist division of the self. Vico could only regret the directness in the relationship between Homer's heroes and their world because of his awareness that this directness had sadly been lost in his own days of the "barbarism of reflection."

5. Final remarks

I want to add one last remark. We must not be mistaken about the nature of this change. It is, in many ways, not at all a big change: it is not something like a war, a revolution, the birth of a new religion, or the discovery of a new and effective weapon. In fact, historical reality as such is not in the least affected by it, it is not even a change in historical reality itself. Rather, it is a change in how Western man decided to look at historical reality, it is a change in perspective, while everything that it observed remained the way that it had always been. Yet, these small and immaterial changes may become irreversible and determine the future fate of humanity. They are like a mutation: somewhere in the union of the genes of one specific animal of a specific genus something may go different on a microscopic scale, and yet, this microscopic event may result in a new phase in the history of evolution, and in a new regime between the victims and the victors in this world. And so it has been with the rise of Western historical consciousness. In the minds of authors like Machiavelli and Guicciardini, the fate of Italy after 1494 was experienced as an irretrievable, irreparable and traumatic loss that caused in them an unendurable pain, the deepest regret, feelings of the profoundest guilt and of the cruelest self-reproach. Nevertheless, it was this historically microscopic event, this "mutation" that would change the face of Western civilization and, by the logic proper to all mutations, several centuries later, of non-Western civilizations as well.

Of course all that I have been saying here is highly speculative: it is just one more way of selecting and arranging a number of well-known facts about the gradual development of historical writing and of historical consciousness since the dawn of mankind. Many other selections and arrangements of these same facts are just as legitimate, or probably even more so. Hence, these musings about the trauma from which the Western conception of the past originated are emphatically not an attempt to state the final truth about the origins of Western historical consciousness or about how that might differ from non-Western historical consciousness.

I do believe, nevertheless, that we should go down to this very fundamental level if we wish to address the issue of the relationship between Western and non-Western conceptions of the past. It is at this level that truth should no longer be our primary goal, simply because the set of shared presuppositions that truth always requires are absent here. But if truth is not attainable here, this should not deter us from asking questions like these. For it may well be that the truly important thing about such questions is that we should discuss them, and go on discussing them, even if we were to know that we will never know the final truth about the issue at stake. As Lessing already argued more than two hundred years ago in his *Nathan der Weise*, it sometimes is more important simply to possess a certain discourse rather than the truths that might be expressed within that discourse—and perhaps this is what I have been talking about all along. Perhaps this is a truth not only about the history of historical writing and about historical consciousness, but about historical writing itself as well. We should always indefatigably and passionately search for historical truth, but never forget, at the same time, that we lose rather than gain something when we actually achieve it.

Notes

1. A movement into the opposite direction can be observed at the birth of the historical novel. For it has been argued that the historical novel resulted from a "historicization" of the literary genre of the "arcadia." Ordinarily, in this genre, invented in sixteenth-century Italy, a company of young lovers make a journey through the countryside while their conversation is not only devoted to love, but also to a learned exposition of the historical antecedents of the towns and villages which they pass. In this way elements of fiction (situated in the present) and history were combined; and it required only the "historicization" of the (contemporary) element of fiction, that is, the location of the Arcadian love story in the past as well, to produce the genre of the historical novel.
2. We may well recall here the lines that Shakespeare put into the mouth of La Pucelle of Orleans when she addressed Philip the Good, Duke of Burgundy:

    > *Look on thy country, look on fertile France,*
    > *And see the cities and the towns defac'd*
    > *By wasting ruin of the cruel foe!*
    > *As looks the mother on her lovely babe*
    > *When death doth close his tender dying eyes,*
    > *See, see the pining malady of France;*
    > *Behold the wounds, the most unnatural wounds*
    > *Which thou thyself hast given her woeful breast!*

    (See First Part of *King Henry VI*, scene III)

    The contrast between Philip the Good and Guicciardini—to whom I shall turn in a moment—is most revealing here. Philip's alliance with England had the same disastrous consequences for France—his own country, that is—as Guicciardini's advice to Clement VII would have for Italy a century later. Yet, while Guicciardini was driven to a paroxysm of desperation by his awareness of what he had done to his country in spite of all his most praiseworthy intentions, Philip could not have cared less. It is this difference that sums up the differences between the medieval and the Renaissance relationship to the past.
3. C. Caruth, 'Introduction', *American Imago* 48 (1991), 417.
4. I am deliberately using this theological term in order to suggest what might be considered to have been the religious origins of modern science and historical writing.

Western Deep Culture and Western Historical Thinking

Johan Galtung

1. Western Historiography as Implication of Western Deep Culture

If I—not a historian—were to try to predict Western historical thought I would use my own general postulates about Western (Christian and secular), or Occidental (including Jewish and Islamic) civilization.[1] I would say, this is what I assume to be the general code for Western civilization, and it is used to explore implications for peace, war, conflict and development, and macro-history,[2] so why not also try it out on historical thought, and as a background for a general theory of Western historiography? Not only are Western historians themselves Westerners, usually applying their craft on something Western. In addition they are usually paid by a Western State (as opposed to Western Capital or Western Civil Society), to teach history at the university, secondary or primary schooling levels; or to do research. Who pays the piper tends to call the tune.[3]

What do I find when I use the first column, "Occident I,"[4] in the following chart, reading downwards through the "spaces" with only one question in mind, how does the column translate into the field of historiography? Being postulates about basic aspects of Western civilization, I could use the column to explore paradigms underlying any scientific pursuit, like economics.[5] But the present exercise is in historiography, asking what we would we expect. In trying to answer I should not draw on knowledge outside this civilizational paradigm, this effort to spell out codes for civilizations. Rather, the implications should have the character of an "unfolding," already hidden in that set of civilizational codes.

Notes for this section can be found on page 98.

The Code of Six Civilizations Expressed in Seven Spaces

	OCCIDENT I	OCCIDENT II	INDIAN	BUDDHIST	SINIC	NIPPONIC
NATURE	Humans over nature	Humans over nature	Humans and sentient life over non-life	Sentient life over non-life	Humans over nature	Humans over nature
	Herrschaft	Herrschaft		*Partnerschaft*		
	Carnivism	Carnivism	Vegetism	Vegetism	Mixed	Mixed
SELF	Weak super-ego	Strong super-ego	Mixed super-ego	Strong super-ego	Mixed super-ego	Stong super-ego
	Strong ego	Weak ego	Mixed ego	Weak ego	Mixed ego	Weak ego
	Strong id	Mixed id	Mixed id	Weak id	Mixed id	Mixed id
SOCIETY	Vertical	Vertical	Vertical	Horizontal	Vertical	Vertical
	Class and gender individual	Caste and gender collective	Caste and gender mixed	*Sangha*, but gender collective	Mixed, but gender mixed	Mixed, but gender collective
	Knots	Knot sets	Knot and net	Nets	Knot and net	Nets and sets
WORLD	Three parts: Center Periphery Evil	Many parts: Each part a center	One part: Unity of Humans	Many parts: Each part a center	Five parts: *Zhong-guo* N, S, E, W *Barbaria*	Three parts: *Nihon* *Dai-to-a* *Recourcia*
	Unbounded	Bounded	Bounded	Bounded	Unbounded	Unbounded
TIME	Self: bounded	Bounded	Unbounded	Unbounded	Unbounded	Unbounded
	Society: bounded	Bounded	Bounded	Unbounded	Unbounded	Unbounded
TRANSPERSONAL	Transcendental	Transc./immanent	Transc./imman.	Immanent	Transc./imman.	Transc./imman.
	One God	One God	More Gods	No God	No God	One/No God
	Chosen people(s)	Chosen people(s)				Chosen people
	One Satan	One Satan	No Satan	No Satan	No Satan	No Satan
	One Soul	One Soul	One Soul	No Soul	No Soul?	No Soul?
	Eternal heaven/hell	Eternal heaven/hell	*Moksha*, Reincarnation	*Moksha*, Rebirth	Rest, Mixed	Rest, Mixed
	Singular/Universal	Singular/Universal	Plural/Universal	Plural/Particular	Plural/Particular	Plural/Particular
EPISTEME	Atomistic	Holistic	Eclectic	Holistic	Eclectic	Eclectic
	Deductive	Deductive	Eclectic	Dialectic	Eclectic	Eclectic
	No contradiction	No contradiction	Eclectic	Contradiction	Contradiction	Contradiction

Some terms in need of clarification: "Carnivism": the tendency to eat meat, much and frequently. *Sangha*: a small Buddhist community, like a monastery, retreat. *Zhong-guo*: Chinese for China, the Middle Kingdom. *Nihon*: Japanese For Japan, the Origin of the Sun. *Dai-to-a*: Japanese for Great East Asia. *Moksha*: spiritual liberation. *Recourcia*: the outside as resource, raw materials and markets. The time curves for self and society reflect the images of what is normal and natural in terms of ups and downs, in personal life and for the society as a whole.

Nature

I would expect the theme nature not to be absent in Western history, but to be *für mich*, not *an sich*. Nature, of any kind, abundant or scarce, would appear as a factor, causing/conditioning or being caused/conditioned by human agency.[6] But the processes of nature as such would not be included; they would be relegated to natural science.

Self

I would expect a strong emphasis on individual agency and on the agency of strong, active individuals, as opposed to the weaker ones, in particular. Categories would appear, weakly organized as collectives or "parties," strongly organized as collective actors, such as the "working class," the "people." But the focus would be on the strong, "colorful," individuals, those who emerge with distinct individualities.[7]

Society

I would expect strong emphasis on the apex of any vertical dimension in the social formation: on men rather than women, on the middle-aged rather than on the marginally young and old, on dominant races, on upper classes—the powerful and privileged—on the "normal" rather than the "deviant," on dominant nations and dominant countries. The others will be "forgotten," suppressed, treated as deindividualized categories with little or no individual agency, or be relegated to nonmainstream branches (like black history, women's history).

World

I would expect world history portrayed as a drama focusing on the West as the center from which good causes emanate, being resisted by Evil in which the bad causes will be ever lurking, and with a periphery in-between, eagerly waiting for the Western message: with God, meaning evangelism, gospels; without God, meaning secularism, "enlightenment," with universal categorical imperatives as God, and modernization as gospel).[9]

Time

I would expect linearity, with progress, as a basic theme. But this irreversibility will be encased in finite time:

- there is a beginning, an identifiable point of origin, a takeoff point from which the process can be said to have started;
- there is an end, an identifiable point of arrival, catharsis or *apocalypsis*, in fulfillment or frustration. But an end.
- in short, time will be seen as bounded, for any actor, for societies, for humankind. There is birth, maturity, decay and death. The task of the historian is to capture that process from beginning to end. Hence, good history should only be written for completed processes, and there is such a thing.[9] This applies not only to the societal level but also to strong individuals, key themes of Western historiography, whether good or evil, meaning that biography as microhistory has to abide by the same basic rules, and then be inserted into mesohistory.

In short, history should be written as a Western drama: a beginning with the presentation of the actors; then something dark happens; then the light comes; there is progress unto a crisis with two possible outcomes, make it or break it, Heaven or Hell, catharsis or *apocalypsis*.[10] If a historian does it this paradigmatic way he may find a public outside the range of colleagues, and even wake up as the author of a best seller.[11]

Transpersonal

Western historiography splits into two, with or without God. With God the basic theme would be history as enactment of God's will or the stage where the fight between God and Satan unfolds, Dichotomous, Manichean, with Armageddon (DMA).[12] Without God there would be a search for one basic secular theme or struggle around which to weave the story, for example, as defined by the four successors to a God sidetracked by the Enlightenment. The successors are:

- to God the omnipotent: the drama of state-building, *via rex gratia dei* as transition figure, and with power as theme.
- to God the omnipresent: capital, market, the drama of the economy, with wealth as theme.
- to God the omniscient: science, the drama of mastering nature through knowledge and technology, with truth as theme.
- to God the benevolent: the drama of the nation as a home, with security as the basic theme.

The sum total, "state-logic plus capital-logic plus science-logic," is known as modernization. As there was only one God, one Satan, one struggle for the soul (Freudian version: one Super-ego, one Id, one struggle for the Ego; Marxist version: one bourgeoisie, one proletariat, one struggle for state and capital), the search for a Leitmotif, *Sinn*, in history could also be guided by Western singularism: pick one. Western universalism would extend that theme to the historical interpretation of non-Western actors.[13]

Episteme

I would expect both an empirical, atomistic focus on details detached from each other, and a theoretical, deductive focus on propositions correctly deduced from a small number of axioms, preferably only one (Leitmotif, *Sinn*). There would be a division in intellectual styles, between the Saxonic style with its focus on empirical data, and the Teutonic-Gallic styles focusing on concepts, contradiction-free theory-building and the tendency to generalize, universalize.[14] The problem with the latter style is to find examples that fit those grandiose theories; the problem with the former is to know what the cases are examples of.

However, the two styles coalesce into eclectic inductive-deductive styles, typical of Nordic intellectualism.[15]

So much for the West interpreted as Occident I. What kind of history, written or oral, as reflected recordings of past processes, would we expect from the other civilizations? The key to the answer is in the last line in the chart, the episteme, as defined by the civilizations. For the other civilizations there is a more or less heavy emphasis on two epistemic elements missing or weak in Occident I: holism (not the same as interdisciplinary studies) and dialectics (not the same as interdependence.)

Typical manifestation in the field of reflected recordings of past processes are, of course, the saga, the tale, the epic; the *Mahabharata*. "*Wie es eigentlich gewesen*" is not the point (nor was it for Ranke, the Christian, who in history saw the unfolding of God's will). The point is to arrive at a deeper understanding, transcending any distinction between "is" and "ought" by showing some whole (*holon*) individual and collective, with its inner fault lines, how they break open, how a new *holon* is arrived at (or not). There would be less attention to detail and the fine tuning and splitting of units and variables, and to theory-building, deducing from some axioms. The focus would be on story as detached from, yet a reflection of, "real" reality. Empirical reality will be tested against, held accountable to that story, not vice versa. This makes the craft of history writing very different, not necessarily superior or inferior.

The basic theme of history as an epic is the unfolding of a projet; as it is for Western history. But the West adds to that concern, fulfilling itself by implanting its projet in others, convinced that "Western history equals universal history," maybe some centuries earlier, paving the way for the rest through sacred and secular evangelization, thereby fulfilling the earth. We would expect the glory of God, whatever His name, to play a major role, like in the sacred West. However, we might perhaps expect a richer, more diverse reflection in polytheist cultures (Indian) and nontheist cultures (Buddhist, Sinic and Nipponic) than in monotheist cultures (Occident II). The hero as the embodiment of collective concerns (like the 47 *ronin* in a major Japanese tale) should be at home in all of them; the individual on a collision course perhaps mainly in Occident I.

In *anatta* (no soul) Buddhism deindividuation may be the rule. We would expect partnership with nature to be emphasized more than in the others. And drama, crisis with catharsis or *apocalypsis* as the outcomes, would be played out more at the individual, and less at the societal levels in the non-West. Society has its ups and downs; inner life is the basic stage.

What is actually being said, then, is that history as a science in the sense known in the West, is a manifestation of Western civilization, and that Western style history writing in other cultures is a part of the Westernization of those cultures. This does not mean that the outcome is necessarily uninteresting. Western methodology/epistemology used by Westerners, or socialized non-Westerners, will capture Western-type processes elsewhere. But it is only one approach among several. And it might be at least equally interesting to have non-Westerners write epics and sagas on the basis of Western history.[16] It also means that non-Western historians trained by the West in their writing will reflect the non-West as seen by the West, and be nonauthentic as witnesses from their own culture because of an overfocus on what can be seen with Western-ized eyes. They have been polluted by the West.

2. Professor Burke's paper on Western Historical Thought

Peter Burke, with a life spent on superbly researched and written history and historiography, has presented "some theses for debate," theses 1-10. So I shall do exactly that, debate them, by comparing them with the seven deep culture the-ses in the chart, codes 1-7. However, I think Burke commits a frequently encountered methodological error, itself a part of Western methodological atomism. Thus, I would never claim Western "peculiarity" or distinctiveness for any one of the codes 1 to 7. A glance at the table, read horizontally, will show codes that are shared across many civilizational divides. What I would claim is holistic specificity, distinctiveness, for the syndrome of the seven code dimen-sions. Civilizations differ, but they—like genders—do not have to differ in all regards to be different. Hence Burke, honest as he is, often gets into difficulties, or doubts, when he claims specificity for any single dimension.

Second, Burke's approach is inductive; mine more deductive, spelling out implications of Western codes for historiography. This provides me with an opportunity to check my own deductions. However, Burke has not examined all history-writing in the West, extracting themes, coding them systematically, tabulating and correlating. He has looked around with very informed eyes and reported his findings, possibly on the basis of a mind-set not that different from the left hand column in the table above. If what he reports coincides with my implications, that does not confirm them, *strictu sensu*; nor does nonreporting disconfirm. These are lists arrived at in different ways. Comparing them we may arrive at more insight in this thing called the West, in general, and as reflected in historical thought in particular.

Thesis 1

Progress, linear view, cumulation and irreversibility. This is similar to code 5b above, noting in passing that Burke seems less interested in the history of one person, biography (microhistory), and particularly inner life, the history of the Self. However, the terms listed above (from Burke), far from exhaust the Western ideas of time. I am missing the concept of closure, not only an end but also a beginning; a basic factor permitting mesohistory (the history of something, any-thing, located between the history of everything and biography). Birth and death are markers for the individual, even if less so in a Hindu-Buddhist context, giving some sense to biography (as opposed to clanography). All beginnings and ends are brutal cuts, and totally unrealistic, but useful for writing history.

Moreover, if Western time is creation-paradise-fall-darkness-illumination-progress-crisis-catharsis/*apocalypsis*, that is, four points of *kairos*, each one followed by one flow of *khronos*, then there is more to look for in Western historical thought than identified by Burke. The obvious hypothesis would be that the biblical drama from genesis to revelation has shaped historical thinking, introducing schemes (not the same as plots) like "equilibrium –disturbance—disequilibrium—light—progress—new equilibrium" as the key to historical drama; like the countless works constructing some medieval equilibrium—then breakdown—then the author's *force motrice*—early modern disequilibrium—one more crisis (like *la grande revolution*)—and mature modernity. The Marxist *Stufengang*, is biblical *á l'extrème*; and the Bible is probably much more important in shaping the West, including Western historiography) than the literary genre types in Hayden White's typology. In short, there is much more to time than progress.

It should be noted that in this more complete presentation of Western time a dichotomous distinction between linear and cyclical time becomes less oppressive. Run the Western agenda only once and the focus may be on only one era of progress. But couple two or more Western agendas in series and we have a cyclical view of history. The Bible runs the agenda only once, but does not proclaim any end of history, only a basic rupture, based on rapture. It takes a Francis Fukuyama (more Francis than Fukuyama) to proclaim one run only; ending in market liberalism.

Thesis 2

Historical perspective, anachronism, past as foreign. Burke finds a sense of cultural distance, that the past is like a foreign country. But he himself seems to have the same doubt as I have about Western specificity. I have not come across any human excursions backwards in time reporting uniformity, except one: the tradition of British social anthropology exploring (for the colonial office) African and other colonial "tribes" with no written language, recording a-chronism, no historicity. On the other hand, a-chronism/synchronism is a question of perspective. In my approach Occident II (the medieval period, manorial and feudal) is certainly a foreign country relative to the two forms of Occident I that flank it. But the basic code is the same, meaning that they are not foreign countries, only different countries with the same basic code. *Plus ça change, plus c'est la même chose.* Sacred-secular, for instance, becomes a minor change of discourse. A focus on codes deprives any point in social space of individual specificity; the craft of the analyst is directed at pattern recognition, not at the specific. The code focus opens for historicity only as unfolding, and threatens any claim to "my period, my country, my tribe."

Thesis 3

Historicism, individuality, idiographic/nomothetic. To stake out a claim for *Einma-ligkeit*, based on syndromes of events and processes rather than on any single one of them, is easy but hardly specifically Western. As Burke himself points out, "the concern with specificity has co-existed with the opposite concern for generality." But this is precisely the whole point about code 7: the coexistence of epistemological atomism with deductivism, exploring the particular, the atom, and hypothesizing the universal, deducting old and new particulars. Missing is holism/dialectics; except for a Hegelian/Marxian countertrend, a trickle relative to the Taoism (mainstream in China) that Leibniz[17] added to the *panta rei.*

Thesis 4

Collective agency, collective agents. Like for human rights, a distinction should be made between "collective" as category (women, workers, blacks, children), as group/organization (families, clans, farms, firms) and as social structure (focus on relations rather than elements). Historians will have to refer to all of this. The basic liberal mind-set, society (and any group/organization) as a set of individuals, prevails. Categories are left to demographers; groups and organizations to sociologists and anthropologists; structures to economists, politologists, sociologists. They would all do better if they added a time dimension, a diachrony. Historians do not have any monopoly on explorations of the human condition with time as parameter. If they did, then Burke is right: there is much study over time, Western or not. But time belongs to everybody. Whether a study of social structure (without names of actors) over time is historical sociology or social history is uninteresting: it is *science de l'homme.* Sans frontières.[18]

Thesis 5

Preoccupation with epistemology. If by epistemology is meant Western atomistic, deductivist epistemology then there is no doubt the West is concerned with itself, including modern (i.e., Western) science. The problem is that epistemological alternatives exist, like Taoism,[19] clearly visible in the writings of, say, a Ssu-Ma Ch'ien. The basic insight of Taoism is not necessarily inferior or superior to a Descartes in *Discours de la Méthode,* but it is certainly both different, much older, and used in other parts of the world. The two epistemologies both fare badly in the eyes of the other; Cartesianism being much stronger on the attention to detail, taoism being much stronger on grasping totalities. There are clearly apodictic elements in both, but both have rules of evidence, in taoism linked to dialectic processes.

Thesis 6

Explanations in terms of causes. This is a specification of the preceding argument about epistemology, privileging causal explanations. The causal paradigm is diachronic, so is history; in principle they should fit each other. *Post hoc, ergo propter hoc*. Regardless of whether we are talking about sufficient or necessary causes, about precipitating causes (events) or cumulative causes (processes)—or make use of the Aristotelian distinction among *causa efficiens* (the push), *causa finalis* (the pull), *causa formalis* (the forms to be completed), and *causa materialis* (the matter through which this takes place)—the basic rule is that the cause precedes the effect. A second rule is to intersperse a dense set of events/processes between cause and effect so as to make the "mechanism" transparent. A chain of falling dominoes is a compelling, mechanistic image of *causa sufficiens/efficiens*.

This is, however, hardly a form of explanation peculiar to the West. Such non-Western macro-historians as Ssu-Ma Ch'ien, Ibn Khaldun and P. R. Sarkar can easily be brought on a causal form even if they do not explicitly use that discourse. That a diachronic representation calls forth diachronic explanations anywhere in the world is hardly astonishing. Burke can limit his thesis as is usually done in Western epistemology today to one of Aristotle's four categories, *causa efficiens*, ruling out "teleology" as some kind of original sin. This curtailment of a rich epistemological discourse to a meager trickle may be peculiar to the West, but not causal paradigms as such.

What would be the alternative to causality? The approach chosen in "Western anthropological thought" was structural-functional analysis,[20] a synchronic approach suited for the "unit of analysis," primitive societies, held to be ahistorical. Rather than tracing causal chains, passing through selected events, with branches and loops, through time, structural-functional analysis operates at the level of the total system, exploring conditions for (dis)equilibrium.

As a paradigm it is at a higher level of abstraction, like a related form of synchronic analysis, taoism.[21] Fault-lines, contradictions, are assumed in any real "unit of analysis," defined by opposing forces of variable relative strength, including parity. When/if parity is obtained for one fault-line, another fault-line opens up as if the *force motrice* jumps from one to the other. These are not causal chains, but properties of reality. Peculiarly Western might perhaps be a single-minded turn to causality narrowly conceived of for explanation, at the expense of other approaches that might shed different light.[22]

Thesis 7

Impartiality, objectivity. There is a case for different epistemological styles, but hardly for different levels of impartiality. Given the number of dimensions available for a description of a human condition, and the uniqueness of a human mind exploring a human condition, "strict intersubjectivity equals reproducibility" hardly holds, but "less strict intersubjectivity equals communicability" may obtain. The set of dimensions describing a country is unbounded. Reducing them to two, like school enrolment and GNP/capital, impartial bivariate, diachronic analysis[23] is possible; strict intersubjectivity (equals objectivity?) may be obtained. But are we still on the historian's turf? And is this specifically Western? Or, is the specificity the Western claim to be objective? A physicist stakes his claim to fame on the combination of an intricate experiment with reproducibility by others; and an historian his claim on intricate and communicable, but hardly reproducible, analysis. Nobody else would have done it exactly that way.[24] Can true originality ever be impartial? Can impartiality ever be original?

Thesis 8

The quantitative approach to history as Western. Burke asks: "Can a similar interest in statistics be found in any other historical tradition?" Maybe not. But numbers often replace names, and the question remains whether history without names is still history or part of a broader tradition of diachronic analysis. Any atomistic, as opposed to holistic approach, lends itself by definition to counting, and hence to arithmetic/statistical analysis. And a holistic approach lends itself to geometric/pattern analysis; not explored by Burke. Maybe the West privileges arithmetics over geometry?

Thesis 9

Literary forms of Western historiography are Western. A historian writes history and in so doing also (often) writes a story, meaning literature. That literature has characteristics that are civilization- and era-dependent has a ring of the obvious; so it is hardly a compliment to Western historiography that it took that long to produce a Hayden White. It is almost inconceivable that similar isomorphisms between the writings of historians and those of other storytellers should not also occur in non-Western civilizations. And, there should be no other science where this is so clearly the case, the discourses of all other social sciences being further removed from any literary genre (not totally removed, though; even mathematics has its "emplotment," that hidden truth, the theorem, being tweezed out of a recalcitrant body of signs).

Thesis 10

Characteristic views of space, not only time. No doubt, the key dimension is center-periphery; within a country and between; Burke mentions Braudel's classic, and work on the U.S., Brazil, Australia. Missing in Burke's discourse is the penchant for world history in Western historiography, with the West as the megacenter. Whether seen as the good cause of good effects (*mission civilisatrice*) or the bad cause of bad effects (imperialism) the West is seen as the center with close to 100 percent of the causation in the world emanating from that center. (West as the good cause of bad effects, or as the bad cause of good effects, introduces more cognitive dissonance than most authors would be able to handle.) The conservative/liberal and Marxist traditions share this centrifugal perspective. Add the time perspective they also share and Western historiography becomes a very important carrier of the Western civilizational code.

3. Comparing the two approaches to Western historiography

Of Burke's ten points, seven can be accounted for by the "deep culture approach," with some reflections added.

Thesis 1

Linearity is only part of Western time cosmology, not only in the sense that there is also cyclicity, but that Western time has several other characteristics to offer. The linear aspect is emphasized at the expense of all others, as a carrier of the theory of progress (when the line tilts upward, that is). But the price of progress, the crisis, is at least equally important, given the drama of what comes next, embedded in deep metaphors of catharsis and apocalypse. The same applies to the idea of finite time. History has to move fast in the West. There is so much drama to enact, and to record as if enacted, when time is bounded, with beginning and end. Hurry up, time is up!

Thesis 3

There is interest both in the specific and the general, as Burke points out, both in the ideographic and the nomothetic. Why not? But I am missing macro-history, devoted to the vast distances in space and time, Ssu-ma Ch'ien and Ibn Khaldun, but then also Smith and Marx, Weber and Toynbee. These are giants capable of seeing more, but with less specificity. They should not be disregarded as philosophers, or, worse, as sociologists. Rather, they have a theme, a Leitmotif, perhaps more projected on, than extracted from, the vast (time, space)-areas they survey; like the micro-historians, the biographers, try to do for the individual lives. Macro-historians tell stories with a morale. They all do that, whether Western or non-Western. In the macro-historians the nomothetic inclination is driven to the extreme, covering "all," generalizing about zillions of "ideographies." But they are as much part of the Western tradition as the latter.

Theses 5–8

They emphasize different aspects of what is usually called the scientific method, and can be seen as explorations of the epistemes of historians. There are sub-cultures, like the Saxonic (more empirical) and the Teutonic (more theoretical) intellectual styles; the ideographic (more atomistic) and the nomothetic (more deductivist) schools. But they are all within the general Western deep culture theme of atomism-deductivism.

Thesis 10

As an important part of Western civilization, historical thought would certainly also be expected to develop distinct perspectives on space, in addition to perspectives on time. Time is the medium in which Western progress and crisis can unfold; space the medium for that major projet: bringing the West to the Rest.

There is an obvious interplay between the two: expansion in space can be interpreted as progress in time. But resistance will then build up, with crisis as the inevitable consequence, and with apocalypse rather than catharsis as the possible outcome.[25] After all, Western empires tend not to last, at least not so long as China has lasted, so far. What this all adds up to is that the center-periphery-Evil aspect of space, with center in the West, is the most important aspect of space, not merely communicative distance. To the West space is not symmetric, but like time equipped with heavy, steep gradients. Then Burke makes three additional points not accounted for by the "deep culture approach"; calling for some reflections.

Thesis 2

takes up the idea of historicity. Any linear approach to history, irreversible and cumulative, will leave the past irrevocably behind, making the past more and more "foreign" as cumulation proceeds. The same applies to cyclical history with one important difference: that foreign country is revisited.

Thesis 4

discusses collective agency, with the ambiguities surrounding the word "collective." If it stands for a category like gender, race, then we are not dealing with an actor, hence not with agency. If it stands for a collective actor, capable of agency, then the focus is probably nevertheless on some strong individual above the collective actor, more than on a collective actor with no individual face. Of course, in a study of some early modern king the point may be made that he was supported/not supported by "the guilds." But the moment the focus is on a specific guild, individuals would appear. "History without names" is still countertrend, hardly mainstream; an aberration from the focus on strong, clearly named, individuals.

Thesis 10

Here, finally, is the reference to different literary styles directing not only the writing, but also the thinking, the entire study, of history. These are interesting specifications of how the individual and the collective (in the sense of the collectivity of a historical "school") subconscious is coded. The searchlight is not on the subject matter, the reality of the past, but on the searchlight on that past—the historian and his craft. The deep culture approach is also in that direction, but focusing on broader categories: civilizational and intellectual, not only literary styles. Hayden White seems to put too much and too precise content into the subconscious, presupposing both exposure to literary styles and some kind of repression of them to make them precognitive. That minds are shaped and set—like in a mind-set, by exposure, including by reading—and that writing is shaped by the mind-set, is hardly characteristic only of the West. More work is needed on cultural differences in literary styles to see how it affects historical styles.

I can incorporate these three points in codes 1–7, but prefer to keep them more separate. Linear social processes by definition leave past social formations behind; so vast distances over time are consequences of historians focusing on irreversible aspects of social processes. History without names is as possible (Marx, *Annales*) as analysis of society without names (sociology). Actors and agency are suppressed; positions and structures are privileged. The sciences of social diachrony and synchrony look more like natural sciences, with individuality and subjectivity abstracted away; and abstraction is a part of Western episteme. And subconscious steering is no news even also when the focus is on the coding of historians in general, not only in particular. But White and Burke certainly add the diversity of subcultures.

Then, how about the dimensions in codes 1–7 not found in Burke? Code 1: In classical Chinese paintings Nature looms much larger than humans; in the West this is reversed. Could this also apply to historiography, as Humans-in-Nature versus Humans-above-Nature? Code 2: The focus on the strong, and different Ego, should make the West more concerned with individual biography as a part of the exploration of social processes. Burke actually mentions this, and a tendency elsewhere to use individuals as exemplars.

Code 6: The transpersonal; Burke mentions God and Progress. But how about the meaning, *Sinn*, of history? To me the meaning of history is the unfolding of the code: the code of the person (personality, micro-history), the nation (culture, meso-history) or the civilization (cosmology, macro-history). Positivist Western historical thought gives the past a loud voice through the "sources," making *telos* more implicit.[26] The epics have the opposite asymmetry. But some *Sinn* is always lurking somewhere.

When Western historical thought is exported/imported to other civilizations and brought to focus on secular unfolding, that is, on the modernization version of the Western code, then the civilizations' basic concerns may be twisted and thwarted. Result: the imposition of a meaning not theirs. And that is, of course, the problem with all such exercises. Strictly speaking, Burke should have been more comparative, offering more contrasts from the "real" non-West, not a non-West trained in or by the West. What Burke is reporting is actually more than Western Historical Thought, namely, historical thought in an age when the West has managed to dominate intellectual life all over the world. But Burke could answer that he is reflecting on "Western Historical Thought," regardless of who thinks that thought and where.

Maybe the contrast should have been made with epics and sagas; "history" typical of Occident I both in the Greco-Roman or generally pre-Christian, Norse, period, and in medieval Occident II. Ibn Khaldun is also Occident, if not West, and like Ssu-ma Chi'en a macro-historian. Maybe both were writing epics? And—maybe that is why they are still being read? And also why the Western macro-historians will probably survive most of the "positivist" micro- and meso-historians, simply because they have a message? And maybe that is what this whole debate is actually about: history with or without message. Not that modern Western history is without message. But it is implicit, and the message is buried in the points theses 1-10 and codes 1-7. The message is what these people—the historians—have in common, whether we arrive at it inductively or more deductively. Maybe the message is not very fascinating. Maybe the authors of epics and sagas simply did better. And so did the macro-historians.

Notes

1. See Johan Galtung, *Peace By Peaceful Means*, London, 1996, Part IV, ch. 2, 211-222, and ch. 3, "Implications: Peace, War, Conflict, Development," 223-240.
2. Johan Galtung, Tore Heiestad, Erik Rudeng, 'On the Last 2,500 Years in Western History. And Some Remarks on the Coming 500', in *New Cambridge Modern History Companion*, Vol. XIII, ed. Peter Burke, Cambridge, 1979, 318-361.
3. In addition, a university professor at a state university often has to commit himself, through the instrument of an oath, to some kind of loyalty to the state. This fact should not be under-estimated, for instance as one factor behind the grotesque servility of German university pro-fessors to the Nazi state. However, one would hardly expect this to become a major theme in research by university professors who themselves have sworn some oath of loyalty. Con-sciously, or subconsciously, the oath would define some constraints on political deviation from the line of the state and, more importantly, on cultural deviations from the line of the nation, and the super-nation, in *casu*, the West.
4. Roughly, Occident I stands for a hard, expansionist (centrifugal) logic, in the West exempli-fied by antiquity (Greco-Roman and Modern); and Occident II stands for a softer, more contracting (centripetal) logic, in the West exemplified by the medieval (manorial and feu-dal)—and (perhaps!) also by the coming postmodern periods. However, the reader is referred to the texts mentioned.
5. See my *Economics In Another Key*, forthcoming, ch. 2.7. ('Culture: Mainstream Economics and Occidental Cosmology').
6. A classic example would be Fernand Braudel's description of Mediterranean nature, and not only during the times of Felipe II, but as a *longue durée* for human and social reality to unfold; wasting no words on the possibility that the human condition is but a brief interlude from nature's point of view.
7. Thus, it would take exceptionally strong personalities, like an Edward Thompson or a Howard Zinn, to produce histories from the "working class" and the "people" point of view. Being already marginally positioned professionally, no wonder that they both also dedicated themselves to the peace movement, standing up against the violent aspects of the hard West, Occident I, unlike most of their colleagues, European or American.
8. Thus, to me "Secularization equals Evangelization," some kind of Christianity without the Holy Family, keeping the underlying code, the "deep culture equals cosmology" intact (*plus ça change*, etc.) and "Modernization equals Westernization," spreading that code to other civ-ilizations, as latter-day missionary activity. The activity, sacred or secular, is not only self-ador-ing, but also self-confirming: if all these peoples and countries really accept these gospels then they cannot be that wrong (as the more perspicacious Westerners, in their better moments, may think).

9. This has one enormous advantage: it is possible, indeed meaningful, to write meso- and micro-history, of the reign of a king, or even of the life of one of his ministers. The historian is not obliged always to write macro-history, about everything, because everything hangs together (as it obviously does). The human condition is constructed in such a way that historical drama can be found and portrayed also in the small. That gives us a lot of histories from the West, but only rarely the wisdom of history.

10. Thus, Hayden White's celebrated *Meta-History. The Historical Imagination in Nineteenth Century Europe*, Baltimore, 1973, spells out what is already in the Western code: this is the Western narrative, the key model being, of course, the span of drama between genesis and revelation in the epic/saga of Western civilization, the Bible. But White's typologies (four "modes of emplotment," four "tropes," four "modes of argument") are, of course, very illuminating and in their specificity far beyond the crude categories explored here as codes. Codes have to be crude, as they are supposed to be internalized by vast masses of people as a collective subconscious, steering their action.

11. As, indeed, happened to the historians/philosophers analyzed by Hayden White: Hegel, Tocqueville, Marx, Nietzsche and Croce, and, perhaps somewhat less, Michelet and Burkhardt.

12. This DMA syndrome can also be seen as a pathology in Western civilization because of the high level of aggressiveness associated with it; see Johan Galtung, *Global Projections of Deep-Rooted US Pathologies*, Fairfax, 1996.

13. Thus, they would all be essentially searching for the same, for power, wealth, truth and/or security; and when they fail to realize any of the above the interpretation may be (1) they are behind, consistent with the theme of "Western History equals Universal History," but centuries ahead of the rest, or (2) they are "ahistorical societies," societies without history.

14. For an exploration of these intellectual styles, see Johan Galtung, *Methodology and Development*, Copenhagen, 1988, ch. 1.

15. I would see the Norwegian professor of philosophy, Arne Næss, as a strong representative of this synthesis, influenced as he was both by Anglo-Saxon and German traditions.

16. As did, indeed, the Ancient Greeks and the Old Norse writers, the West before the West (in the sense of the Biblical, the Abrahamic West; and, of course, thereby also shaping that West).

17. *Die Denkweise der Chinesen.*

18. Of course I have in mind that Mecca for social scientists from all national and all intellectual territories: *Maison des Sciences de l'homme*, 54 Bd Raspail, Paris, and the debt we all owe to Fernand Braudel for his conceptualization.

19. See Johan Galtung, 'Una epistemologia daoista para las ciencias sociales?', in *Investigaciones teóricas: Sociedad y Cultura Contemporánea*, Madrid, 1995.

20. For an exploration of how structural-functional analysis can accommodate conservative, liberal and revolutionary thought see Johan Galtung, *Methodology and Ideology*, Copenhagen, 1977, ch. 6.

21. To some extent picked up by C.G. Jung in his writings about synchrony.

22. Thus, the field theoretical approaches explored by a Sheldrake may one day rule the ground. The cosmology/codes approach used here may be said to belong to that family: the code is not a cause but the name, and description of a field operating through the collective subconscious, aligning human action in certain directions peculiar to that civilization rather than in other directions.

23. Galtung, *Methodology and Ideology*, (see note 21), ch. 4.

24. Of course, it is possible to retrace the steps of a historian; checking his sources and references et cetera. However, given the complexity of human reality and our thinking about human reality the very act of checking will bring up so many new perspectives that the result will hardly ever be the same: "Why didn't he pay attention to the next file in the archives?" The laboratory of the physicist is so sanitized that the serendipity factor, the unplanned discovery (known to everybody browsing in a library/bookstore) should be less important.

25. The end of the Crusades in Acre, Syria, in 1291, with a whimper rather than a bang, would come to mind as an example.

26. In the approach of the present author *telos* does not enter as some abstract entity beckoning from a position in the future, but as a code, a cosmology, internalized in the collective sub-conscious.

What is Uniquely Western about the Historiography of the West in Contrast to that of China?

GEORG G. IGGERS

I.

A few words of introduction: It is striking that at a time when the world is becoming increasingly interconnected in the process of globalization, virtually no attempts have been made at a transcultural approach to historical thought and historical writing. The few comprehensive histories of historiography in the modern period which exist—Fueter (1911), Gooch (1913), Barnes (1938), Thompson (1942), Breisach (1983) and Iggers (1997)[1]—limit themselves to the West, and except for Gooch who also deals with Eastern Europe, Scandinavia, and Spain, to the English, French, German, and occasionally Italian literature. Perhaps this is inevitable because of the historians' lack of acquaintance with other languages. In part this attitude reflects an arrogance wide spread in the nineteenth century, when Hegel, Ranke, Marx, and Macaulay all agreed that only the West thought historically; in part it exemplified a parochialism that showed little interest in the intellectual life of the world beyond the limits of the Western world or even of one's nation. Jörn Rüsen in a series of colloquia held at the Center for Interdisciplinary Research in Bielefeld has sought to initiate a comparative, intercultural study of historical consciousness. Yet such a comparison, he recognized, could only proceed if there existed an agreement on what was to be compared. Without such a definition, as Donald Kelley has suggested, "the comparison between two subjects adds nothing to the separate accounts; one history plus one history equals nothing more than two histories."[2] To initiate a transcultural study of historical thought and writing, Rüsen had Peter Burke present a paper, "Western Historical Thinking in a Global Perspective—10 Theses," and to ask what is indeed Western in historical thought generally in the West, and more specifically, what characterizes the assumptions of working historians in the West which distinguish their histories from those of non-Western historians. Rüsen then asked a number of persons to react to these theses for a volume that will be published in German as well as in English. The present paper constitutes a very tentative formulation of my contribution to these volumes. Fully aware of the "problematic nature of the concept Western," Burke nevertheless in his ten theses seeks to offer an "ideal type" of Western historical thought, serving heuristic purposes, while fully aware that such a "model … necessarily exaggerates the differences between Western and non-Western historians and minimizes intellectual conflict within the Western historical traditions." Burke stresses that he "see(s) the Western historical thought not as a series of unique characteristics but rather as a unique combination of elements each of which is to be found elsewhere, a pattern of emphases, which themselves vary by period, region, social group and individual historian."

This careful formulation raises the question whether in fact it is possible to formulate an ideal type that can aid in the definition of Western historical thought, or whether the mere use of the ideal type distorts our understanding of the subject to be defined. Admittedly there is a great variety of traditions in the West, defined by ideological differences, national diversities, and different temporal settings. Nineteenth-century historiography assumed that a grand narrative was possible that endowed the Western world with an identity through time and set it sharply apart from other cultures. Postmodern thought has challenged the notion of a history and replaced it by the notion of many narratives, each of which in turn can be told in many different ways.[3] Burke carefully treads a middle road but nevertheless holds on to the idea that there are sufficient communalities in Western thought since classical antiquity to permit the formulation of an ideal type. Although Weber is not mentioned specifically, the West is essentially seen in Weberian terms. "Only the West," Weber writes, "knows the rational organization of work," "rational calculation of capital," and the "rational state," and only the West has a "rational" system of science, law, music et cetera.[4] This is not to deny that elements of science, legal system, or bureaucratic organization do not exist in other cultures, but for Weber they do not form a consistent system and do not constitute a coherent outlook.

For Burke the most important, or at least the most obvious characteristic of Western historical thought is its stress on development or progress, in other words its "linear view of the past." Connected with the idea that history moves onward, that it is irreversible, that "you can't put back the clock," is the "Western concern with historical perspective," the recognition of "each historical period having its own cultural style, its own individuality," also the notion that history has to deal with unique individuals. This combination of "development" and "individuality" constitutes the core of the historical outlook that Meinecke declared to be the "highest point in the understanding of things human."[5] Burke avoids such an ethnocentric claim, but nevertheless sees in this combination the quintessence of Western historical thought. From this combination derive the other characteristics that mark Western historical thought. The interest in individuality spurs the occupation with biography; biographies are approached in terms of the development of the individual personality in a temporal context. Also connected with the awareness of individuality, is the fact that while "histories of states or empires or dynasties are common in various parts of the world ... the most distinctive collective agents in Western historiography are groups smaller than the state, people or nation. Among these smaller groups one might single out social classes and voluntary associations, which appear to have played unusually important roles in Western history." Weber similarly has seen in the autonomous towns a key factor in the formation of uniquely Western patterns of thought and social organization.[6]

A further crucial distinction of Western and non-Western historical thought rests for Burke in the preoccupation with epistemology and with the problem of historical knowledge that he considers "distinctive" of Western historiography. Here again a Weberian note is apparent when Burke writes: "Historians in most if not all places and times have been concerned with practical criticism ... in order to choose what appears to be the most reliable version of events. What appears to be distinctive in the Western tradition is the concern with this problem at a general as well as a specific level." While attempts at historical explanations are universal, the couching of these explanations in terms of "causes" is a distinctively Western characteristic. Connected with this is the commitment to objectivity, which he sees as a specifically Western notion, and the quantitative approach that he terms "distinctively Western." Finally on a very different plane, there is a distinctively Western form of writing history that is grounded in Western literary traditions such as the novel.

I can go along a considerable way with Burke, but find his characterization of Western historiography problematic on three levels. Before proceeding with my critique, I would like to point at a serious shortcoming in both Burke's and my background, which leaves us insufficiently prepared for this comparison. Neither of us is adequately knowledgeable in the historiography of non-Western traditions. Burke stresses that to discuss what is distinctive in Western historical thought, it is absolutely necessary "to have a good knowledge of other historiographical traditions, such as the Chinese, Japanese, Islamic, African, indigenous American and so on," which neither of us possesses. Considering the limited intercultural training of almost all experts in historiography today, a comparative study of historiography is possible only through the cooperation of historians in different cultural fields. Burke briefly touches on Chinese and Islamic historiography, but Chinese historiography for him means Ssu-ma Ch'ien, and Islamic Ibn Khaldun, both great historians but not necessarily representative of traditions spanning millennia. Moreover there are problems with an approach that isolates ideas from a broader social and historical context. Western historiography must be seen within the context of Western culture and society undergoing change through the ages.

II.

I am not fully convinced that ideas which Burke considers to be essentially Western do not occur in the Far Eastern and Islamic historiographical traditions. For him the quintessential core of the Western tradition is a view of history which links the idea of linear development with that of a historical perspective recognizing the distinctiveness of every historical period. This is connected with a conception of historical science which strives for methodologically rigorous inquiry with the aim of attaining "objective" knowledge. Yet none of these ideas is absent in Far Eastern or Islamic historical thought, as Burke recognizes. Very early Chinese historians began to write universal histories that were in fact histories of the Chinese world, but then Western universal histories, like Ranke's *Weltgeschichte*, were histories of the Western world. Ibn Khaldun's *Magaddimah*[7] certainly is universal in its historical scope and much more transcultural than the classical Chinese or the nineteenth-century Western presentations of universal history. Nor are Chinese or Islamic conceptions one-sidedly cyclical. One key concern in East Asian universal histories and in the *Magaddimah* is the transformation of primitive nomadic cultures into highly developed urban civilizations. Classical Greek and Roman historical outlooks have also commonly been described as cyclical, but recent studies have pointed out that Hellenic, Hellenistic, and Roman writers were quite aware of progress in certain fields such as medicine and technology.[8] Concepts of development, however, did not exclude historical pessimism, as in the notion, which we find in Lucretius,[9] that development also undermines traditional values and confronts civilized man with the meaninglessness of existence. A striking example of the merger of an idea of progressive development and deep pessimism is Thucydides' famous "archeology"[10] at the beginning of his book on the Peloponnesian wars.

Nor is it true that Chinese and Japanese thought was not aware of the striking differences between historical periods. Painting and sculpture are good indications of this, as Burke realizes, and in China and Japan frequently portray differences in custom and style. On the contrary, Western art in its portrayal of the past is remarkably ahistorical not only in the Catholic Middle Ages but well into the eighteenth century. Renaissance art portrays biblical scenes in the dress of the Renaissance period; on the stage modern costumes predominate in the Elizabethan and post-Elizabethan periods. But also East Asian historians were aware that past historical epochs have their own character. There appears to have been a tension in both Chinese and Western thought between conceptions of universal norms that govern all historical periods, and a keen awareness that every historical epoch is different. The Western idea, present in ancient classical as well as in humanist and Enlightenment thought, of history as a *magistra vitae* was also present in Chinese thought through the ages which "considered [the past] to be a repository of lessons which not only illuminated present problems but also applied directly to the present."[11] In the West there was the tradition of natural law both in secular and religious thought.[12] In East Asia, in the Confucianist but also the Taoist traditions, there was the notion of "Heaven (*t'ien*), principle (*li*), the Way (*tao*) and human nature (*hsing*) as but varied manifestations of one essential order."[13] Similarly there existed in both Western and Chinese thought a countervailing tendency, which On-Cho Ng in a recent article described as a form of historicism. Ng sees the emergence of a historicist attitude in seventeenth- and eighteenth-century Chinese thought in the writings of three leading historians. They recognize the priority of "principle" that provides a degree of permanence through the ages, but also recognize that "principle was by no means transcendent and ineffable; it was embedded in concrete material force (*ch'i*) and manifested in actual conditions." Ng cites the seventeenth-century historian Wang Fu-chih: "Conditions become different when times become different; principles also become different when conditions are different."[14] In a similar tone Ma Tuan-lin wrote in the thirteenth century: "It has always been my observation that periods of order and disorder, of rise and fall of different dynasties are not unrelated. The way the Ch'in dynasty came to power was not the same as the way the Han dynasty came to power, while the fall of the Sui dynasty was quite different from the fall of the T'ang dynasty."[15]

The recognition that individuals differ is also found in China. When I saw the excavations near Hsi'an (Xian), I was struck how every soldier looked different in contrast to the stereotypical representation of persons in Byzantine and medieval Catholic art. Very early in Chinese historiography, beginning with Ssu-ma Ch'ien's "Records of the Historian," biographies form an important genre. In fact, they occupy a much more central place in Chinese than in Western historiography. While most of them were the work of official historians attached to the history office and told little about the personality of the biographee outside his official functions, there were also non-official biographies. As D.C. Twitchett noted: "The details in such works were naturally somewhat more intimate than those in centrally compiled histories, and since the intention of the author was normally to delineate character rather than to illuminate an official's career, their subject matter is nearer to that of Western biography."[16] Nevertheless, Twitchett would agree that on the whole "whether the subject is a monk or an artist, his biography will very seldom give any hint of the personality spreading beyond his professional function."[17] Finally causal explanation is by no means as absent in East Asian historiography as Burke supposes. I am thinking of the analysis of economic conditions in Ssu-ma Ch'ien's history and his examination of the effect of monetary supply on prices, with their effect on politics,[18] which has no parallel in Western historiography until the nineteenth century.

Now to the crucial question to what extent the occupation with the problem of knowledge was unique to the Western tradition. Undoubtedly in regard to the critical treatment of texts, in Charles S. Gardner's opinion "the Chinese are not a whit behind Western scholarship in the exacting domain of textual or preparatory criticism, that domain that is concerned with the authentication, establishment, and meaning of texts," although, as he concedes, "not with their historical appraisal and utilization."[19] Beginning as early as Ssu-ma Ch'ien, the questions of the authenticity of texts and of the techniques of textual criticism are much more highly developed in China than in Europe until the age of humanism.[20] But this is the area of external criticism that sought to establish the authenticity of the sources. In the field of internal or historical criticism, which sought to test the credibility of sources, Chinese scholarship made fewer advances. Benjamin Elman in a recent work[21] has argued that in the eighteenth century an academic community came into existence in Central China that developed highly sophisticated methods of historical criticism. Not unlike the intellectuals in Europe at the time but independently of them, scholars in this community set themselves the task of finding and verifying knowledge. They began to apply linguistic and philological methods and geographic and astronomic knowledge to verify or to controvert important elements of the Confucian legacy. "This change in outlook," Elman writes, "was most obvious in the application of systematic doubt to the ageless Classics and their historicization, that is demotion to the status of historical sources."[22] Although in Elman's opinion, the decisive influence of Western scholarship on China in the seventeenth century should not be underestimated, in eighteenth-century China a rigorous scholarly orientation came into being so that "the critical research carried out by contemporary Chinese scholars is not due to the influence of modern Western social and natural science alone."[23]

III.

Burke is right that the characteristics he associates with the historiography of the West are less developed in other traditions of historical thought and historical writing, including those of East Asia. Again referring to China, there is very little of an idea of historical development. History is not seen as a continuous unit presenting a master narrative. Instead, a scissors and past approach dominates. This lack of development is even present in the official and generally also in the unofficial biographies in which the functions of the biographee are listed, but little is said about his personality. The critical approach to the sources is well developed in Chinese historiography, and similarly also in Japanese historiography;[24] but what is lacking is a well-formulated theory of knowledge, although manuals for the critical treatment of sources exist. Chinese historians in their critical approach of the sources are well aware of anachronisms and are by no means oblivious of the fact that different times are different. Nevertheless the faith in a transcendent *tien* leads to the conviction that certain basic norms maintain their validity permanently and universally. In brief, the historicism that various Western thinkers[25] have seen as the essential feature of historical mind-edness is only very partially developed in Chinese thought.

Yet this historical mindedness is even less present in Western thought prior to the modern period. Burke identifies Western historical mindedness with a certain mind-set which Weber identifies with rationalism, the ability to reduce the multiplicity of events and phenomena to a rational system and the commitment to approach the world with rational tools. The latter, as we saw, are incompletely developed in Chinese thought, but they are even less developed in premodern Western thought. Thus the Chinese were much further advanced in textual and historical criticism as were also the Moslems. As to the latter, I am thinking of Ibn Khaldun's critique of the exodus story in the Bible. A similar attempt at the critique of canonical writing did not occur in Western Christian thought until the eighteenth century. Not only the "English Universal History"[26] but even an Enlightenment historian such as Gatterer in his world history[27] still accepted the Biblical historical account without criticism. Critical methods were little developed in classical Greek and Roman historical writing, even if Thucydides in sharp contrast to Herodotus, for example, sought to establish the truth of what happened and excluded the supernatural. While official historians in China often sought omens in the past to illuminate the events they were portraying as Western medieval historians had also done, many Chinese historians preferred wherever possible   find human explanations for human events.[28]

In brief the characteristics that Burke identifies as Western are in fact modern. Key to them is Max Weber's conception of rationality. Rationality involves the questioning of authority. On-cho Ng refers to a recent, much acclaimed work by Jeffrey Stout in which Stout characterizes modern Western thought as "flight from authority," born in the early seventeenth-century crisis of authority generated by the Reformation and the attending religious conflicts.[29] In this period a historical and a scholarly outlook emerged in the West, which in basic elements corresponded to Burke's conception of the Western historical outlook. But it was only in the eighteenth century, and then only partially, that this outlook gained hold in historical scholarship. This new outlook was by no means as free from myth as it proclaimed, and in fact created new myths and authorities. A key notion, which gained dominance in the course of the Enlightenment, is that of a grand narrative that gives history unity and direction. In the place of the many historical accounts that compose history, the idea emerges that, of course, there is a history (*die Geschichte*): the history of the evolution of mankind, which finds its highpoint in the history of the modern West, as it does in Hegel's philosophy of history, or in an only slightly modified form in Marx's dialectic.[30] Undoubtedly the place of teleology in the Western Judeo-Christian historical outlook has in its secularized form had a deep influence on the conceptions of world history as a directional process. Marx too, despite his avowed atheism, sees history in eschatological terms. This eschatological note is lacking in East Asian but also in classical Greek and Roman thought. In medieval Christian and Islamic thought it is restricted to the otherworldly sphere. For the modern West it provides a convenient tool for bringing coherence into the multiplicity of historical events and situations. Burke is right in pointing at the literary character of this new history, its similarities to the novel. The classical novel of the nineteenth century also told a coherent story in which the actors were individuals with coherent personalities. The great histories of the nineteenth century thus structured their stories in similar ways as the great novels. But this is specifically modern and not a generally Western phenomenon. And new authorities emerge. The professional scholars of the nineteenth century, whether Droysen or Michelet, go into the archives to construct myths of the national past. Outside the West, modern Western conceptions of the coherence of the historical process penetrated conceptions of history. In China, as Elman and Pulleyblank suggest, Chinese historical thought had moved independently in similar directions that facilitated the reception of modern Western ideas.[31] From a postmodern perspective this coherence and the preeminence of modern culture has been emphatically questioned.[32]

Finally Burke remains too narrowly in the sphere of the history of ideas neglecting the social and institutional character in which the writing of history takes place. The political structures in China and the Christian West were different, with much greater decentralization in the West and with the greater autonomy of towns in classical, medieval, and modern times. Burke thus points out that the most distinctive collective agents in Western historiography are groups smaller than the state, people or nation." This is true although in China too there was a great deal of local history. Moreover, the fundamental changes that took place in Western societies in the modern period and differentiate it fundamentally from traditional societies should not be neglected. The historiography that Burke describes as characteristically Western was possible only under conditions of modern society very distinct from those of the medieval or the classical world. One striking difference between China and the West is, of course, the bureaucratic character of the former through the ages. Dynastic histories, written after the end of each dynasty, occupied a great deal of Chinese historiography. Although there were private histories, a major part of historical writing was carried out by official historians. Beginning with the reunification of China and the establishment of the T'ang dynasty, the composition of standard dynastic histories was no longer the work of single individuals but of groups working in the history office. Chinese history was thus written "by bureaucrats for bureaucrats. Its purpose was to provide collections of the necessary information and precedents required to educate officials in the art of governing."[33] Chinese historiography thus served different social purposes and functions than did that of the West. A comparative history of historiography must therefore take note of the social context of historical writing and an important part of the social context in China as well as in the West, and, as we see even in its emphatically secularized form in the case of Karl Marx, has to be understood in conjunction with the religious traditions that have effected historical thought: Judaeo-Christian in the West and Confucian in the East.

Notes

1. Eduard Fueter, *Geschichte der neueren Historiographie*, Leipzig, 1911; George P. Gooch, *History and Historians in the Nineteenth Century*, London, 1913; Harry Elmer Barnes, *History of Historical Writing*, New York, 1962; James Westfall Thompson, *A History of Historical Writing*, 2 vols., New York, 1942; Ernst Breisach, *Historiography. Ancient, Medieval, Modern*, Chicago, 1983; Georg G. Iggers, *Historiography in the Twentieth Century. From Scientific Objectivity to the Postmodern Challenge*, Middletown, 1997.
2. Unpublished essay.
3. See Lutz Niethammer, *Posthistoire. Has History Come to an End?*, London, 1992; Iggers, *Historiography in the Twentieth Century* (see note 1); Allan Megill, 'Grand Narratives and the Discipline of History', in *A New Philosophy of History*, eds. Frank Ankersmit, Hans Kellner, Chicago, 1995, 151-173.
4. Max Weber, *The Protestant Ethic and the Spirit of Capitalism*, New York, n.d.; 'Author's Preface', ibid., 13-22.
5. Friedrich Meinecke, *Die Entstehung des Historismus*, Werke, vol. 3, München, 1965, 4;
6. Max Weber, *The City*, New York, 1958.
7. Ibn Khaldun, *The Maqaddimah. An Introduction to History*, Princeton, 1981.
8. E.B. Dodds, 'Progress in Classical Antiquity', in *Dictionary of the History of Ideas*, New York, 1973, vol. III, 623-633; L. Edelstein, *The Idea of Progress in Classical Antiquity*, Baltimore, 1967.
9. Lucretius, *De rerum natura*.
10. Thucydides, *The Peloponnesian War*.
11. George M. Logan, 'Substance and Form in Renaissance Humanism', *Journal of Medieval and Renaissance Studies*, 7 (1977), 18, cited in On-Cho Ng, 'A Tension in Ch'ing Thought: Historicism in Seventeenth- and Eighteenth-Century Chinese Thought', *Journal of the History of Ideas*, 54 (1993), 566.
12. Friedrich Meinecke, *Historism: The Rise of a New Historical Outlook*, New York, 1972.
13. Ng, 'A Tension in Ch'ing Thought', 565.
14. Ibid., 568.
15. Wm. Th. de Bary, et al., eds, *Sources of Chinese Tradition*, New York, 1960, 500-501.
16. D.C. Twitchett, 'Chinese Biographical Writing' in *Historians of China and Japan*, eds W.G. Beasley and E.G. Pulleybank, London, 1961, 99.
17. Ibid., p. 112.
18. See 'The Treatise on the Balanced Standard', in *Sources of Chinese Tradition*, eds Wm.Th. de Bary et al., eds, 79-106.
19. Charles S. Gardner, *Chinese Traditional Historiography*, Cambridge, Mass., 1961, 18.
20. See E.G. Pulleybank, 'Chinese Historical Criticism. Liu Chih-chi and Ssu-ma Kuang', in *Historians of China and Japan*, eds W.G. Beasley and E.G. Pulleybank, London, 1961, 135-166.
21. Benjamin A. Elman, *From Philosophy to Philology. Intellectual and Social Aspects o Change in Late Imperial China*, Cambridge, Mass., 1984.
22. Ibid., xix/xx.
23. Ibid., 256.

24. See Beasley and Pulleybank, eds., *Historians of China and Japan*, London, 1961.

25. See Georg G. Iggers, 'Historicism. The History and the Meaning of the Term', *Journal of the History of Ideas*, 56 (1995), 129-151.

26. *An Universal History from the Earliest Account of Time. Compiled from Original Authors and Illustrated with Maps, Cuts, Notes, etc.*, London, 1736-1765.

27. Johann Christoph Gatterer, *Abriß der Universalhistorie nach ihrem gesamten Umfange von der Erschaffung der Welt bis auf unsere Zeiten*, Göttingen, 1761; see also Hans Peter Reill, *The German Enlightenment and the Rise of Historicism*, Berkeley, 1975.

28. Pulleyblank, 'Chinese Historical Criticism', (see note 20), 145.

29. See Ng, 'A Tension in Ch'ing Thought', (see note 11), 581; Jeffrey Stout, *The Flight from Authority. Religion, Morality and the Quest for Autonomy*, Notre Dame, 1981.

30. On the emergence of the notion of *a* history, see Reinhard Koselleck, *Future's Past. On the Semantics of Historical Time*, Cambridge, Mass., 1985.

31. Elman, *From Philosophy to Philology*, (see note 21), xiv.

32. See Iggers, *Historiography in the Twentieth Century*, Middletown, 1997; Lutz Niethammer, *Posthistoire. Has History Come to an End?*, London, 1992.

33. Beasley and Pulleyblank, 'Introduction', in *Historians of China and Japan,* (see note 20), 3, 5.

The Westernization of World History

HAYDEN WHITE

We must be grateful to Peter Burke for essaying the task of setting Western historical thinking within a world perspective. It is an important project, because what we mean by a "world perspective" is determined in large part by what we mean by a distinctively Western notion of history. I shall not quibble with him over matters of fact or detail. His is a task of conceptualization. And so it is that our task must be, like his, to conceptualize the Western idea of history and ask what relation it bears to other ideas of history met with in the rest of the world.

I confess to some uneasiness with the term "perspective" when it is qualified by the substantive "world" functioning as an adjective. I can imagine a "world perspective" on the geography of the earth, but I cannot conceive how one could take up an equivalent position with respect to the many different ideas about history generated in the cultures of the world over the last four millennia. As a matter of fact, it turns out that, by the term "world perspective," Peter Burke means a *Western* perspective, which is to say, his is a *Western* perspective of what a "world perspective" on historical thinking in the world might be. Burke's basis for comparing Western historical thinking with that of other cultures in the world is also troubling. He begins by suggesting that historical thinking or historical consciousness is the same thing as a general "interest in the past." In my view, this is questionable, since an "interest in the past" can be said to be a component of any number of different kinds of consciousness or modes of thought, many of which are (in the Western tradition) conventionally conceived to be ahistorical or even antihistorical. Such is the case, for example, of mythic or religious thinking, of traditionalist thinking in general, and of certain kinds of literary fiction, such as the epic and the historical novel.

A general interest in the past, in memory or commemoration is conventionally contrasted with a distinctively historical (or as Heidegger would have had it, a "historiological") kind of thinking. In fact, it is arguable that a specifically historical interest in the past stands over against, and always serves as a corrective, to the kind of interest in the past that informs memory or tradition. When nineteenth (and even some twentieth) century Western historians spoke of primitive peoples as peoples "without history" or as being "prehistoric," they did not suggest that these peoples had no interest in the past or awareness of the differences between past and present. What they meant to say—and often said—was that these peoples did not have the kind of interest in the past that, in the West, had been elevated to the status of a specialized mode of inquiry, turned upon a specific kind of object in the past, utilizing a specific kind of evidence (written), and requiring conformance to certain practices and procedures for the study of this evidence. Indeed, insofar as many historians and philosophers of history defined historical thinking in *opposition to* mythical, literary or poetic, and onto-theological thinking, "history" was—as Burke mentions—a distinctive construction of the West, a construction that contributed to the West's construction of its own cultural identity. It is this move, against a *general interest* in the past in favor of a *specific* interest in a *specific* aspect of the past—that aspect of it that was accessible by way of the study of a written evidence—which distinguishes Western culture in general from other cultures that in general appear to have different kinds of interest in their pasts.

That Burke's world perspective on historical thinking is actually a Western perspective is indicated in his suggestion that in our time there has finally appeared "a global community of professional historians, with similar if not identical standards of practice." But what "global community" does he refer to, if not that congeries of historians from various cultures who have adopted the "standards of practice" of Western professional historians? Can one suppose that the standards honored by the "global community" are a product of contributions made by non-Western as well as Western historians? Or is it more likely that this "global community of professional historians" is an exact counterpart of the "global community" of physicists or chemists, which is to say, a community made up of those who have accepted standards of practice for their disciplines that developed exclusively in the West?

Peter Burke posits a "phase of convergence" between Western and non-Western historiographical traditions in the nineteenth and twentieth centuries in which the "specific qualities of Western historiography" tended "to weaken if not to dissolve." Is this to suggest that the historical thinking of "the global community of professional historians" was as much a product of non-Western as it was of Western practices? Or was it a matter of non-Western scholars adopting Western historiographical practices along with Western science and technology, Western economic institutions and practices, and in some cases Western religions, architecture, urban design, engineering, painting, and so on?

Burke speaks of a worldwide interest in the "Western paradigm" in the nineteenth and twentieth centuries, an "encounter" between that paradigm and the indigenous tradition in Japan, and a "meeting" between Spanish and Incan cultures in the age of Garcilaso de la Vega. But he cites no case of a constitutive *contribution* by a non-Western culture to the thinking of the modern "global community of professional historians." To be sure, he distinguishes between professional historians and "general historical culture" and denies to the latter anything like the kind of homogeneity he finds in the former. Here, he suggests, the situation is rather like that which obtains in the "global culture of professional artists," wherein a number of different "styles" circulate. But his examples of the styles in question are all Western in origin: "intellectual history," "microhistory," and "quantitative history." So how has the Western mode of historical thinking been "dissolved" or otherwise attenuated by its encounter with indigenous traditions? It is difficult to say. Perhaps this is why Burke abandons his survey of contemporary historical thinking from a "global perspective" and recurs to an effort to define ten "peculiarities" of Western historical thinking.

Burke claims that historical consciousness (identified with an awareness of a past), is shared by all cultures everywhere. However, according to Burke, different cultures combine *the elements* of this shared historical culture in different ways and with different *emphases*. To him this means that Western historical thought has no "unique characteristics." So what is distinctive about the West, he concludes, is its "unique combination of elements ... and pattern of emphases." To be sure, these combinations and emphases "vary by period, region, social group, and individual historian" and this variation is what constitutes the differences to be found within "the unique combination of elements" that comprises a distinctive tradition of Western historical thinking. It is because all cultures share a general historical culture but in different combinations of its elements and different emphases that we can see a pattern of convergence and divergence in the histories of historical thinking in "global perspective."

In other words, Burke recognizes that the question "What is distinctive about *Western* historical writing?" is meaningful to the extent that the West or European civilization constitutes a distinctive cultural bloc. Whence his insistence on linking Western historical writing with Western religions, sciences, literatures, legal institutions, and economic practices (especially capitalism). It is not surprising, therefore, that, in his treatment of this question, what turns out to be distinctive about Western historical thought is equivalent to what is distinctive about Western culture in general. But then, this means that what we must mean by a "Western" conception of history depends upon where and when we mark the beginning of a distinctively "Western" civilization.

I go along with Burke in his suggestion that neither the Greeks nor the Romans can be said to belong to "the West." In my estimation, he is quite right to consign both Greece and Roman to another, Mediterranean cultural ambit which begins to come apart sometime in the fifth or sixth century A.D. A distinctively "Western" culture can be said to crystallize only much later, in a different place (transalpine Europe) and time (roughly between the eighth and eleventh centuries A.D.). In a word, Western Europe takes shape in (what is only much later called) "the Middle Ages," and it follows therefore that what we must mean by a distinctive "Western" historical consciousness can only have crystallized during or after that time.

This means that Greek and Roman thought about the past must be recognized less as an origin of Western historical consciousness than as a resource for the latter's articulation, in much the same way that Greek and Roman architecture or urban design were "forms" into which a Western European "content" could be distilled—rather than "contents" in themselves that could be imported into the West and adapted to modern needs. Greek and Roman historical works provided an array of genres for representing the events of the past and modes of conceptualizing the relations between the past and a present into which the radically different contents of both medieval and modern historical realities could be distilled.

Whence the similarities between Greek and Roman historiography, and much of the historiography of the period between the Renaissance and the middle of the nineteenth century in the West? These similarities are not genetic, which is to say, they are not a consequence of a material process of evolution from an earlier to a later generational affiliation. They are, rather, a consequence of a retrospective choice by cultural groups or their representatives to treat themselves as descendants and heirs of earlier ones and to tailor their discourses to the standards and values of those old Greeks and Romans for specific ideological purposes.

Hobbes hit the point when he linked "sedition" to the reading of old Greek and Roman histories that celebrated the deeds of tyrannicides and seemed thereby to valorize rebellion against any sovereignty. But the function of the Greek and Roman models for the proper representation of historical reality changed in the nineteenth century, as historiography became indentured to the newly forming national state polities. Those models in their Renaissance incarnations were ill adapted to the needs and interests of the commercial middle classes and had to be attenuated into little more than ornaments of a historiographical style, which, in order to claim authority amongst the newly forming social sciences, had to feign a scientificity of its own. With the result, if might be added, that what passes for professionally respectable historiographical practice today in the West bears no resemblance whatsoever to its putative Greek and Roman prototypes: as little resemblance as it does to its Christian, or medieval predecessors.

The seeming continuity of modern Western professional historiographic practice—with its putative (but in my view purely constructed remote) past—is typically justified by appeal to the macromodels of linearity and cycles to characterize two modes of construing temporality equally "mythical" in nature, over against which a properly "historical" notion of time can be set. Burke finds in the Western idea of "progress" a modern Western version of the myth of linearity, which, in his view, distinguishes Western culture in general from its non-Western, traditionalist counterparts. "Progress," in his view, is a "secular" form of religious ideas indigenous to Judaic and, later, Christian notions of "fulfillment," "consummation," "messianism," and "millenarianism." He locates in these the origins of later, specifically historical notions of "modernity," "revolution," "evolution," "irreversibility," and "development"—all of which he finds to be more typical of Western historical thinking than of its non-Western counterparts. But amongst the "community of professional historians," which he distinguishes from those possessed of a "general historical culture," such still mythical notions are further attenuated in the analytical techniques they bring to bear upon their data, and the modulating style of their writing—which resists excessive generalization, reductive explanations, and the hyperbolical style of the epic (à la Churchill, for example).

Western conceptions of history—considered as both mode of being in the world and as an object of a distinctive scholarly enterprise—originated within the conditions of medieval feudal culture; and they have changed as Western modes of social production and reproduction have changed. It is the experience of these changes that has made possible the many different "perspectives" on history that "the West" has produced since its formation in transalpine Europe sometime between the Fall of Rome, at one end, and the constitution of the Holy Roman Empire, at the other. In other words, there remain in modern Western culture as many different potentially usable "perspectives" on history as there are models circulating in our culture for symbolically representing humanity's relations to nature as mediated by different modes of production.

Historical scholarship is a cultural means of social reproduction and it can have as many modalities of articulation as there are modes of production available to any particular social formation. It would follow that the "Western" perspective on history represented by modern professionalized historical researchers would take root outside the West precisely in the extent to which the most modern Western mode of production, that is, multinational corporate capitalism, had spread beyond the confines of the West itself.

Viewed in this light, the "professionalization" of historical studies, which Peter Burke takes to be the hallmark of Western historiography, must be apprehended as one with the general professionalization of work that accompanies the transition from feudalism to capitalism in "the West." In short, the distinctively "Western" perspective on history understood as that of the now globalized "professional" historian's perspective, must be seen as another manifestation of the commodification of the world and our knowledge of it effected by capitalism in its most advanced phase. And if this perspective now aspires to a global reach or scope, this aspiration itself must be seen as another manifestation of the global reach of Western, capitalist economic institutions and the techno-scientific mode of production that has made that reach possible.

I think that Burke has (like Marx) opted for the absolute superiority of the capitalist mode of historical thinking over its feudal counterparts. Indeed, in his account of what is "distinctive" about "Western historical thinking" he singles out precisely those attributes that allow us to identify it as belonging to a cultural superstructure informed by a capitalist mode of production. Thus, he identifies as distinctively Western such attributes of historical thinking as: 1. the linear model of development and belief in the irreversibility of time; 2. the search for causal explanations; 3. quantitativity; 4. an individualist bias; 5. a preoccupation with epistemology and an intimate relation with Western "nomothetic" (or law-seeking) science; and 6. the experience of colonialism as determinative of its specific notions of spatiality. By contrast, those aspects of Western historical thinking that over the course of its development it has shared with other cultures are such "traditionalist" notions as (1) a cyclical notion of time; (2) awareness of changes in cultural style; (3) a "hermeneutic" bias that seeks "meaning" rather than "causes" in its study of the past; and (4) certain literary forms used for the writing of history.

To be sure, Burke recognizes that older, premodern or traditionalist conceptions of history have continued to exist alongside of these "distinctive" attributes of Western historical thinking. In fact, he notes that a cyclical view of time and evolution has been "normal" over the whole course of "Western" historiography since the Greeks. And he attributes the Western idea of linear development ("progress") to the secularization of Christian notions of eschatology and the millennium. So, too, he points out the continued popularity in the West of notions of integral period styles, a hermeneutic interest in "meaning" rather than "causality," and the perseverance of certain literary forms (such as "tragedy") in Western historiographical practice. But this is to say only that the older, feudal modes of historical consciousness continued to exist alongside of, and in opposition to, the modern, capitalist mode—just as the feudal mode of production continued to exist alongside of, and in opposition to, the capitalist mode well into the modern period. But it is *these* aspects of historical thinking that "the West" shared with the non-West until very recently; and if the non-West has finally adopted the Western "professional" ways of thinking about history, it is because and only in the degree that non-Western societies have adopted the modes of production and forms of life of Western capitalism. Indeed, it no longer makes very much sense to call capitalism "Western," since it has genuinely undergone mutation into a multinational or international form. It turns out to be just as adaptable to (and just as solvent of) local socio-cultural conditions as Western science, mathematics, and technology.

Burke holds that Western historiography is distinctive in its preoccupation with epistemology or the problem of historical knowledge. Yet it is questionable whether such epistemological preoccupation has been characteristic of either "working historians" or those elements of the laity marked by a general "interest in the past." For most of its history, and even in the Middle Ages, historical writing was considered to be a branch of rhetoric. Only in the early nineteenth century, did historical writing become dissociated from rhetoric, in the interest of establishing its seriousness (either scientific or poetic) and indicating its necessity to become a morally responsible servant of the political order and especially the nation-state. Only then was history's relation to science taken seriously—

although the *kind* of science that history was supposed to be remained a subject of debate throughout the nineteenth century and well into the twentieth. But who or which historians in the West have displayed a marked interest in "epistemological" issues? Does he mean "methodological" or "conceptual" issues?

Burke lays out the *aporias* of historical thought that characterize the period from its professionalization in the early nineteenth century to the present. Prior to the early nineteenth century, historical writing was an amateurs' activity: retired military men, jurists, gentlemen of means, clergymen, court orators, antiquarians, and the like. In the nineteenth century, historical studies moved into the university, to render service to the nation-states taking shape during this period and charged with the task of providing for these new nation-states an appropriate genealogy. This "incorporation" of historical studies was accompanied by the establishment of professional associations for the licensing of historians, journals and periodicals for the reporting of findings in various fields, and a strict division between professional and what would be considered henceforth to be "merely" amateurish work in the field.

Thus, historical studies were professionalized without having gone through anything like a "scientific revolution." In the nineteenth century, history's claim to the status of a science was purely conventionalist; it was by a fiat of incorporation that historical studies were translated from a branch of rhetoric into a new kind of "science." And it was this conventional criterion that prevailed as the mark of history's scientific status down to about 1950 or thereabouts, when certain philosophers of history finally turned to the question of history's authority as a science.

The above remarks suggest a chronology slightly different from that which informs Burke's account of that "Western historical thought" which he wishes to observe "in world perspective." Moreover, it implies a different notion of that "Western historical thought" which he wishes to relate to other aspects of Western culture. Burke never mentions the long association of historical studies or at least historical writing with rhetoric. And this suggests that he has accepted somewhat uncritically the idea that history, historical consciousness, historical thought, and historical writing share some essential trait or attribute that appears at a certain time and place, undergoes certain vicissitudes but continues to develop, enters upon a phase of realization or comes into its own at a specific time, and finally achieves a kind of consummation in our own age and place. Thus, although Burke rejects the view that Western historical thought is superior to the historical thought of other cultures and actually identifies the notions of development, consummation, fulfillment, and the like as "themes" of a purely Western historical thought, he casts his own account of the evolution of that kind of historical thought in the same terms that he attributes to it.

But what if we were to consider the evolution of Western historical thought as a series of discontinuities and displacements that have occurred in culturally dominant notions of the past, the past's relation to the present, and the ways in which we ought to comprehend these, rather than as the unfolding of a single mode of comprehension of a single entity (the past)? Burke himself distinguishes among the attitudes of the professional ("working") historian, the philosopher of history, and the general lay public. And he stresses the difficulties encountered by historians trying to relate to other domains of Western cultural life, such as religion, science, politics, literature, economics, and the like. At the same time, he speaks of a convergence of interests in the twentieth century between professional historians of the West and professional historians of other cultures in which, as in the situation of painting, everyone has access to all of the different styles, genres, and modes of historical comprehension developed in the modern age for a general understanding of the past. Burke does not suggest that this convergence of interests might be a function of Western political, economic, and cultural imperialism in which a distinctive Western notion of history has gained hegemony over other "nativist" notions. On the contrary, he accepts the idea of "professionalism" as a transcendental perspective in which the advance of knowledge of the past is held to be a good in itself.

Burke speaks of the possibility that much of modern Western ideas about history may be secularized equivalents of a religious inheritance. He notes that "stress on development or progress," a "linear view of the past ," the notion of the "irreversibility" of time, the ideas of modernity, revolution, evolution, and development , and so on, may well be derived from Jewish and Christian ideas of "fulfillment," "consummation," "messiah," and "millenarianism." And the notion of "progress," which he takes to be central to the Western idea of history, may well be, he says, the "secular" form of these religious notions. At the same time, however, he seems to sever that part of Western historical thought which might have been evolved from religious ideas from its current "secular" incarnations—such as "quantitative history," scientific ideas of causality, and the ideal of history as a science of "facts"—which serve as the ideals governing the practices of the professional historians not only in the West, but around the world.

The crucial consideration here has to do with the extent to which modern Western historical thought can be said to converge with or veer away from the concept of knowledge pursued by the natural sciences. For, in point of fact, the one and only aspect of Western knowledge that has proven to be exportable to other cultures *without compromise* is the modern physical sciences. There is no possibility of "adapting" Newtonian or Einsteinian physics to "local" traditions. If one wants to make airplanes that fly or build an atomic bomb that explodes, one has to use Western physics. And so it is with Westernization in culture. If you want to westernize, you have to adopt Western historical thinking, for it precedes rather than follows all those other aspects of our culture that comprise its Western-ness.

Western Historical Thinking from an Arabian Perspective

SADIK J. AL-AZM

I approach the task of commenting on Peter Burke's paper with some fear and trembling considering that the historian's craft is foreign to me by training. This is not to say I am not interested in history, historians and historicism, but to say that I am very conscious of my shortcomings and limitations when expressing myself on his theses. I, therefore, present my thoughts and observations in pretty much the same spirit of tentativeness, openness and generality that he assumes in the whole of his paper. I also take seriously his judicious reminder that in these preliminary investigations emphasis should fall on description in the hope that we may eventually arrive at some explanations.

Peter Burke mentions (without adopting) Hans Baron's thesis about "the 'awakening' of historical thought at a particular moment"—the early Renaissance—and then notes the important consequences that such European cultural and social movements as the Renaissance, Reformation, Enlightenment, Romanticism, Positivism, and so on, have had on modern European historical writing and on shaping its distinctive characteristics ("uniqueness"). This formulation immediately brings to my mind the very similar manner in which twentieth century Arab intellectuals in general and historians in particular implicitly (and often explicitly) conceive of themselves, their origins, vocation, role, mission and practice in terms of an awakening and/or renaissance. Deep down they all pretty much agree with a local version of Hans Baron's thesis to the effect that the awakening of Arab historical thought occurred (after a long period of sleep) at a particular moment, the Arab Renaissance in the second half of the nineteenth century. This fateful event is now universally seen as a natural consequence of Bonaparte's occupation of Egypt in 1798, and of the massive "shock of modernity" (and a very rude shock at that) it administered to the heartlands of Islam.

Notes for this section can be found on page 126.

The local image would be something like the Seven Sleepers waking up on a jolt to continue their course under greatly altered circumstances.

The mainstream position holds that this awakening is neither an absolutely fresh beginning, nor a simple reassertion and extension of the classical Arabo-Islamic historiographical tradition, but a superior mediation of the two. This is not very different from the old argument about whether the European Renaissance is merely a resurrection and reassertion of classical antiquity or a genuine new start on all counts. This either/or approach culminated in Europe in the famous "*querelle des anciens et des modernes*," a version of which continues unabated to this day in the Arab world. The superiority of the above-mentioned mediation is seen to reside, by mainstream Arab historiography, in its claims of scientificity, demythologized categories, secular explanations, more critical methodologies, the accuracy and objectivity of its approaches, and a pervasive sense of teleological optimism.

One major complicating difference in this analogy is the fact that the shock of modernity administered to Christendom in general was an indigenous European development, while in the Arab world and Islamdom in general it arrived in the form of an alien external and hostile force of penetration, invasion, conquest and domination. It would be a major mistake to underestimate the historical, social, psychological, political and ideological consequences of this fact for the making of the modern and contemporary Arab world, Middle East and Muslim world in general.

There is general agreement also that this Arab Renaissance/awakening compressed in itself a Muslim theologico-legal reformation, an Arabic literary-intellectual revival, a cultural-rationalist enlightenment of sorts and a socio-political and ideological *aggiornamento* as well. Consequently, both Arab and Western scholars and historians refer to it in such terms as a "religious reformation," an "enlightenment," " Muslim modernism," "the liberal age, "a revival of Arab thought, culture, spirit" et cetera.

Obviously, then, the basic approaches and assumptions of modern Arab historiography, and of its conception of the recent past and present, echo European modes of historical writing, philosophizing, conceiving and explaining on the one hand, and genuinely respond to major local socio-economic, legal and cultural developments on the other. The Arab Renaissance also had its rationalist, evolutionist, positivist, romanticist, materialist and scientistic currents and forces that left their imprint on the historiography of the day and its later evolution. Why all these European echoes on our side of the Mediterranean? Why all these resemblances and close analogies? I will venture an answer in the following considerations:

The more advanced and influential Arab historians, intellectuals and authors consciously sought to imitate and adopt European historiographical models, methods and approaches because they seemed far more vivid, powerful, efficient, effective and fruitful than any alternatives available to them. In other words, the European paradigm seemed to give its owners such superior hold on

social and natural reality that one ignored it only on pain of total marginalization if not extinction. For example, the history of philosophy in all Arab universities is now divided into the traditional European schema of Ancient,
Medieval (i.e., classical Islamic philosophy) and Modern. The title of a widely
read and influential book by a colleague of mine at Damascus University speaks
of "Arab Thought in the Medieval Period."[1] Similarly, the division of Arabo-
Islamic history into Ancient, Medieval and Modern has become pretty standard
practice, and in spite of all kinds of protestations.

It should be evident by now that the relationship between the Arab and
European historiographical traditions does not fit Peter Burke's minimalist pattern of the "increasing divergence between Western and other historiographies
from the Renaissance onwards ... followed by a phase of convergence in the
nineteenth and twentieth centuries." In other words, there is a lot more to the
relationship than this intentionally weak statement of the model implies. Peter
Burke attributes this convergence to the worldwide interest in the Western paradigm "resulting from its encounter" (in the most benign sense of encounter)
with indigenous historiographical traditions." He then notes that this encounter
issued in the weakening, and even dissolution of, "the specific qualities of Western historiography" in favor of "a global community of professional historians,
with similar if not identical standards of practice." This diagnosis sits badly with
the Arab case I am discussing because:

(a) The Arab "encounter" with the Western paradigm was never benign
     as relations of relative strength, hostility and enmity figured heavily
     in it. In fact it is precisely the power of that paradigm, which made it
     so attractive to Arab emulators since the end of Bonaparte's Egyptian
     adventure.

(b) Far from leading to a long-term weakening of the Western paradigm,
     the "encounter" issued in a total displacement of the indigenous
     historiographical traditions; and what the paradigm may have lost
     by way of local dilutions was more than compensated for by its
     extension to and absorption of other histories. The standards of the
     resulting global community of professional historians belong, in
     essence, to the core of the dominant Western paradigm. The same
     applies to painters and the situation of the art of painting in the Arab
     world of today.

(c) The forces that have been shaping and reshaping Arab life for the last
     150 years or so are, in every instance, of European origin and
     provenance, such as capitalism, nationalism, colonialism, secularism,
     liberalism, populism, socialism, communism, Marxism, modernism,
     developmentalism, evolutionism, the idea of progress, scientific
     knowledge, applied technology (both civil and military), modern
     nation-state building with all the attendant structures, institutions and

apparatuses (I will not attempt to establish a hierarchy of primacy and relative importance among these forces for the moment). And since these forces respect neither political, nor ethnic, nor cultural nor religious borders and boundaries their impact on outside regions is bound to generate similarities to and echoes of the phenomena first produced in their original European fields of action. In other words, the connections of the noted similarity between Arab and European historiography to Western capitalism, imperialism, science and law are not mere possibilities, as Peter Burke hints, but formative realities.

(d) When these forces attacked the Arab heartlands of Islam, they did not work themselves out in societies and cultures that are as alien, other and different from the original European breeding grounds of these forces as the inherited enmity between Christendom and Islamdom would seem to suggest. Suffice it to mention that Islam not only is, but also conceives of itself, as an offshoot and development of the Judeo-Christian tradition on which Europe prides itself, and is heir to the Greco-Roman heritage to which Modern Europe attributes itself. Furthermore, Islam descended on Byzantium and a culturally Hellenized Christian Middle East, while Hellenism underlay in varying degrees: the scholastic reason of Eastern Christianity, the scholastic reason of Western Christianity and the scholastic reason of Islam. They all shared Plato, Aristotle, Plotinus, Adam, Abraham and Moses as well. This is another reason why the relationship between Arab and European historiographies cannot quite fit into Peter Burke's mere "divergence/convergence," model and its implications and applications.

One crucial question that needs to be pursued further may be formulated in the following manner: Peter Burke very deftly and accurately defined the distinctiveness of the modern Western historiographical paradigm, not by naming some unique characteristic or set of characteristics, but by identifying a unique combination of a lot of elements and characteristics common to the historiographical traditions of all cultures and civilizations. Now, why should this specific combination and no other prove to be so powerful, efficient, productive, fertile and influential at all levels of theoretical explanation, empirical research and the practical manipulation of reality?

Peter Burke correctly states that "the assumption of progress or development has not been a constant feature of Western historical thought." On the contrary, "it has its own history." What he leaves undecided is when did that history begin? Here, I would venture the claim that before the European Renaissance, history was never really conceived as progress except nominally. For example, in the Christian idea of history "progressing" towards a divinely preordained goal, "progress" means no more than that the distance between the world-process and the preordained goal is getting shorter and shorter. It does not imply the notion of "cumulative change," the defining characteristic of "progress" in the nontrivial sense of the word. The religious ideas of fulfillment, consummation and of the end of history and the world would remain fully valid on a cyclical and/or regressive conception of history. Unlike Peter Burke, I would, therefore, risk my money on the assertion that "the idea of cycles is normal and that of progress is exceptional" in all premodern cultures, including that of Europe, and of the West in general.

Peter Burke's mild insistence on making "progress" a distinguishing characteristic of European and/or Western historiography (to the exclusion of all the other traditions) is really a suitably diluted version of the old Hegelian thesis to the effect that real historical thought or historical consciousness is a monopoly of the West. For purposes of discussion, debate and clarification, I prefer Hegel's robust, full-blooded and provocative assertion to the kinder, gentler and more sensitive version that seems to silently underlay a lot of contemporary European historical writing.

Western historians have of course taken for granted many similar propositions. For instance, underlying all the historical scholarship that we find in Bernard Lewis' volume *The Muslim Discovery of Europe*[2] is the unexamined and unarticulated belief that only the West is capable of the disinterested pursuit of the truth about alien cultures and other civilizations. When Muslims embark on such a pursuit it is always interested, pragmatic, tied to the mundane affairs of war, conquest and commerce. In other words, seeking knowledge of other cultures for knowledge's sake, pursuing discovery of other civilizations for discovery's sake, understanding other peoples for understanding's sake is the distinguishing attribute of Western culture and the European mind. Philosophy begins in wonder and only the Greeks wondered for the sake of wondering. "All men by nature desire to know" and only the Greeks and their European descendants desired knowing for its own sake et cetera. Nonetheless, I can safely say, on this score, that Arab historians, scholars and intellectuals agree implicitly and in practice—but not always explicitly and in theory—with D.E. Brown's assumption about the superiority of the Western style of historical writing today over all other alternatives.

The deep assumption of all classical and traditional Muslim historiography is that history moves towards its preordained end regressively from an absolute charismatic golden moment : the revelation of the Koran. On this view, after every previous revelation (e.g., Moses') history would resume its decline until a fresh revelation (Jesus') would arrest temporarily the process and momentarily alleviate the fallen condition of mankind. But since the Koran is the last revelation ever, the course of history would have to continue on its downward spiral until the day of judgment: a supra- and extrahistorical occurrence.

It was this decline and fall conception of history that collided head on with the imported European idea of progress at the very dawn of the Arab Renaissance. The big surprise was how quickly the more advanced Arab intellectuals, historians and scholars of the time managed to adapt and adopt the new idea of history as progress. The "shock of modernity" must have been so profound and pervasive that it facilitated the said transition with the minimum of pains and efforts. Since then the idea of history as progress never ceased to play a dominant and guiding role in Arab culture, thought, philosophy, history-writing and politics.

It is interesting to note in this connection that the radical critics of the idea of progress in Europe today revert back to a conception of historical change that is strikingly similar to the classical Muslim one. The most prominent and telling instance, of course, being Martin Heidegger. Via his critique of modernity he replaces history and progress with the religiously derived Fate and Destiny. According to him also, after the revelations of the Being of Beings to the pre-Socratics, history went into a decline that reached its nadir—via the barbarous Latins—in the Waste Land of a twentieth century populated by Hollow Men, by Stuffed Men. In the contemporary Arab World, the radical Muslim fundamentalists adopt exactly the same stance through their conception of the twentieth century as a total "*Jahiliyyah*," that is, as an age of idolatry, ignorance and paganism duplicating Arabia's condition before the revelation of the Koran.[3]

The following are additional comments elicited by some of Peter Burke's theses and explanations. Thesis number 3 defines individuality in terms of "awareness of and interest in the specific." I would argue, here, that individuality is equivalent to specificity only in the trivial sense of "individuality," that is, the sense of a thing being what it is and no other.

There is nothing particularly Western and/or European about "awareness of and interest in the specific" as such. Individuality in the nontrivial sense, and as we tend to understand it today, is actually—a product of European modernity. This is why I would hold that the kind of individuality that the Romantic era was interested in has little to do with individuality in the mere sense of specificity. I would argue, therefore, that Peter Burke's third thesis is really a diluted reassertion of an old Eurocentric presumption to the effect that only Western culture—starting with the Greek Miracle—showed an impulse for considering human beings as individuals per se, and not merely as parts of some collectivity, or as expressions of some totality, or as mere members of some community. It is this old impulse that is supposed to have finally triumphed in the rise of modern European individualism and of its accompaniments, such as individual human rights, liberties and prerogatives. I suspect that thesis 3 is another polite attempt at retrospectively finding ancient roots and respectable ancestry for a major modern bourgeois development and achievement.

In pursuing my argument further, I would say also that the "idiographic" approach is much more characteristic of premodern historiography than the "nomothetic" one. The latter approach is very modern and makes no sense outside the novel idea of the flux of phenomena being subject to discernible universal laws (the uniformity of nature, for example). Therefore, I understand Guicciardini's and Hyde's criticisms of Machiavelli and Hobbes, for their lack of awareness of the specificity of events, to be an attack on the tendency of these two great political theoreticians to substitute a nomothetically-centered paradigm for the traditional idiographically-centered one when observing, describing and explaining certain human phenomena. The contemporary radical critics of modernity attack vehemently all nomothetic approaches to phenomena even in the natural sciences and strongly favor a return to the premodern idiographic paradigm in all matters and affairs.

I have no independent means of ascertaining the accuracy and/or veracity of Peter Burke's thesis 5. I find it acceptable only if classical Muslim historiography and allied fields of scholarship are included in the statement: "Western historiography is distinctive in its preoccupation with epistemology, with the problem of historical knowledge." For Muslim scholars were certainly extremely interested in the "practical criticism, ... evaluation of and discrimination between the particular stories about the past which they heard and read," in order to choose what "appeared to them the most reliable version of events."

The origins of this interest and practice go back to the attempt of early Muslim scholars to sift through the huge mass of continually proliferating traditions and sayings attributed by later generations and warring factions to the Prophet Muhammad himself. This gave us the monumental science of *Hadith* and the great classical compendia of the Prophet's most likely authentic sayings and traditions. In this movement to evaluate, select and codify the most correct sayings of the Prophet (and not just all the reported and/or attributed sayings) all the general and specific problems bearing on the question of historical knowledge were raised, thoroughly debated and answered in one manner or another. As would be expected in such an endeavor, the problems of "sources," "evidence" and "testimony" became particularly acute, pressing and highly contentious among Muslim scholars, historians, philosophers, theologians and *faqihs*. Islam had its Pyrrhonists, skeptics, sophists and naysayers not only vis-à-vis the possibility of historical knowledge, but vis-à-vis all certain knowledge in general as well. The evolution of Shariah Law (against a background, of Jewish and Roman law) influenced highly these researches, debates and polemics and was influenced by them beyond doubt.

Apropos of thesis 6, I would like to point out that classical Arab-Muslim thought witnessed a very major debate on the questions of causality and the place of causal explanations in human affairs, historical occurrences and natural events. The two great poles in this polemic were (1) the master theologian Al-Ghazali who denied causal efficacy in the world in favor of divine intervention at all times and places, thus adopting an occasionalist position similar to the one formulated many centuries later by some post-Cartesian thinkers, most notably Malebranche. In other words, God is not only the creator of the world, but also its sustainer from one discrete moment of time to another through perpetually fresh acts of creation. And (2) Averroes, who argued, on Aristotelian grounds, that to reject causality in the world is to reject all reason and knowledge at the same time. Scholars have often compared this debate with the much later polemics and controversies generated by David Hume's famous attack on causality. The thoroughly debated relevant question in classical Muslim thought is whether human beings are the real authors (in the causal sense) of their actions or not.[4]

Only further research and investigation can tell us something about the impact of the causality debate on the Arabo-Islamic historiographical tradition; or, conversely, about how embroiled was that tradition in the controversy over causality and causal explanations of human actions in general and human historical actions in particular. We need further research as well to ascertain the influence, if any, of the categories and explanations employed by Arabic medicine on the problem of causality (Averroes was a practicing physician).

On the implicit assumption that causal explanations are unique to Western historiography and thought, some European scholars of Islam have arrived at the conclusion that the Muslim mind is inherently atomistic, occasionalistic, disjointed, views "life and the universe as a series of static, concrete and disjunct entities," recognizes "no necessary consequences and no natural laws or causes" and conceives of "every event in every atom of time as the result of a direct and individual act of divine creation." For example, the atomicity thesis is very starkly stated in one of the most widely used introductory textbooks to Arab history in the English speaking world, Bernard Lewis' *The Arabs in History*.[5]

My last observation pertains to thesis 7. Here, an investigation of Shi'i historiography becomes very relevant and interesting considering that its absolutely central and dominant event remains to this day the tragedy of Al-Hussein, the son of Ali and grandson of the Prophet, brutally massacred by the Omayyads of Damascus.

Notes:

1. Tayeb Tizini, *Project for a New View of Arab Thought in the Medieval Age*, (in Arabic), Damascus, 1971.
2. Bernard Lewis, *The Muslim Discovery of Europe*, New York, 1971. See also his essay 'Muslim Perceptions of the West', *Comparative Civilizations Review*, no. 13 and 14, Nov. 1986.
3. The Classic Work on the *Jahiliyyah* doctrine is by the brother of the master theologian of contemporary Muslim Fundamentalism Sayyed Qutb: Mohammed Qutb, *The Jahiliyyah of the Twentieth Century*, (in Arabic), Cairo, 1964. The most lucid and up-to-date exposition of the concept is to be found in Judge Abdul-Jawad Jasin, *Introduction to the Fikh of the Contemporary Jahiliyyah*, (in Arabic), Cairo, 1986.

4. For an excellent summary and exposition of the great debate see Majid Fakhri, *Islamic Occasionalism and its Critique by Averroes and Aquinas*, London, 1958.
5. Bernard Lewis, *The Arabs in History*, New York, 1967, 140-143. Note also the following assertion by one of Europe's greatest scholars of Islam and its history: "The oriental thinker, though he is apt to press an argument to conclusions by what seems to us an excessive reliance on the method of logical deduction, is not disturbed by inconsistencies between the conclusions so derived from accepted postulates. With his habitual distrust of human reason, he is content to accept the standing for a fact of ultimate truth which can be completely synthesized only in the Divine mind." Cf. H.A.R. Gibb, *Mohammedanism. An Historical Survey*, Oxford, 1970, 96.

Cognitive Historiography and Normative Historiography

Masayuki Sato

A feature of historiography is that it is not determined by the combination of its elements. Rather, the nature of each part, and thus the nature of the combination of these parts, is determined by the position and role of historiography within a culture as a whole. Even if the nature of the parts changes, the character of the whole can be preserved. As an example of this principle, European historiography has remained fundamentally cognitive in nature over the past four centuries, while East Asian historiography has retained its normative, publicly authorized character during the past century and a half despite its adoption of the cognitive historiographical methods of the modern West.

1.

It is thought that there are two general methods for studying historiography. One is to speak of it in purely theoretical terms, while the other is to discuss it using cultural differences as the point of departure. The theoretical approach to historiography is based in the tradition of what we call philosophy of history. Most recently, it has been thought of as the "analytical philosophy of history." In this approach, the level of abstraction is usually very high; therefore, it is conducted in terms of theoretical arguments. However, we must acknowledge that this tradition itself is a highly Western tradition; "theoretical" does not necessarily mean "trans-cultural."

The assumption that (Western) theory does in fact transcend culture was born in the scientific revolution that began in seventeenth-century Europe. The worldwide acceptance of Western science, when interpreted broadly, brought with it an acceptance of the universality of Western learning in general. And if we think of the history of historiography as a part of the social history of sci-

---

Notes for this section can be found on page 140.

ence, we find that the revolution in historiography occurred two centuries after this revolution in the natural sciences. Specifically, in the second half of the nineteenth century, German-born positivistic history, coupled with the birth of the university, gave rise to the professional historian. These Western historical methods also spread to non-Western cultural areas. All over the world, countries began to use these methods to construct their own past as history.[1] Surprisingly, China—which had its own two-thousand-year-old historiographical tradition—also converted to Western historiography.

The Western method of historical research that spread throughout the world in the nineteenth century was actually, above all, the technique of historiography. In fact, the book that played a central role in spreading Western historical methods to Asia was Bernheim's *What is History?*, which was itself more a book on the technique of historical research than on theory or philosophy.[2] Of particular interest to East Asian historians were chapter 2, "The Jurisdiction of Historical Research," and chapter 3, "The Steps of Historical Research." For example, Kumezo Tsuboi and Liang Ch'i-ch'ao took chapters 2 nd 3 of Bernheim's book and transplanted them into Japan and China, respectively, practically adopting these chapters wholesale and incorporating them into their own works on historical research.[3] In Japan, the style employed in this book continued to be used until the onset of social history in the early 1970s.

However, long before this, the study of historical theory in East Asia began with Liu Chih-chi's *Shih t'ung* (*The Comprehensive Historiography*), written in China in the eighth century (708). However, aside from a few exceptions,[4] this work has been ignored. Why is this? Whenever I think of this problem, a comparison between La Popelinière and Liu Chih-chi comes to mind. And when I compare them, I actually perceive a more theoretical posture in Liu's *The Comprehensive Historiography* than in Popelinière's *L'histoire des Histoires, avec l'Idée de l'Histoire accomplie* (Paris, 1599). That is, La Popelinière's argument on objectivity emerged as a historiographical triumph over a historical reality peculiar to the West: the religious conflict between Catholics and Huguenots. In contrast, Liu Chih-chi's argument is more universal, because he focuses on the actual *mentalité* of the historian. For example, Liu's argument on "objectivity" is dealt with in terms of "classification and evaluation," "truthful writing," "falsification," "discernment," et cetera.[5]

As the language in these chapter titles prove—and this point is crucial to remember—theory is bound by culture. From our perspective, when we read Liu's *The Comprehensive Historiography*, we probably have the impression that the "universality" of Liu's theory of history was in fact based simply on "the East Asian World selected by Chinese-style history"; that is, a "universality" that was in fact limited by time and space. To use another expression, we cannot extricate ourselves from the particularity of our geography and our past. "Geographical particularity," in Liu's case, means that his historical vocabulary itself was proscribed by its historical world. "Past particularity" means that the world system that formed the background that produced *The Comprehensive Historiography* is long extinct.[6]

What I want to point out is that, as the complex of politics, culture, society, thought, and way of life we call the "Western system" diffused throughout the world in the second half of the nineteenth century, Western historiography spread as a part of this complex. Therefore, it became necessary that the various regions of the world, having placed their new point of reference on this new mode of existence, reconstruct their own past. A perfect example of such a reconstruction is the postwar dominance of the "feudal system" debate in both Japan and China.[7] This conversion from an East Asian to a Western world system was not always a smooth one. There are a number of examples of cultural friction and discord worthy of mention, some of which have continued throughout the past century into the present. Therefore, to inquire about historical consciousness and historical cognition, we must eventually proceed with a cultural anthropological approach.

2.

In order to research the comparative history of historical thought, many scholars have compared the founding father of East Asian historiography, Ssu-ma Ch'ien, with those of Europe, Herodotus and Thucydides. But in doing so, we must question whether in fact history occupied the same position and role in the East Asian cultural context as it did in Europe. For what we must think about first is precisely the position and role of historiography within each particular culture. Only after that is it wise for us to compare the historiography of different cultures.

For the most part, the task of historical compilation in East Asia was a state-run project. The "official history" produced by that compilation, along with materials collected for the purpose of compilation, became the core of a historiography. Historiography was the primary cultural undertaking in East Asia. Thus, in considering the comparative position and role of historiography in different cultures, the problem I must raise next is whether there existed in other cultural regions any "primary cultural undertaking" equivalent to the historical compilation that occurred in East Asia.

Let us enter this discussion from the case of China. For two thousand years, Chinese historiography centered on the "official history," compiled by each successive dynasty as a state enterprise. Later generations positioned Ssu-ma Ch'ien's *Records of the Grand Historian* as the first official history, and since then, twenty-four official histories have been compiled. A characteristic that is found in these official histories is that they have an encyclopedic tinge to them; that is, we can say that the body of the work originated by Ssu-ma Ch'ien brought one entire culture—its politics, economics, society, culture, technology et cetera—into a unified structure. History was written as a means of comprehensively describing such a cultural system.[8] However, to one degree or another, it is a fact that countries outside of East Asia have also undertaken historical compilation as a state enterprise.

In the West, biblical commentary and Roman law are perhaps equivalent to such a "primary cultural undertaking." When we think of it from the perspective of the accumulation of a tradition of grand commentaries (a tradition built on the accumulation of grand commentaries), the sacrality of the narrative found in such biblical commentaries surely rivals that of the Chinese official histories. Likewise, in my estimation, the *Corpus Iuris Iustanianus* (compiled under the initiative of Emperor Iustinianus) also rivals the official histories of China, for it spoke of all aspects of life and thus transcended the boundaries of a work of mere law, becoming an encyclopedic description of Roman society as a whole. And in India, does not the *Laws of Manu*, written at the same time as Ssu-ma Ch'ien's *Historical Records*, occupy a status equivalent to the official histories of China? This work on ancient India touches upon everything from caste restrictions and the life of the Brahman to the role of God, redemption, and salvation. Consequently, rather than simply a book of law, it is better to call it an encyclopedia, a comprehensive description of ancient India as a "system." In the Muslim world, there is the Koran, which starts with a discussion of the concept of God and then proceeds to touch on all aspects of the world, from marriage to inheritance to commerce. Likewise, the laws of Islam, which were built on the foundation of Koranic norms, tell us exhaustively about the Islamic "system."

As we can see, even though in many cultures and states the position of "primary cultural undertaking" is occupied by law, in East Asia that position is occupied by historiography; it is crucial that we call attention to this peculiarity. It is clear that in the pre-nineteenth-century West, the "primary cultural undertaking" was not historiography. In fact, ironically, it was the collapse of Roman Law as the "primary cultural undertaking" of European society that made possible the "historical revolution" in seventeenth-century Europe.

3.

Now I shall move on to investigate historiography itself. In the elements of traditional Japanese historiography (as well as in that of China, Korea, and other East Asian countries), we find analogues to the ten historiographical elements posited by Peter Burke.[9] Burke is of the opinion that this combination of elements as a whole is more important than the individual elements themselves. That is an important point, and we should not overlook the fact that from this observation, we can obtain a glimpse of the role played by the past in our present.

But on the other hand, when I think of the context of East Asia—or, strictly speaking, that of Japan—I feel there is another major issue that exists in the background of this combination of elements. For example, unlike in Europe, in Japan the concepts of "history" and "legal judgment" never combined to produce the notion of historian as judge. If we inquire as to why, we must look no farther than to the fact that historiography is inextricably linked with the role it plays in a particular society and culture.

I think I can summarize my thesis as follows: "The unique feature of historiography is that it is not determined by the combination of its elements. Rather, the nature of each part, and thus the nature of the combination of these parts, is determined by the position and role of historiography within a culture as a whole. Even if the nature of the parts changes, the character of the whole can be preserved." What must first be interrogated is the social/cultural/political role played by historiography, for the role played by "the past" in different cultures is quite diverse. Having said this, it is important to actually compare individual cases. And in doing so, we must begin by recognizing the fact that "history" or "the past" occupied an entirely different position and role in Japan and China than it did in the West.

I should start by explaining two features of traditional Chinese historical study, which formed the prototype for East Asian historiography. First of all, historiography was mainly the work of the state, with most histories being written at a government-run Office for Historical Compilation. This task of conducting a new historical compilation with each successive dynasty began with the collection and preservation of historical documents. With each dynastic shift, this responsibility was assumed by the next dynasty. Then, using these documents, the Office for Historical Compilation would compile an official history of the previous dynasty. Beginning with the *Historical Records* in the first century B.C., this practice has continued without exception until the present; now there are twenty-four (or twenty-five) such official histories of China.

Secondly, for what purpose was history written? For the clarification of historical facts, and the recording of all human action. And this record of human action was important because it served as the authority for human judgment. Unlike Christian society, China, a Confucian society, was not monotheistic; therefore, historical fact alone formed the basis for all human judgment. This was an idea common to all the countries of East Asia that incorporated Confucianism as a state ideology. Therefore, historiography had to be accurate and objective. This concept is expressed clearly in the words of Confucius (552–479 B.C.): "All the empty words I want to write down are not as clear and startling as seeing [their meaning] in action."[10]

This idea was incorporated by Japan as well, as we can see in the following passage from the *Taiheisaku* of Sorai Ogyu (1666-1728):

> Nothing excels scholarship in producing men of talent. The path into scholarship is a knowledge of one's letters, and for this one should employ the study of the successive histories … For they contain the facts of the successive dynasties, the Way for governing the country, the facts about the [great] military campaigns, and the

goings-on of the world at peace, as well as the accomplishments of loyal ministers and dutiful officials. Rather than [merely] hearing about the Principle [governing the world], nothing will move one like observing the effects [of these actions and events through the reading of history].[11]

In this way, history occupied a crucial position in East Asia. In the case of China and Korea, as a rule, the historical materials collected at the Office for Historical Compilation were destroyed after each official history was completed. This was to guard against the rewriting or changing of this single, sacred official history, published under the name of the government. Indeed, in order to bestow a biblical-type status to the official history, destroying the original materials was a reliable method. In Yi dynasty-Korea, the materials were actually incinerated after the compilation was complete.

On the other hand, in what seems at first glance to be a contradiction, in Japan we observe a curious phenomenon: a strong adherence to the preservation of primary materials. The most conspicuous example of this is the *Classical Collection of Japanese Classics and Documents*, compiled from 1786-1822 by Hanawa Hokinoichi. It is no exaggeration to say that this work rivals the *Monumenta Germaniae Historica* and the *Rerum Italicarum Scriptores*. Among East Asian countries, this idea of preserving primary historical materials is a phenomenon unique to Japan.

There are various interpretations as to why Japan, among all East Asian countries, was the first to successfully adopt modern German historical methods. However, one obvious factor is that, as a kind of latent prerequisite, Japan had been compiling huge documentary collections before the introduction of modern Western historical research. This tradition would eventually gave rise to the major historical subfield of "Documentary Research."[12] In this, we can say that early-modern Japan possessed a historiographical experience closely resembling that which occurred in nineteenth-century Europe. Thus, in Japan's large-scale primary source compilations and its extensive field of documentary research, we have found an unexpected similarity to the "techniques of documentary management," which were the selling point of modern German positivist history.

4.

From the various perspectives discussed above, I will try to examine a number of Peter Burke's arguments within the context of East Asia, and especially Japan.

4.1. Historical Research and Legal Judgment

As Burke points out, the analogy between historical research and the legal judgment was probably the idea of a Westerner. If pre-nineteenth-century East Asian historians could have read Carlo Ginzburg's *Il Guidice e lo Storico* (Torino, 1991), which describes the historian as one who delivers judgment upon the mundane

affairs of society, it would undoubtedly have sent them reeling, thinking, "historiography can't be such a puny thing!" Then, however, they probably would have
rethought it in this way: "The historian … judges the people of history? Oh, he
must be a judge who, under special authorization by the government, passes
judgment upon the great men of history." For in Japan, and even more so in
China, historiography was a task far more important than that of legal judgment.
History was the reconstruction of the past. This is a much greater thing than the
mere act of judging the individuals or groups involved in a particular incident.

If we read the works of early modern Japanese historians, this analogy
between historian and judge does not appear, and rarely can we detect the influence of that sort of thinking on their historical research. Because Japanese historical research at this time had indeed articulated the notion that tracing
historical cause and effect is very much like solving a mystery, one would expect
that the analogy to legal judgment would emerge. However, in Japan, as well as
in China, one finds no trace of such an analogy.

The long history of Japan's system of trial law would again lead one to
expect to find an analogy between judge and historian. Japan's tradition of a
legal trial system extends back to the seventh century; furthermore, in the
twelfth century, verdicts on land suits were delivered based on the authenticity
of documentary evidence (for at the time, there were many false documents).
However, this practice was never connected conceptually with historical
research.[13] It was after the Meiji Restoration in 1868, when Japanese historical
study switched from the traditional Chinese historical approach to a Western-
type historiography modeled after Ranke, that the consciousness of the "historian as judge of the past" emerged for the first time. A typical example of this
consciousness is found in Shigeno Yasutsugu, nicknamed "Doctor Massacre" or
"Doctor Obliteration." By applying the method of "history as judge" to Japanese history, he reexamined the *Taiheiki* and proved that the fourteenth-century
military commander Kojima Takanori never existed.[14]

That these kinds of references occurred after the introduction of Western
historical methods is related to the shrinking of the official/state role played by
historiography and to the narrowing of history to a single academic field within
the university. That is, in order for historians to survive at this new "university"
setting, each historian had to have his own "specialty." So, in order to distinguish
oneself from amateur historians, university historians created the specialties of
"documentary studies," "cause and effect," and "source criticism." The appearance of "documentary research" as a part of historical research was a phenomenon that also occurred after the introduction of Western-style historical
research. In the West, the "occupationalization" of historical research merely
resulted in the transformation of history into an independent academic field.
However, for East Asia, the introduction of modern Western historical research
heralded the end of the East Asian-style historiography which aimed at a comprehensive description of the entire world.

4.2. Hermeneutics

From Burke's discussion of hermeneutics, it appears that traditional East Asian historical research was similar to this Western interpretational tradition. Let me explain by using the Japanese historiographical tradition as an example. As in China, the compilation of historical works in Japan developed with the government playing a central role. This tradition began with the *Chronicles of Japan* in 720, and has continued ever since. Even the Meiji government, which began in 1868 as a "modern" government, tried to continue this tradition, establishing a department for historical study in the cabinet.[15]

Within this tradition, we can observe similarities to Western hermeneutical studies of the Bible, particularly in the "Lectures on the Chronicles of Japan." These study meetings on the *Chronicles of Japan*, held from the early eighth century through the late tenth century as a public event of the imperial court, were attended by many courtiers and officials under the prime minister. The focus of these lectures was not to interrogate the veracity of the *Chronicles of Japan* or to debate its meaning and significance; rather, it was merely to establish an authorized, fixed reading of the text. When we look at the three-volume *Private Commentaries on the Chronicles of Japan* in which these lectures are recorded, we can see that the focus was not so much to critically investigate the *Nihon Shoki*, but rather—as if it were a Western biblical commentary—to recognize the *Nihon Shoki* as the singular authority and to discuss how to interpret its fundamental truths.[16]

However, the hermeneutical study of official histories (as in the *Private Commentaries*) should not actually be considered "history"; rather, in the East Asian tradition, this falls under the category of "history reading." In contrast, the actual task of constructing the official history was much more than hermeneutics; it was the permanent construction of the past. When the government compilers in East Asia wrote the official history of the previous age, they did so with the intention of replacing a body of historical facts. By destroying the historical materials used to write the official history, historians were effectively denying any future access to historical fact, and submitting in its place an official history, which they thought could possess the same ontological status as historical fact. All that remained was the official history; any link with the realm of historical fact was severed after the official history was in place. Thus, the aim of traditional East Asian historiography was not merely to interpret or discover the past, but to construct it—and to preclude any future re-construction. In turn, the subsequent study of these official histories would be relegated to the status of mere hermeneutics, of "history reading."

4.3. Objectivity

Within the East Asian historiographical tradition, objectivity (or "impartiality," "freedom from bias," etc.) was pursued with the utmost vigor. However, we must remember that just as historiography is regulated by the particular civilization that produces it, the conception of objectivity, too, is not absolute; in the normative tradition of East Asian historiography, as well, "objectivity" conformed to the cultural and historiographical context in which it operated.

For example, in the official histories of East Asia, the compilers of biographies first of all related what they considered to be "facts." Then, afterwards, these facts would be followed by the historian's commentary. The two endeavors—relating facts and adding commentary—were rigidly distinguished from each other in separate epistemological categories. In keeping with this principle, commentaries added to the texts of *The Comprehensive Historiography* and the *History of Great Japan* would necessarily be signified with a stamped character that would clearly identify the section as a commentary, so as not to sully the "factual" nature of the official history with the historian's interpretation. This was the unique way in which East Asian historiography provided proof of its impartiality. In contrast, in the cognitive historiographical tradition of the early modern West, objectivity meant a release from religious and/or political factionalism. However, in East Asia, as a fundamental rule, the notion of using history as a tool in political strife did not exist. In China, history was about dynasties that were already extinct; in Japan, too, history did not deal with current issues.

In East Asia, the ethos of objectivity placed extensive demands upon the individual historian. The following anecdote from medieval Korea captures this East Asian spirit of objectivity. In 1437, just before the completion of the *Thae-Jong-Sil-Rok*, Emperor Se Jong wanted to see it. However, a minister admonished him: "This work of history is written in order to tell about the things of the past to future ages; they are all facts. Once your highness sees it, we cannot rewrite it. If future kings continued that sort of practice, historians would become unable to write truthfully. If that happened, how on earth could we communicate facts to future generations?" Upon hearing this, the emperor ultimately withdrew his request.[17]

5.

Here I would like to devote some time to answering Burke's question, "Do Japanese historians emphasize the "nobility of failure" which is such a favorite theme in Japanese literature?" This discussion will also serve as a commentary on Ivan Morris' book on this subject, *The Nobility of Failure*.[18]

Before that, however, I will say a few words about literary forms of historiography. Concerning the relationship between history and literature in Japan, one fundamental point to remember is that history was written in Chinese, and literature in Japanese. This tradition continued up until the nineteenth century. Within the body of literature, Japan has produced many novels—beginning, of course, with *The Tale of Genji*. Among these novels, many take history as their subject matter; in fact, a number of literary genres of historiography (such as war/military chronicles, etc.) have emerged from within this literary tradition. However, what we must remember about these works is that, even though from our perspective they are splendid works of historiography, at the time they were not considered to fall within the boundaries of history. At the time, "history" was the exclusive realm of chronicles of those affairs of state worthy of record. In the narrow sense in which it was conceived at the time, history was "official history," and its narrative form was fixed. Nevertheless, alongside these works, historical fiction advanced greatly in its own right.

This relationship between literary and "official" historiography is closely related with the Japanese notion of the "nobility of failure." The ethos of admiring those who fail, even today, permeates the Japanese character. There is even a special word in Japanese—*hangan biiki* (or *hogan biiki*)—to express this concept. *Hangan* refers to those of official rank in old Japan, and it alludes specifically to the tragic hero Minamoto no Yoshitsune, who held this rank; nowadays the word is used to speak of a sympathy for a tragic hero and/or sympathy for the weak.[19] Yoshitsune himself was a twelfth-century figure who was killed by his older brother Minamoto no Yoritomo, Japan's first shogun who unified Japan in the twelfth century and established the Kamakura government. Ivan Morris introduces this story in the fifth chapter of his book.

In Japan, the failures and the vanquished (such as Yoshitsune) are admired; sometimes, people even build shrines in honor of such failures and worship them as gods. It is no accident that three of the great masterpieces of Japanese Puppet Play (called *Joruri*, one of the forms of traditional Japanese theater) deal with the nobility of failure: *Yoshitsune Senbonzakura*, *Kana Tehon Chushingura*, and *Sugawara Denju Tenarai Kagami*. Each of these plays ran for over two centuries. The immense popularity of such plays speaks to the "aesthetic of failure," which is so deeply rooted in the heart of the Japanese people.

However, what is interesting is that, as a research topic for university historians, Yoshitsune has been the subject of nothing more than a few biographies. On the other hand, the Joruri and Kabuki play in which he is the main character, Yoshitsune Senbonzakura, has done a thriving business, and is one the Kabuki plays that attracts the widest audience. It is quite interesting to observe from a historical perspective why this gap emerged. The origins of this gap lay in the professionalization of history that began in the second half of the nineteenth century. In keeping with the German-style positivist history practiced at the time, historians sought diligently to specify what they considered to be "facts." As a result, that which could not at least be surmised from historical materials was to be discarded, thus allowing the formation of modern historical study.

And, what has probably been most neglected by such professional historians is the area of individual biographical study. A central cause of this neglect was the popularity of Marxism, which gave rise to the "faith" that proper nouns could be excluded from "academic" history. This precipitous decrease of the weight of biographical research among university historians is a crucial characteristic of modern Japanese historical study. However, just as the burden of proper nouns was being discarded by professional historians, "nonprofessional" historians who worked outside of the university system stepped in to take on this mantle. This relationship between professional and non-professional historiography is related closely to another of Burke's questions: "Do indigenous literary genres play the same role of conscious or unconscious models in the work of historians, as White suggests they do in the cases of Ranke, Burckhardt, Tocqueville, etc.?"

Japanese historians baptized in this modern form of historical study were deeply influenced by such historians as Ranke, Burckhardt and Tocqueville, and in fact modeled their own research after these Europeans. However, in reality, Japanese historiography proceeded in the opposite direction. That is, when the Japanese historical field began in the second half of the nineteenth century to divide itself between the two camps of "academic historiography" and "nonacademic historiography" (or, alternatively, between "public historiography" and "private historiography"), the "nonacademic historiography" side modeled itself after the historiography of men like Guizot and Buckle. But since most of them were not salaried employees of a university, their work was derogatorily termed "nonacademic" history. After World War II, this nonacademic tradition was carried on through the efforts of so-called historical novelists. The realistic depictions found in Erich Auerbach's *Mimesis* were the kind of stage on which such historical novelists excelled. However, compared to those writers who were considered "historical novelists" in the West, the Japanese historical novelists maintained strict standards of documentary historical research and faithfulness to historical reality. According to Japanese sensibilities, works like those of Jules Michelet who was considered a historian by Westerners were relegated to the status of historical novels. In fact, Japanese historical novelists aimed at descriptions that adhered more closely than Michelet's to historical facts. By Western standards, it is perhaps safe to say that the historical novelists of Japan would be considered historians, or maybe historical essayists; it is merely the structure of the Japanese historical profession and the East Asian normative tradition that has positioned them outside the realm of academic history. But ironically, these very historical novelists have, alongside the historical instruction received by Japanese people in primary and secondary schools, profoundly influenced the historical consciousness and sensibility of most Japanese people.

6.

One direction in which these various arguments converge is in the social, cultural, and political role held by historiography. When comparing East Asian historiography with that of Western Europe, this is an unavoidable issue. And when we think of the role of history within a particular culture, we almost always return to Marc Bloch's fundamental question: "What is the use of history?"[20] To gauge Japanese feelings regarding this issue, I handed out a questionnaire to 126 college students majoring in history, asking them the question: "Why do we study history?" In response, thirty-eight of these students answered, "To learn from the past." Of these thirty-eight, nineteen answered by quoting the words of Confucius. The proverb reads: "Try to find a guide into tomorrow by taking lessons from the past."[21] What is interesting is this idea, proposed by these Japanese students of history, that history is "for the benefit of the future." For ever since the late-nineteenth century, university-based historical study has been established as an independent discipline precisely on the premise of separating itself from a moralistic view of history. Yet, even now, these students are unable to justify their own discipline on anything other than this.

To be sure, in East Asia as well as in Western Europe, "the past" is understood in terms of a "mirror." This forms a powerful current in our consciousness of history, and it would be a mistake not to think about this particular meaning of history. However, as I said previously, it is very dangerous to apply to East Asia the "history as a mirror of humankind" interpretive framework, embedded as it is in a Western society steeped in the revelationist religion of Christianity.[22] It is dangerous because, as I mentioned earlier, history in the East Asian world was the single foundation for human judgment; in short, "the sole mirror for humanity."[23] In traditional Japan, before the changes of the mid-nineteenth century, it is no exaggeration to say that over 90 percent of all intellectuals were historians.

Here I would like to pull together my argument concerning the transformation of the old moralistic view of history into a new historiographical framework. The confrontation between the two is what I have termed "Cognitive Historiography versus Normative Historiography." Before this confrontation history was a cognitive field of study in the West, while it was a normative one in the East. However, long after this confrontation, East Asian historiography continues to fundamentally retain its normative character. History in East Asia has always constructed political, social, and cultural norms. Therefore, whenever a particular form of historical work (such as biography or chronology) emerged, it became fixed, and the historical writings of successive generations passed along these same tracks. These models were preserved, and sanctioned publicly by the government, precisely because they were viewed as norms. And, as a result, this normative tradition would persist, despite the fact that Japanese have actively adopted Western cognitive historical techniques ever since the mid-nineteenth century. This is what I stated in my initial thesis: "even if the nature of the parts changes, the character of the whole can be preserved." In the case of Japan, despite the historiographical changes of the past century and a half, the tradition of historical compilation by a public institution—and, in fact, the tradition of normative history in general has continued uninterrupted, and flourishes even today. To observe this phenomenon, one needs only to consider the history textbooks or local histories being produced today, with their rigidly fixed form and their explicit "authorization" received from central (or, in the case of local histories, local) governments.

In contrast, since the sixteenth century, historical research in the West has constructed itself as a cognitive field of study in opposition to the other academic fields of the time. The new "cognitive method," which sought to make sense of the events of the time within their historical context, emerged in nineteenth-century Germany. If we think of the emergence of works on historiography (in which La Popelinière was a pioneer) as an early sprout of the cognitive view of history in the West, then the flood of works on historical theory in nineteenth-century Germany can be seen to signify the establishment of history as an independent, cognitively defined discipline.[24]

East Asia was a culture of the written word, and at its core was historiography. But why is it that, in proportion to the great number of historical works produced in East Asia, works of cognitive historiography were so sparse? I have been thinking about this question continuously for the past twenty years. My present answer is this: norms value form, while form precludes the possibility of cognitivism. However, twentieth-century East Asian historiography is clearly the site of a confrontation between normative historiography and cognitive historiography. I believe that a metahistorical examination of normative historiography will clear the way towards a new horizon in cognitive history.

Notes

1. Georg G. Iggers, 'Geschichtswissenschaft im 20. Jahrhundert. Einige Überlegungen', *Shakai Keizai Shigaku* 60-2, 1-23.
2. Ernst Bernheim, *Einleitung in die Geschichtswissenschaft*, Berlin, 1905. The Japanese translation was first published in 1922, but before that, Bernheim's *Lehrbuch der Historischen Methode*, Berlin, 1889, was also widely read among Japanese historians.
3. Kumezo, *Shigaku kokyuho*, Tokyo, 1903; Liang Ch'i-ch'ao, *Chung-kuo Li-shih yea-chiafa*, 1922.
4. Naito Konan, *Shina shigakushi*, 1949; Tanaka Suiichiro, 'Liang Ch'-ch'ao no rekishi kenkyuhoh' in id., *Shigaku ronbunshu*, Tokyo, 1900, 347-385.
5. See vol. 7 of Liu's *Shih t'ung*.
6. Burton Watson, *Ssu-ma Ch'ien: Grand Historian of China*, New York, 1958, 104.
7. Suzuki Shun, Nishijima Sadao, eds, *Chugokushi no jidai kubun*, Tokyo, 1957).
8. Tsuneo Matsui, *Chugokushi*, Tokyo, 1981.
9. However, we must wait until the first half of the nineteenth century for the appearance of the quantitative approach.
10. See Ssu-ma Ch'ien, *Shih chi*, ch. 70.
11. Sorai Ogyu, 'Taiheisaku', in *Ogyu Sorai* [vol. 36 of the *Nihon Shiso Taikei*], Tokyo, 1973, 485.
12. Juichi Igi, *Nihon komonjyogaku*, Tokyo, 1995, 18-37.
13. Shin'ichi Sato, *Komonjyogaku nyumon*, Tokyo, 1971, 4-5.

14. Yasutsugu Shigeno, 'Kojima Takanori', in *Shigeno hakase shigaku ronbunshu*, vol. 2, Tokyo, 1938, 577-590.
15. Toshiaki Okubo, *Kindai nihonshigaku no seiritsu*, Tokyo, 1988, 70.
16. Shojiro Ota, 'Jodai ni okeru Nihonshoki kokyu', in *Honpo shigakushi ronso*, Tokyo, 1939, 367-422.
17. Suiichiro Tanaka, *Tanaka Suiichiro shigaku ronbunshu*, Tokyo, 1900, 510-512.
18. Ivan Morris, *The Nobility of Failure*, London, 1975.
19. Tadao Sato, *Nihonjin no shinjyo*, Tokyo, 1976.
20. Marc Bloch, *Apologie pour l'Histoire ou Metier d'Historien*, Paris, 1949, introduction.
21. This quote originates from Confucius' *Analects*. However, what is more interesting is that the original meaning of the proverb was something like, "If one study over and over again the things he has learned in the past, he can arrive at a new interpretation. Such a person can perhaps become a teacher." This passage conveys the meaning that interpretation is the primary duty of the scholar. This original meaning has disappeared from the minds of most Japanese.
22. For example, see J.H. Plumb, *Death of the Past*, London, 1969.
23. This makes one think of J. Huizinga's 'Over Historische Levensidealen', in *Verzamelde Werken*, vol. IV, 411-432.
24. Jörn Rüsen, *Studies in Metahistory*, Pretoria, 1993, 97-128.

Western Uniqueness?

Some Counterarguments from an African Perspective

GODFREY MURIUKI

Peter Burke has deftly examined European historical thought from the classical period to the present. He recognizes that interest in the past appears to have existed everywhere in all periods. However, he contends that European historical thought is distinct due to a unique combination of elements. Nevertheless, he readily admits that his model exaggerates the differences between Western and non-Western historians while at the same time underplaying the intellectual conflict inherent in the Western historical tradition itself.

His model then looks at ten features that he considers to cumulatively make Western historical thought unique. All in all, these are provocative propositions that render the chapter worth reading. Indeed, there is much that one agrees with. For example, the stress on epistemology, quantitative approach and historical explanation in terms of "causes" seem to be peculiar features of the Western historiography. Others, however, do not appear to be that clear-cut. Consequently, this commentary intends to examine a few of his propositions in order to test the validity of his overall argument and thesis.

Take, for example, the idea of progress. The view that change is cumulative would seem to go beyond the Jewish and Christian traditions mentioned by Burke. The germ of the idea was planted in the Fertile Crescent, particularly in ancient Persia. In the Persian religion—Zoroastrism—the struggle between Ahura-Mazda, the wise lord, and Ahriman, the hostile spirit, was expected to culminate in a final struggle whereby goodness would triumph over evil. The cumulative effect of all this would be a final judgement before entry into eternal paradise. Equally, Burke proposes that anachronism is a unique feature of the Western historical thought. He contends that he finds it difficult "to find examples of historians in other parts of the world (and uninfluenced by Western paradigms), who demonstrate the acute interest in the individuality of epochs, regions or persons." This view is debatable to say the least.

In recent years, students of African history have carried out historical studies using oral traditions or narratives and descriptions about the past orally transmitted from generation to generation.[1] These studies have provided ample evidence to demonstrate that there existed "a sense of individuality" for epochs, regions or even individuals who played a prominent historical role in their society. For instance, in many African societies initiation—normally through circumcision—was a widespread phenomenon. This was considered to be both a private family affair as well as a public ceremony. The importance attached to it arose from the fact that it was a rite of passage during which the youth graduated into adulthood. Indeed, the allocation of public responsibilities to, and the acquisition of privileges by, individuals could only be done after undergoing such a ceremony. For example, a young man could only be married after initiation and having served the community as a warrior for a prescribed period of time. With modifications, the same rule applied to young women.

As Jacobs and Muriuki[2] have shown, initiation constituted one of the most important rituals in an individual's entire life. Moreover, it was rigidly controlled by the community, which considered it to be a public or communal affair rather than a private one. It was for this reason that the community dictated when or whether initiation could take place or not. In the case of the Kikuyu and Maasai of Kenya, there was a closed period during which no initiation was allowed to take place. This was meant to allow the youth to mature so that on initiation he would be physically developed enough to shoulder the public responsibilities expected of him. In this respect, a major consideration was whether or not he would be capable of carrying out his military duties. After the prescribed closed period, initiation was then allowed to take place before another enclosed period was imposed. Depending on the community and locality, a closed period lasted nine years and an open period five or vice versa. Thus one cycle normally took about fourteen years.

All those young men who were initiated at a given open period of initiation formed an age or warrior set. Moreover—and important for our purposes—they considered themselves to be coevals. Not only did they consider themselves to be brothers, but they had a high degree of solidarity. Their sense of mutual interest was so high that, when visiting each other, it was not uncommon for an age set mate to be offered hospitality that included the sharing of sexual favors of each other's wives. That, I am sure, is incomprehensible to the Western world. But to these communities, this constituted or was indicative of a valuable social bond.

Above all, each age set was given a name that encapsulated the most important events that occurred immediately before, during or after its initiation. In this way, the names of age sets were invariably associated with the major historical events that were considered to be peculiar to their time or epoch. Hence these names commemorate wars fought, famines and diseases endured, or significant social—economic trends. In short, the names are a summary of communal history as remembered. From this perspective, each age set was considered to be unique. And by extension, both the Kikuyu and Maasai had thus a distinct concept of the uniqueness of each age set or epoch. Furthermore, each one of them was remembered not only for its "uniqueness" but also for its "individuality." Amongst the Kikuyu, for example, the mere mention of the name of an age set evoked particular historical characteristics in the collective memory.

Furthermore, the Kikuyu were, and still are, deeply attached to their land. They regard this as a bequest from their ancestors, which must be safeguarded at all costs. It is for this reason that, during the colonial period, the cry for a return of the alienated land became an irresistible battle cry against the British government. Thus their patch of territory was more than just a piece of land.

Equally, collective agency does not appear to be necessarily peculiar to the Western historical thought. Once again., in Africa oral traditions lay a special emphasis on "collective agency." African societies place a special value on mutual social responsibility in contrast to the individualism espoused by the Western world. For this reason, historical narratives have a special function of enhancing "collective agency." Moreover, historical narratives constitute living history as they are essentially a record of what people think is important about their past.[3] Take the Kikuyu as an example. Their history indicates that their ancestors were a disparate group of people. To weld them together into a community, they evolved a legend that claims that they are all descendants of the eponymous Gikuyu and his wife Mumbi. The couple is supposed to have procreated ten daughters whose descendants eventually became the ten Kikuyu clans. In a nutshell, here is a manipulation of oral traditions to suit a particular set of historical circumstances. Here historical narratives have been modified to suit a particular conception of history. However, this is not an extraordinary phenomenon.

Manipulation of tradition is a tool that is often used by rulers and leaders in their endeavor to legitimize their positions. Some historians would call this phenomenon "the invention of tradition."[4] For example, Trevor-Roper shows how Macpherson and Stuart fabricated the Scottish bagpipe, kilt and the association between the tartans and clans. And they claimed that these were old Celtic cultural items in order to boost Scottish nationalism or individuality. Similarly, Ranger shows that Europeans had to invent traditions to define and justify their colonial roles. In the mines, for example, they created rituals of craft unionism in order to exclude Africans. At the same time, in order to ensure that there was a reasonably contented colonial civil service, the British establishment was at pains to sell the glamour of serving the empire and participation in the noble cause of spreading the blessings of Western civilization to benighted Africans.

These examples illustrate that the concept of collective agency is by no means a monopoly of Western historical thought. Western historiography may lay emphasis on the family, city, church or the army. Elsewhere the focus will be on different social categories or institutions that are specific to these societies and reflect their local mores. In Africa, these will be the extended family, the

clan or age set. Though different in many respects, these social groups or institutions in the Western world and Africa play an important socializing role that
has important historical implications.

This brings me to the final comment. In the last three decades, there has been
an upsurge of interest in the social history of daily life. This has led to the use of
oral sources in the production of historical knowledge even in the Western world.
The resurgence of interest in the oral sources is the culmination of a struggle that
has been successfully waged by African historians, amongst others. It should be
noted that from the Renaissance period written sources increased rapidly, a feature that saw a corresponding decrease in the use of oral sources. The upshot was
that by the nineteenth century oral sources had become virtually obsolete as
sources of history in the Western world. It was then even claimed that the basis of
history was the existence of written sources. Consequently, it was argued that for
Africa, which lacked written records until the arrival of Moslems and Europeans,
there could be no history worth bothering about. Hence, emphasis on literacy
encouraged contempt for the so-called primitive people and went some way to
justify conquest and partition of Africa. In other words, Africans had no history
worth talking, or writing, about before the arrival of foreigners who acted as a catalyst for whatever subsequent developments were discernible in the continent.

Students of African history took issue with that contention, particularly
from the 1960s. Fired by the euphoria of the coming of independence, they
contended that Eurocentric historians had misunderstood the nature of historical evidence and seemed obsessed by the written word. To Eurocentric historians, the crucial factor was what was meant by the phrase "historical evidence,"
which they interpreted to mean any shred of material that could be used to offer
a glimpse of the past. And if that were the case, resoned students of African history, then this need not be necessarily written documents: it could be artifacts,
legends, myths, poetry, songs and dances. Can a people exist without a history,
they wondered aloud? "No," they thundered back, because the maintenance of,
and continuity in, a society demands some form of collective memory or history. It was equally clear to students of African history that the attempt to control knowledge about the past was a deliberate and calculated move designed to
ensure an efficient control of the colonized peoples. Above all, this formed an
essential element of the Westernization process that was intended to produce a
compliant populace under the guise of the white man's burden.

For this reason, since the 1960s there has been a flurry of academic activity aimed at reconstructing the African past by whatever tools have been available to students of African history. In particular, they have paid attention to
arguments advanced against the use of oral sources. Critics of this genre of
sources have questioned the reliability of oral testimonies, which are at the
mercy of the unpredictable vagaries of the human memory. Furthermore, they
have pointed out that historical narratives have a social function to perform in
every society and hence are subject to distortion, selectivity and subjectivity.

In their turn, African historians have pointed out that the use of oral sources is nothing new. It is the oldest known method of transmitting historical knowledge as evidenced even in the Western world.[5] They are particularly fond of reminding the skeptics that in Africa this is living history—since oral traditions are alive—not dead history as is the case in the Western world. Even more, they add, nonliterate societies have a big capacity for memory. In any event, a lot of care was taken to ensure that these traditions were carefully transmitted by experts, such as the griots of West Africa. In other situations, oral traditions were taught by renowned experts during initiation ceremonies when the youth became adults. Coming at such a critical and impressionable stage, the neophytes could hardly forget those traditions throughout their lives. Finally, African historians point out that the major historical sins—of distortion, selectivity and subjectivity—do not only afflict oral sources. They are inherent in the discipline of history and equally plague written documents.

The debate about the viability of oral sources has raised interesting questions about the nature of history and historical knowledge. Historical narratives and personal reminiscences have been viewed as an effective tool in re-creating the past, particularly the neglected or "excluded past."[6] Some historians vehemently believe that this development has given the ordinary people a chance to participate in the reconstruction of their past that has hitherto been the preserve of the academic elite. Many a historian has thus welcomed this democratization of historical knowledge.

But it would be erroneous to assume that the use of oral sources has been confined to African historians. The bug has spread to the Western world where, if one may be allowed to surmise, it is bound to have an appreciable impact on Western historical thought, particularly in the field of methodology and epistemology. A few examples will suffice. The London School of Economics and Political Science established a British Oral Archive of Political and Administrative History in 1980. Moreover under the auspices of the History Workshop an appreciable work has been carried out amongst the ordinary people, such as the Welsh miners, using personal reminiscences as a research tool. And in the United States significant studies, based on oral sources, have recently been carried out particularly among African Americans. Even further back, historians at Columbia University in the U.S.—such as Allan Nevins—and the School of Oriental and African Studies of the University of London have maintained a healthy respect for oral sources since the 1940s. In short, then and as of now, there have been many intersections between Western historical thought and others. This feature would seem to call into question the "uniqueness" of the Western historical thought. Perhaps the problem lies in the fact that, comparatively, a lot more is known about the Western historical thought than those of the non-Western cultures. The hiatus, therefore, may very well revolve around the "excluded past."

Notes

1. J.Vansina, *Oral Tradition as History*, London, 1985.
2. A. H. Jacobs, 'A Chronology of the Pastoral Maasai', in *Hadith* I, B.A. Ogot, ed., Nairobi, 1968, 11—31; G. Muriuki, *A History of the Kikuyu 1500—1900*, Oxford, Nairobi, 1974.
3. UNESCO, *General History of Africa*, London, 1981, vol. I.
4. Eric Hobsbawm and Terence Rangers eds, *The Invention of Tradition*, Cambridge, 1983.
5. Cf. D. Henige, *Oral Historiography*, London, 1982; Trevor Lummis, *Listening to History. The Authenticity of Oral Evidence*, Totowa, 1987; J. Tosh, *The Pursuit of History. Aims, Methods, and New Directions in the Study of Modern History*, London, 1984; UNESCO, *General History of Africa*, London, 1981, vol. I.
6. P. Stone and R. Mackenzie, eds, *The Excluded Past. Archaeology in Education*, London, 1990.

Historical Programs
A Western Perspective[1]

MAMADOU DIAWARA

Peter Burke's equally bold and well-documented essay deals with historical thinking in its global sense. From the very beginning the author makes it easy for the commentator: He articulates theses that are explicitly marked as being a matter of discussion. Burke relies on the following presuppositions:

— In opposition to hypotheses of philosophers such as Hegel or Hans Baron, the interest in history is universal.
— Distinguishing the special character of European historical thought calls for a good knowledge of other historiographical traditions: of Chinese, Japanese, Islamic and African historical thinking as well as of the thought of the "autochthon" in America. What is more, Burke articulates the idea that the Occident is not given as such, but is rather a historical construct.

Very carefully, without losing sight of his main argument, but also without hesitation, the author writes about the peculiarities of European historiography and about the search for the common grounds of the differences, which he does not consider as a number of equal characteristics, but as equal combinations of elements, each of which can be found somewhere else as well. Implicitly the Cambridge historian defines an occidental space of analysis ranging from the most noble of the European ancestors, the Greeks, to the "Neo-Europeans" of the "New World." Although the author can never be accused of directly relying on dichotomies, this space is set against China and Japan. Also the Arabic world, represented by the great Ibn Khaldun, is not left aside. This roughly complete list calls for some remarks.

Reducing Western historical thinking to a fixed unity remains not without consequences for its depth and heterogeneity. To oppose this singular unity to other unities, disregarding of their origins, represents at least a dangerous way of thinking. Does not the search for the common denominator of so-called historical thinking inevitably lead to the discovery of the respective ways of thinking of a particular geographical and cultural region? Already the example of Europe reveals that it is merely an arbitrary construction. The historian's list dangerously tends to rely on a "Europe" as being "the West" and on a certain image of Asia. This is understandable if one considers the specific method of academic research: You can ground your hypotheses only on what already exists. One has to start from some point! On the other hand, this does not legitimize relying exclusively and de facto upon written historical accounts. The discourse of a nation's past that is primarily based upon oral traditions remains thereby almost unacknowledged. It can be found in only a few of Burke's sentences such as:

— "The awareness of changes in cultural style is not uniquely Western." (thesis 2.3.)
— "Ruler-centered historiography is of course common in many cultures ..." (thesis 3.3)
— "Attempts at historical explanation are universal ..." (thesis 6.)[2]

To support his case, one could say that the author is simply not very familiar with those kinds of historical sources. But studies on that subject are so common that the absence of any comment calls for an explanation. Characterizing European history, one could add, calls for an explanation of the author's scriptocentrism. History begins with writing, everything before is prehistory! That leads me to my next point: the Ping-Pong System.

The Field of Action

In earlier times, Burke brilliantly points out, the thoughts of Hegel and other authors were valid. Today a new and more open tradition has originated and asserted itself. Still the historian is bound to a civilization that is primarily based on writing. There used to be civilizations and nations without history; today there are civilizations with or without writing. Western experts of the past start accepting those Others, when they are beginning to write as the historians do. Who has no written tradition remains on the other side of the line. What does the academic history, written by a handful of members of the historical profession, represent for the everyday life of those men and women who are the subjects of that history? One can ask the same question regarding the relationship between historians of Africa and the people who represent the object of that historical research. Already Cohen and Vansina[3] from different perspectives, have made that point. When accepting this as a problem, one can also question the following of Burke's statements:

My impression is that the situation in historiography is rather like the situation in painting. Visual cultures differ from region to region, but superimposed is the global culture of professional artists, whose international exhibitions correspond to the international congresses of historians.

The international community of historians might actually represent the entire association of "specialists for the past"; but does it represent history? For the history of nations whose past has been subject of a primarily oral tradition, such a view is considered as a mutilation of reality. A handful of writers cannot be representative. The essential (of the history of those nations) takes place somewhere else, and that location should be noticed more closely through the recognition of local knowledge.[4] The younger historiography of Africa is quite conscious of this, as recent debates about this question have shown.[5]

The attempt to apply Western analytical and conceptional tools onto others by searching for the peculiarity of occidental historical thinking in its relation to other continents, runs the risk of falling into a trap. To use a striking expression of the China expert Francois Jullien, one could say that an academic field—that of Western historiography—becomes applied upon another field, without realizing the possible originality of those other fields. In thesis 8, Burke gives an illustration of this with the headline statement: "The quantitative approach to history is distinctively Western"; and with the rhetorical question: "Can a similar interest in statistics be found in any other historical tradition?"

Which Field to Study?

The author remains on a programmatic level. I can only follow him into this field by suggesting an alternative in the form of a program that the title of my essay indicates. I wish to enforce a sensitization for the history and culture of different continents and their plural character,[6] calling programmatically for an increased international use of social sciences. In order to strengthen what we already have—the Western "tools," which themselves have to be improved—I completely agree with Burke's idea when he writes: "Only after we have made the inventory of differences between historical thought in the west and in other parts of the globe will it be possible to make a systematic investigation of the reasons for these differences." The structural ordering of the differences is the first step of an enterprise that is not aimed at substantializing those differences but at constructing an inner coherence for a field of study[7] on which the profession usually projects the perspectives of the West. What has to be described are the processes that produce the different or equal perspectives in the first place. As one of those processes the practice of local knowledge has to be considered as well.[8] The circulation of knowledge, and the thematization and study of its transformations, is more important than the search for peculiarities.[9]

This is my modest contribution to the fascinating and ambitious program of Peter Burke for our common study of history.

Notes

1. For a critical reading of the German version I wish to thank Gottfried Müller.
2. My emphasis (M.D.)
3. David William Cohen, 'The Undefining of Oral Tradition', *Ethnohistory* 36 (1989), 9-17; id., *The Combing of History*, Chicago, 1994; Jan Vansina, 'Some Perceptions on tnhe Writing of African History 1948-1992', *Itinerario* 1 (1992), 7-91; id., *Living with Africa*, Madison, 1994.
4. Clifford Geertz, *Local Knowledge*, New York, 1983.
5. Conference on 'Words and Voices. Critical Studies in African Oral History', International Institute, University of Michigan, Ann Arbor, Winter 1997.
6. See Karine Chemla, *Qu'attendre de l'histoire des sciences dans les aires non-occidentales*, Paris, 1996, 8.
7. See François Jullien, *Le détour et l'accès. Stratégies du sens en Chine, en Grèce*, Paris, 1995.
8. See the convincing observations on the study of history by Chemla (see note 7).
9. Ibid., 9.

4. The Difference of the Others

Reflections on Chinese Historical Thinking

Yü Ying-shih

With a historiographical tradition as long and variegated as China's, any attempt at a sweeping generalization of Chinese historical thought with a view to clearly distinguishing it from its Western counterpart is hazardous. To suggest that there are essential determinate characteristics in Chinese historiography that are wholly absent in the West is to lapse into a false essentialism. The more I know about the history of Western historiography, the less I am sure about the possibility of drawing a sharp distinction between the two traditions. As far as the individual component parts of Chinese and Western historiographies are concerned, they appear to be more similar than dissimilar. On the other hand, however, the shapes of the two traditions do look different when viewed historically. I am inclined to believe that the differences lie in constellation and emphasis, which, if further investigated, may turn out to be, to a large extent, culturally determined.

Peter Burke's ten-point characterization of historical thought and historical writing in the West provides me with a good starting-point for some reflections on the Chinese tradition in a comparativist light. In what follows I shall choose to discuss only a few interrelated ideas that may be considered central to traditional Chinese historiography.

Burke is quite right to suggest that the most important characteristic of Western historical thought is its stress on development or progress, which originated in the Judeo-Christian notion of Destiny or Providence. E.H. Carr also pointed out, "It was the Jews, and after them the Christians, who introduced an entirely new element by postulating a goal towards which the historical process is moving—the teleological view of history."[1] Burke further notes, citing Karl Löwith, that "modern concepts of historical development may be viewed as

---

Notes for this section can be found on page 170.

secular forms of these religious ideas." However, I wish to make the observation that it is precisely in its secular forms that this Judeo-Christian idea of "development" or "progress" has exerted its greatest influence on modern Western historiography. Hegel's *Geist* and Marx's "mode of production" are clearly latter-day successors to the "plan of God." Paradoxically, the idea has also found its most powerful ally in modern science, which has inspired the intensive search, since the eighteenth century, for universal laws governing the development or progress of history. Thus Marx, in his "Preface" to *Capital* speaks with great confidence of "the natural laws of capitalist production" working "with iron necessity towards inevitable results." Even the American modernization theory in the 1950s and 1960s was also formulated on the assumption of a single process of economic development for all societies. This universal model, needless to say, was built on the Western historical experience since the Industrial Revolution.

The reason I begin my discussion of Chinese historical thinking with this peculiar Western idea of "development" or "progress" is twofold: First, the notion that human history is an irreversible process guided by some transhuman forces such as Divine Providence or natural laws is wholly alien to indigenous Chinese historiography; but, second, it is none other than this strange idea disguised as "science" that has captivated Chinese historical imagination in the twentieth century. Especially, with the establishment of Marxism-Leninism as state ideology in 1949, this teleological view of history has become a Procrustean bed on which Chinese history, in all its aspects, must be placed at all times. A central task set for historians by the Party is to periodize their national history according to the five-stage theory of social development. While the Marxist approach to history may be credited with discovery of interesting historical data in areas previously neglected in traditional historiography, its total impact on Chinese historical scholarship is rather disastrous: Chinese history has been falsified, misinterpreted and distorted on a massive scale. As a result, today a new generation of Chinese historians is beginning to question practically every large generalization about Chinese history established during past decades. There are also signs of a revival of interest in traditional historiography in its own terms.

In the last three or four years a noticeable intellectual movement is growing in China to celebrate the first generations of historians who made a systematic attempt to reorganize Chinese classical and historical scholarship in a modern way in the early decades of this century. These Great Masters of National Learning, as they have now come to be called, relied primarily on their traditional training in textual and philological studies to make important new historical discoveries, even though conceptually they had been enlightened by the Western learning of their own day, including natural and social sciences. It has been generally recognized that the great achievements of Chinese historical scholarship in the early Republican period was a direct outgrowth of the indigenous historiographical tradition, which reached its full maturity in the course of the previous three centuries. The contribution of Western learning during this period lay rather in the widening of general intellectual horizons than in providing Chinese historians with specific historical theories and methods. On the contrary, when the Chinese historical mind in the post-May Fourth period gradually turned away from its own tradition, and looked with ever-growing veneration theories and practices in Western historiography for guidance, the quality of historical research and writing in China began to deteriorate markedly.[2]

In the "Preface" to his last book, *The Origins of History*, Herbert Butterfield identifies science and historiography as two of the most distinguishing features of Western civilization. According to Butterfield, the only known parallel to it in both respects is to be found in early China. However, the scientific revolution and the historiographical revolution that took place in Europe in the seventeenth and nineteenth centuries, respectively, have left China far behind. As a result, "in both fields the Chinese themselves have had to become the pupils of the West."[3] I do not disagree as much with Butterfield's statement as I would like to qualify it by making a further distinction. It is true that the Chinese of this century have, of their own accord, become "the pupils of the West" not only in science but in historiography as well. However, Chinese acceptance of Western historiography is fundamentally different from that of Western science. In the latter case the acceptance is total. As we know only too well, modern Chinese have simply ignored the existence of their own past scientific achievements (as reconstructed in Joseph Needham's multivolume *Science and Civilization in China*) and started completely anew by following the Western model to its minutest detail. This has been possible because scientific and technological studies in traditional China had been confined to a small coterie of specialists, but never a part of the general Confucian curriculum. By contrast, for over two thousand years the Chinese elite had been molded by a type of Confucian education centered around classics and history.

Moreover, from the twelfth century to the eighteenth, Confucian scholars made a series of methodological breakthroughs in historical research as their critical reexamination of classical and historical texts gradually deepened with time. Writing in 1937 Charles S. Gardner rightly pointed out: "Within the past two decades there has grown up in China a new school of history, new in inspiration, new in historical technique. This school seeks and finds one side of its ancestry among China's past historians ... During the seventeenth and eighteenth centuries especially, important advances were made towards the scientific method."[4] It is this background that accounts, to a large extent, for the astonishing readiness with which Western historiography was accepted by Chinese historians in the early decades of the twentieth century. As clearly acknowledged by Hu Shih (1891-1962), a leading member of what Gardner calls "a new school of history," he was able to feel at home "in the new age of modern science" because he had come from "a scientific tradition of dispassionate and disciplined inquiry, of rigorous evidential thinking and investigation, of boldness in doubt and hypothesis coupled with meticulous care in seeking verification."[5] He may have somewhat exaggerated his case about the "scientific tradition" in early China, but his inner experience is nevertheless amply borne out by his diary written during his student years in the U.S. (1911-1917).

So, unlike in science, when modern Chinese became "pupils of the West" in historiography they did not, and could not, come to embrace it with minds as clean as *tabula rasa*. Instead they looked at Western historiography through the lens of their own tradition assimilating the "scientific method" to "evidential thinking and investigation" developed by Ch'ing philologists. They were willing to become "pupils of the West" because they believed that this "scientific method" had been developed to a most advanced state only in the modern West. However, in actual practice the first generation of Chinese historians were still largely following their own research tradition with only limited innovations and modifications of Western origins.

At this juncture let me return to the recent rediscovery of the Great Masters of National Learning by a new generation of Chinese historians, mentioned above. I take it as symptomatic of an awakening on their part that the time has finally arrived for Chinese historians to take stock of what has really happened during their long apprenticeship in Western historiography. From hindsight it appears very paradoxical that the first generation of historians who were exposed to Western influence only in a limited way have produced historical scholarship now generally judged to be far superior to that of the later generations who are obviously much more sophisticated in their application of the so-called scientific method. This immediately calls into question the validity of Western historiography as a universal model on a par with natural science. Here, too, the very idea of "scientific method" may well have played a role more negative than positive. Excessive obsession with "scientific method" has been particularly characteristic of scientism in modern China.[6] But method has turned out to be neither ideologically neutral nor clearly separable from the context in which it originated. As a result, historical terms, categories, and theories unique to Western experience have also been indiscriminately transferred to Chinese historiography along with the so-called scientific method. As rightly observed by Arthur F. Wright, "twentieth-century Chinese historians borrowed methods, then concepts, and finally systems from the West."[7]

Now, as the twentieth century has drawn to a close, historiography in the West, or at least, in the U.S. has lost its original "vision of a unified and cohesive historical discipline."[8] In this allegedly "postmodern" culture of ours in which "chaos" reigns supreme, the historical profession is said to be describable in the last verse of the Book of Judges: "there was no king in Israel."[9] History as an academic discipline finds itself in a similar situation in China today. Inspired by a postmodern critique of Orientalism on the one hand and the post-Cold War struggle for recognition of non-Western cultures on the other,

Chinese intellectuals are also beginning to search for spiritual resources in their own tradition. Since the early 1990s, there has been much talk about "Chinese humanist spirit" and "New Confucianism." It is in this new climate of opinion that historians have first rediscovered the Great Masters of National Learning and then, through them, moved further back to reexamine the Chinese historiographical tradition in an affirmative mood. This trend is much in evidence in recent Chinese publications.

If we compare traditional Chinese historiography as a whole with theories and practices of history developed in the West since the eighteenth century, the differences are truly striking. Moreover, the comparison inevitably casts the former in an extremely unfavorable light. This is precisely why the eminent historian, Liang Ch'i-ch'ao (1873-1929), proposed in 1902 that the "dynastic history" paradigm in the Chinese tradition be swept aside in order to make room for a "New History" based essentially on Herbert Spencer's interpretation of the course of human development as evolution. For he was utterly overwhelmed by the Western style of historical writing as he encountered it while an exile in Japan.[10] However, if we take a concrete and analytical approach by comparing two of the earliest Chinese historical works (say, Confucius' *Spring and Autumn Annals* with its later commentaries, and Ssu-ma Ch'ien's *Records of the Grand Historian*) with two of the earliest works in the West (say, Herodotus' *Histories* and Thucydides' *History of the Peloponnesian War*), the picture that emerges from the comparison would be quite different. As far as underlying assumptions, principles and methods are concerned, there appear to be as many similarities as differences between the Chinese and the Greek texts.[11] For example, an important principle Herodotus followed in his recording of events is the distinction between what he has seen and what he has heard. Thucydides, too, "first trusted his own eyes and ears and next the eyes and ears of reliable witnesses."[12] We find the same principle in Confucius' *Annals* and Ssu-ma Ch'ien's *Records*. According to tradition, Confucius distinguished between three types of sources: What he has seen, what he has heard and what he has learned through transmitted records.[13] This is corroborated by his *Analects* where he deplored that he was not able to discourse on the rites of the Hsia and the Yin dynasties because there are "not enough records and men of erudition" to support him with "evidence" (III. 9). Ssu-ma Ch'ien also always reports what he has seen and what he has heard from eyewitnesses in addition to the vast amount of written documents at his disposal.[14]

To give one more example, A. Momigliano takes great pride in what he calls "critical methods" of Greek historians, especially Herodotus and Thucydides. By "critical methods" he means that "the user, after reflection and study, was satisfied as to their reliability."[15] He even goes so far as to assert that "no historiography earlier than the Greek or independent of it developed these critical methods."[16] But similar critical methods seem to have been already present in Chinese historiography in the time of Confucius (551-479 B.C.). Ssu-ma

Ch'ien tells us that in preparation for his *Spring and Autumn Annals*, Confucius not only made extensive investigations of old historical records of the royal house of Chou and edited the texts but also established "meaningful principles" and laid down "methods of writing."[17] Confucius' guiding "principle" for recording of events, according to the *Ku-liang Commentary* to the *Spring and Autumn Annals*, was to "transmit what is reliable as reliable and what is doubtful as doubtful."[18] True, we can by no means be sure about the accuracy of these statements as descriptions of the *Spring and Autumn Annals* because they may well have been attributed to Confucius by Confucians of later centuries. Nevertheless, there can be little question that Confucius did exhibit a general critical attitude towards learning along the lines indicated above. In the *Analects* he has the following to say to a student: "Use your ears widely but leave out what is doubtful; repeat the rest with caution and you will make few mistakes" (II.17). At any rate, by the fourth century B.C. at the latest, a critical consciousness with regard to the reading of historical texts was already highly developed in China. This is nowhere more clearly shown than in the words of Mencius: "If one believed everything in the *Book of History*, it would have been better for the *Book* not to have existed at all. In the *Wu ch'eng* chapter I accept only two or three strips" (*Mencius*, VII, Part B.3).

There is no need to elaborate on Ssu-ma Ch'ien's *Records of the Grand Historian* in which historical criticism can be detected in almost every part of the book. It suffices to quote a few sentences from his famous letter to Jen An: "I have gathered up and brought together the old traditions of the world which were scattered and lost. I have examined the deeds and events of the past and investigated the principles behind their successes and failure, their rise and decay, in one hundred and thirty chapters."[19] Clearly, the *Records* qualifies as *historia* in the sense of "inquiry," "research," or "investigation."[20]

We can certainly push this kind of parallelism between the two historiographical traditions down to recent centuries. The philological movement and its revolutionary impact on historical research in early and middle Ch'ing period, for instance, bears a remarkably high degree of resemblance to the rise of philology in Europe since Lorenzo Valla.[21] Burke raises the interesting question about legal metaphors in the Western historiographical tradition and wonders if historians of other traditions, including the Chinese, have also taken over assumptions from their indigenous legal system. My reply to this question is in the affirmative. As Hu Shih has convincingly shown, Chinese historical methodology known as *k'ao-cheng* (evidential investigation) was developed out of the legal system from the twelfth century on. Terms like "evidence," "judgment," "witness," are all borrowed from the practice of law. Confucian scholars while serving as local officials often had extensive experience in the administration of justice. Chu Hsi (1130-1200) stated repeatedly, and in no uncertain terms that a scholar must deal with his texts as if he were a judge struggling with a very difficult and complicated litigation. He must listen with an open mind to the presentation of all sides and check the legal documents carefully with special attention given to the possibilities of forgery and anachronism, the two methods often decisive for reaching a reasonable judgment in lawsuit.[22] Even in the highly speculative domain commonly called "philosophy of history," parallelism also existed between China and the West. Chang Hsüeh-ch'eng (1738-1801), for example, developed ideas about history that may be fruitfully compared to those of Vico and Collingwood, though the historical and intellectual contexts are vastly different.[23]

Now, let me turn to the other side of the coin, namely what are some of the central features that distinguish Chinese historical thought from its Western counterpart. The differences are many and fundamental. However, due to space and time, I can only offer a few general observations without elaboration. To begin with, I wish to stress the point that the differences cannot be located in the historiographical domain itself. Instead they may be shown to have been deeply rooted in the two distinct cultural traditions of China and the West. In this connection I wish to say a word about the origins of historical writing in ancient China. Butterfield was impressed by the fact that as early as well before 1000 B.C., the character *shih* (historian) already appeared in China. *Shih* could be translated in many ways such as "scribe," "archivist," "historiographer," "astrologer," depending on the text in which it appears.[24] The discovery of thousands and thousands of oracle bone inscriptions datable roughly between 1300 to 1100 B.C. has amply confirmed this early origin of *shih* as a "scribe" or "archivist." The practice of divination involved several individuals: the *chen-jen* who made the inquiry on behalf of the king; the *pu-jen* who carried out the divining act; the *chan-jen* or prognosticator who specialized in the interpretation of the cracks on the burned bones or shells; and, finally, the *shih* scribe or archivist, who inscribed the notations.[25] However, at this early date the function of *shih* was clearly religious and it cannot be interpreted as "historiographer." It was probably in the late seventh century B.C., at the latest, that the *shih* was gradually transformed from an archivist in charge of religious matters to a court historiographer. Confucius, for example, praised one such *shih* who had, in 605 B.C., shown the moral courage of recording the truth at the risk of his own life. He was, Confucius said, "a good historiographer of old time: his rule for writing was not to conceal."[26] From the above account, a few observations may be made with a view of distinguishing the Chinese historiographical tradition from its Western counterpart: First, Chinese historiography began at a very early date and grew up in a remarkably long and continuous tradition. Second, it was from the very beginning inseparable from official archives and documents. Third, the office of *shih*, already in existence as a hereditary and prestigious institution by western Chou times (1027?-771 B.C.),[27] placed the court historiographer in the very center of the Chinese political world.

In light of these unique beginnings of Chinese historical writing, it is little wonder that historiography occupied a central place in Confucian learning throughout the traditional period. This contrasts sharply to the Western cultural context in classical antiquity in which historiography was accorded a secondary place at best. The following succinct characterization of the Greek attitude towards historiography by Momigliano is worth quoting for the purpose of comparison:

> The Greeks liked history, but never made it the foundation of their lives. The educated Greek turned to rhetorical schools, to mystery cults, or to philosophy for guidance. History was never an essential part of the life of a Greek—not even (one suspects) for those who wrote it. There may be many reasons for this attitude of the Greeks, but surely an important factor was that history was so open to uncertainties, so unlikely to provide undisputed guidance.[28]

I am tempted to extend this characterization to cover the cultural tradition of the West as a whole, needless to say, only for the purpose of sharpening the contrast between China and the West. Very impressionistically speaking, it seems to me that the Western mind has always been looking to philosophy or religion for spiritual guidance. It turns sometimes more to philosophy and sometimes more to religion, but most of the time a combination of both. Since the seventeenth century, of course, science has been ever-increasingly made the foundation of lives of the Westerners, even though it has not succeeded completely in replacing religion and philosophy altogether. In this regard, however, science may also be viewed as continuous with religion and philosophy in the sense that all three are ultimately concerned with the search for "certainty." So far as my limited knowledge goes, Western historiography over the many centuries has advanced by being nourished and enriched by the religious, philosophical and scientific developments at every new turn. By contrast, Chinese historiography has grown together with Confucian classical scholarship and literary art. But I must hasten to point out that the intellectual emphasis on holistic approach in the Chinese tradition has made the trio practically undifferentiated and undifferentiable; the relationship between them can by no means be understood in terms of the Western system of classification of knowledge. Of the so-called Six Classics, two are clearly historical and one literary in nature, if we follow the Western system. The idea "all classics are history" had long been in currency before Chang Hsüeh-ch'eng gave it a definitive reformulation.[29] The point I wish to emphasize here is that any fruitful comparison between Chinese and Western historical ideas must, of necessity, take into full account the two different cultural traditions in which they originated and grew respectively.

To the best of my judgment, fundamental to Chinese historical thought is the centrality of human agency in the making of history. By this I do not mean the naive view that man, and man alone, makes history as he wills. It is rather the principle that whatever other forces, natural or supernatural, may have been at work in the course of history, the historian's chief attention must always be directed at the human factor. For it is his business to find out which individuals or groups were responsible, positively or negatively, for certain states of affairs, especially, at some critical moments in history such as the rise or fall of a state or dynasty. This special emphasis on the role of human agency in history was in all likelihood related to the rise of what is generally referred to as the rise of Confucian humanism during the sixth century B.C. In 524 B.C. a senior contemporary of Confucius made this famous remark: "The Way of Heaven is distant, while that of man is near. We cannot reach to the former; what means have we of knowing it.."[30] It is generally accepted today that this casual remark had a profound influence on Confucius' thinking, which is amply borne out in the *Analects* (V.13; VI.22). I would like to quote the following conversation between Confucius and Duke Ting of Lu (r.509–495) to illustrate the former's view about the role of human agency in history:

> Duke Ting asked, "Is there such a thing as a single saying that can lead a state to prosperity?"
>
> Confucius answered, "A saying cannot quite do that. There is a saying amongst men: 'It is difficult to be a ruler, and it is not easy to be a subject either.' If the ruler understands the difficulty of being a ruler, then is this not almost a case of a saying leading the state to prosperity?"
>
> "Is there such a thing as a saying that can lead the state to ruin?"
>
> Confucius answered, "A saying cannot quite do that. There is a saying amongst men: 'I do not at all enjoy being a ruler, except for the fact that no one goes against what I say.' If what he says is good and no one goes against him, good. But if what he says is not good and no one goes against him, then is this not almost a case of a saying leading the state to ruin?" (*Analects*, XIII.15)

I quote this conversation in full because it was taken so seriously by later historians that they, as a rule, recorded in their writings words with consequences uttered by important individuals. It is quite illuminating to note that Confucius, in both cases, used "cannot quite" and "almost" to modify his statements. This clearly suggests that while he would definitely hold man's words and deeds responsible for what happened or might happen, he was also fully aware that factors beyond human agency matter to history as well.

According to tradition, Confucius was the first historian to establish the principle of praise and blame in Chinese historiography, which, needless to say, is logically implicit in his fundamental notion about the reality of human freedom in history. Of course the didactic function of history can also be found in many other historiographical traditions including the Western. But none has developed it to so central a place, with such pervasiveness and continuity, as in China. What is even more remarkable is that it not only penetrated to, but also grew luxuriantly in the fertile soil of popular culture. Through historical novels and plays such as, especially, *The Romance of the Three Kingdoms*, the principle of praise and blame had reached countless readers and audiences since the twelfth century, if not earlier. In the *Romance*, for instance, it is easy to see the author's conscious intention to condemn some of the major characters while honoring others.[31] Although later historians, fearing that excess in moral judgment would impair historical objectivity, from time to time counseled restraint, the principle has never been wholly rejected in Chinese historiography even to this day.

In the Chinese case, the historiographical principle of praise and blame served not only a didactic function but, perhaps more significantly, a critical one as well. Speaking of why Confucius wrote the *Spring and Autumn Annals*, Ssu-ma Ch'ien said,

> Confucius realized that his words were not being heeded, nor his doctrines put into practice. So he made a critical judgment of the rights and wrongs of a period of two hundred and forty two years in order to provide a standard of rules and ceremonies for the world. He criticized the emperors, reprimanded the feudal lords, and condemned the high officials in order to make known the business of a true ruler and that was all. Confucius said, 'If I wish to set forth my theoretical judgments, nothing is as good as illustrating them through the depth and clarity of actual events'.[32]

This statement probably represents more Ssu-ma Ch'ien's view than Confucius'. Understood in this way we may say that history writing in the Chinese tradition is an act of political and moral criticism. The quoted saying of Confucius surely reminds us of the famous rhetorical formula of Dionysius of Halicarnassus, "History is philosophy teaching by example." Perhaps in our case the term "philosophy" should be replaced by "theory of morality." There can be little question that Ssu-ma Ch'ien intended his *Records* to be also a work of criticism. Through a variety of literary devices, he criticized not only the powerful and the rich of past and present but also the reigning emperor—Wu Ti—and some of his policies. This is precisely why in A.D. 192 a high official in the Han court called the *Records* "a defamatory book."[33] As late as the Ch'ing period, when the Manchu court launched large-scale political persecutions against the Chinese intelligentsia, it was the historians who took the heaviest toll since they were generally under the suspicion of using their enormous critical power to question the legitimacy of the Manchu rule in China.

Throughout the traditional age, Chinese historians were able to perform this critical function to a greater or lesser degree sometimes even in extreme adversities. The noted historian Liu I-cheng (1880-1956) takes this function to be a unique feature in the Chinese historiographical tradition and proudly calls it "the authority of the historian."[34] Thus history may be understood as having provided Confucian scholars with a much needed critical distance. But the historian as critic in traditional China may best be understood as what Michael Walzer calls a "connected critic" or "an insider":

> He is not a detached observer, even when he looks at the society he inhabits with a fresh and skeptical eye. He is not an enemy, even when he is fiercely opposed to this or that prevailing practice or institutional arrangement. His criticism does not require either detachment or enmity, because he finds a warrant for critical engagement in the idealism, even if it is a hypothetical idealism, of the actually existing moral world.[35]

This critical tradition is so strong that it continues to linger on even to this day. In modern Western thinking, however, moral judgment in history has long been rejected as an obstacle to scientific objectivity. Isaiah Berlin's powerful defense of praise and blame in his *Historical Inevitability* four decades ago seems to have fallen on deaf ears. In this connection, then, a question inevitably arises, namely, what was the Chinese historian's attitude toward what we call objectivity? Our answer is that in its own way Chinese historiography was also very much concerned about the Rankean notion of "What had actually happened?" Truthful recording, as a Chinese historiographical principle, can be traced to pre-Confucian antiquity. Paradoxically, from the Western point of view, value judgment and truthful recording are taken as two sides of the same coin rather than two conflicting principles in the Chinese tradition. Thus, for example, the statement "A minister murdered his king," if true, expresses a moral judgment and conveys a historical truth at the same time. To state otherwise, such as "The king died," is to distort a historical fact despite the objectivity of the language. Similarly, when the case is established on evidence, the traditional Chinese historian would say "Hitler exterminated millions of Jews out of racial hatred"; not "Millions of Jews died during the Second World War." In order to guarantee truthful recording, a remarkable tradition was established in imperial China that the emperor must refrain from reading the diary of his own reign kept by a court historian.[36] Obviously, this historiographical practice was intended to accord the historian the freedom to record "What had actually happened." Needless to say, tensions of various kinds did exist between the principle of moral judgment and that of truthful recording in the Chinese tradition. But, on the other hand, the Chinese case also suggests the possibility of reopening the issue whether moralizing history and historical objectivity are as mutually exclusive as has been generally assumed on the model of the natural sciences.

As suggested above, traditional Chinese historiography does recognize the fact that natural or trans-human forces are also at work in history even though its general emphasis has been placed on human agency. It is now necessary to pursue this problem a little further in connection with the absence of the teleological view of history in the Chinese tradition. In his famous "Letter in Reply to Jen An," Ssu-ma Ch'ien describes his *Records* thus: "I wished to examine into all that concerns Heaven and man, to penetrate the changes of the past and present, completing all as the work of one family."[37] A reading of the *Records* can easily bear him out. There are many cases in the *Records* that suggest that its author (or authors if we include his father) is constantly weighing factors pertaining to human agency on the one hand, and those pertaining to *t'ien* or "Heaven" on the other, in his search for answers regarding "changes of the past and present." But as scholars generally agree, Ssu-ma Ch'ien is notoriously vague about the role of "Heaven" in history and he seems to move freely between the two poles of "Heaven" and "Man." In some cases he assigns the rise or fall of a state or dynasty to the work of "Heaven" and in the other cases to human responsibility.[38] This is also true for traditional Chinese historiography as a whole. As Lien-sheng Yang rightly points out,

> in traditional terms, the factors were often vaguely grouped into those belonging to *T'ien* "Heaven, or Nature" and those belonging to *Jen* "Man." The human factors cited in tradition are usually based on common sense and consequently are easy to understand. The *T'ien* factors, however, are rather slippery for comprehension, often in terms of such semi-mystical concepts as the Five Elements, *ch'i-yün* "vitality and fortune" or *ch'i-shu* "vitality and number."[39]

A reasonable explanation for the vagueness of the Chinese conception of "Heaven" as trans-human forces in history, seems to lie in the general belief that Heaven, in its supernatural sense, does not directly interfere with human affairs. Whatever role it plays in history, it is still played through human agency. Mencius already made this point very clear when he said that "The Emperor can recommend a man to Heaven but he cannot make Heaven give this man the Empire." Mencius then quoted a passage from the *Book of History*, saying "Heaven sees with the eyes of its people. Heaven hears with the ears of its people." (V, Part A.5) This quoted saying is obviously a Chinese version of "The voice of the People is the voice of God." However, unlike Western God, Chinese Heaven has no "divine plan" for mankind to carry out in history. Nor would Heaven strike down a state or dynasty out of wrath. Heaven is seen as only passively waiting to review human proposals accepting good and rejecting bad ones. Thus the notion of Providence can find no place in Chinese historical thought. Neither Ssu-ma Ch'ien nor later historians showed any inclination, as Herodotus did, "to persuade the reader that history conforms to a divine plan."[40]

Following the example of Confucius not to speak of prodigies and gods (*Analects* VII.21), Chinese historians generally refrained from making references to the supernatural. A most remarkable example is provided by Ssu-ma Kuang's (1019-1086) *Comprehensive Mirror for Aid in Government* (Tzu-chih t'ung-chien), a general history in chronicle form covering the period from 403 B.C. to A.D. 959. In such a long chronicle we rarely encounter reports on strange occurrences of a supernatural kind. On the contrary, when evidence is available he does not hesitate to expose the so-called auspicious omens faked by court flatterers. In a letter to his research associate, he gave specific instructions concerning the inclusion or exclusion of "strange and uncanny happenings" in the early draft of the *Comprehensive Mirror*. For instance: "Prophecies ... which gave rise to slaughter and rebellion should be retained. Ones which wantonly try to show coincidences ... need not be recorded." "If uncanny occurrences give warnings ..., or if as a result of them something is started, ... They should be retained. The rest need not be."[41] Clearly, he intended to keep "strange and uncanny happenings" to a minimum even in the first draft; only those that had produced actual consequences in history were to be retained. However, a check of this letter against the *Comprehensive Mirror* as we now have it further shows that some of the specific "happenings" originally listed for inclusion were also dropped in his final draft. In this long chronicle, as in the *Records of the Grand Historian*, we cannot find a slightest trace that history is going somewhere— toward a predestined end. Indeed, some elements of "providence" can be detected in Chinese popular religions, early and late, but they have failed to penetrate into the domain of historiography.

As I have pointed out in the beginning of this essay, it is the providential view of history in its modern secular forms that has captivated the Chinese historical mind since the turn of the present century. Ideas such as "progress," "evolution" and "development" have been generally accepted by Chinese historians as what Collingwood calls "absolute presuppositions" for the study of history. It is therefore also desirable to direct my reflections on Chinese historical thought to this modern version of historical teleology.

It seems to me that the modern idea of "progress" is different from its original, religious version in one essential way: The "end," "goal" or "purpose" of history is no longer imposed from outside by a transcendent force called God. Instead it is immanent in history and ceaselessly seeks self-realization from inside. It makes little difference if this prime mover inside history is called "spirit" or "matter." As long as it pushes to fulfill its own "end," history moves forward in one, and only one, predetermined direction. As a result, the whole process of history must of necessity take a definite shape or exhibit an overall pattern. In this irreversible process individual human beings and their personal intentions and beliefs are of no importance. For they are not fundamentally different from molecules and their consciousnesses are false. They exist only as means for this prime mover to realize itself in history.

If we take the modern teleological view of history as thus caricatured, then we must say that it is just as alien to the Chinese historical mind as the idea of providence, discussed above. In this connection, however, a brief mention of the Chinese understanding of "impersonal forces" in history seems very much in order. At times I find it difficult to resist the temptation to interpret what Ssuma Ch'ien calls "Heaven" in his *Records* as a vague reference to "impersonal forces," which may also involve human agency as a collectivity as well. For example, when he referred to the unification of China in 221 B.C. by the First Emperor of Ch'in as commanded by Heaven, he may well have had in mind a vague sense of change generated by a historical trend too vast for individuals to stop or resist. For want of an adequate term he could only resort to the traditional concept of Heaven. In later times, however, a new term *shih* was adopted to explain historical changes involving "impersonal forces." Speaking of the same event of 221 B.C. in institutional terms—the change from "feudal system" to "prefectural system," Liu Tsung-yüan (773-819) takes as his explanatory concept, not the old idea of *t'ien* or heaven, but the new notion of *shih* which may be rendered as "condition," "situation," "trend," "tendency," et cetera, as the context requires. (It is to be distinguished from the character *shih*, mentioned earlier, meaning "scribe," "archivist," or "historiographer.") According to him, the Chinese "feudal system" (*feng-chien*) did not come into existence purely by human design as tradition says. It was not the case that ancient sages invented this idea and then established it as a political system. Nor was it the case that the First Emperor of Ch'in arbitrarily abolished it for the convenience of centralization of power. On the contrary, the beginning and end of the system were both necessitated by the "conditions of the times" (*shih*). Here, Liu clearly perceived what we would call "impersonal forces" in history.[42]

After Liu, the term *shih* has become firmly established as a category of historical analysis. Two outstanding examples will suffice to illustrate our point. Wang Fu-chih (1619-1692), particularly, made an extensive use of the term in his philosophical discourse on Chinese history. He often appealed to the notion of *shih* when he tried to give an account of why certain major historical changes had occurred. In a manner very reminiscent of Liu, he also attributed the abolition of the "feudal system" and the emergence of the "prefectural system" under the Ch'in to the operation of forces generated by the historical "condition of the times" (*shih*). He even went a step further to raise the question of the possibility that there may have been "principles" (*li*) governing impersonal forces of change in history. As one of his formulations says, "Historical conditions (*shih*) change with the times while principles (*li*) vary with historical conditions."[43]

In his best-known essay "On the *Tao*," Chang Hsüeh-ch'eng also used *shih* to explain the evolution of the *Tao* (Way) in history. True to the spirit of his age, Chang historicized the *Tao* to a point dangerously close to the borderline of his Confucian faith. In his conception, as the *Tao* gradually evolved in history, it took forms in human society through all kinds of institutional developments, political, social, economic as well as cultural. It was a process of evolution in the sense that the *Tao* began in the simplest form of the family ("three persons living together in one house"), and then grew more and more complex with the increase of population and the ever-increasing differentiations of social functions. What particularly interests us here, however, is how Chang brings "impersonal forces" to bear on this evolutionary process. The emergence of many great institutions in pre-Confucian antiquity, the above-discussed "feudal system" among them, marks the earliest breakthrough in the evolution of the *Tao*. According to the Confucian tradition, these institutions were created by a long line of sage-rulers ending with the Duke of Chou for whom Confucius showed unbounded admiration. Like Liu Tsung-yüan before him, he argues against this traditional Great Men theory, but in a more systematic and sophisticated way. In his view, even with the "sagely wisdom" as enormous as Duke of Chou's, the Duke could not have accomplished so much had it not been for the fact that he happened to live in the times when all necessary conditions converged to make such institutional creations possible. As aptly expressed by David S. Nivison, "A sage cannot 'create' just anything. What he achieves is strictly limited by the possibilities of the historical moment."[44] In his discussion of ancient institutions, he invariably attributes their origins to historical situations (*shih*) that he describes as "inevitable." But he goes beyond Liu to suggest that these inevitable historical situations or conditions arise, ultimately, from "the daily activities in human relations" (*jen-lun jih-yung*) of the unreflective common people, which he identifies as none other than the *Tao* itself. This is why he says that only by "learning from the common people" can the sage seek to know the *Tao*.[45] This idea is not exactly new in the Confucian tradition. But Chang is certainly the first Confucian thinker to apply it to the study of history thereby making more explicit what he means by "inevitable historical situations."

From the middle of the seventeenth century on, Chinese historiography underwent a significant change due partly to the rise of evidential scholarship and partly to external factors that cannot be discussed here. For our purpose here I wish only to mention three important developments. First, historians moved beyond political history and their research branched in all directions. Second, they tended to focus their attention on special topics and problems and began to present their new findings in a proto-monographic form. I say "proto-monographic" because their favorite medium of scholarly communication was the highly condensed "note," which is capable of being developed into modern monographs or dissertations. As a matter of fact, many twentieth-century Chinese historians have indeed used these "notes" as starting-points for their monographic research. The leading authority on Chinese religious history, Ch'en Yüan (1880-1971), once made an interesting analogy: An insightful "note" by a Ch'ing scholar may be compared to a spoonful of milk powder, which with boiling water will make a full cup of milk.[46] Third, the philological turn in the early Ch'ing made scholars increasingly aware of the historical changes of language. A central concern common to both classicists and historians was to discover the changing meanings of words and terms from the times of Confucius down through the centuries. As a result, scholars' horizons were broadened, research specialized and historical sense sharpened.

Both Wang's and Chang's ideas about historical changes must be understood in light of these intellectual reorientations. Among practicing historians there was also a growing interest in origins, evolution or changes of particular aspects of Chinese civilization as diverse as kinship system, religious rituals and beliefs, philosophical ideas, civil service examination, poetry, art, music, printing, and footbinding, to give only a few examples. Some (like Chao I, 1727-1814) even ventured to offer general observations on patterns of change in longer or shorter historical periods and explore their possible causes. None of us will probably go so far with Liang Ch'i-ch'ao to assert that "the Ch'ing scholars' pursuit of knowledge was based solely on the inductive method and a scientific spirit."[47] Nevertheless it is undeniable that some of the important elements of modern (Western) historical scholarship were beginning to emerge in Ch'ing evidential research. It is probably safe to conclude that on the eve of the coming of the West, Chinese historiography reached its own peak both conceptually and methodologically. It cannot be purely accidental that at exactly the same time, in the last years of the eighteenth century, Chao I, in his *Notes on Twenty-Two Histories* (*Nien-erh shih cha-chi*) proposed a fundamentally new way of reading Chinese history, while Chang Hsüeh-ch'eng in his *General Principles of Literature and History* developed theories and ideas about history in a systematic fashion. To the best of my judgment, Chang's is the only work in the long Chinese intellectual tradition truly worthy of the name of "philosophy of history" in its several senses. The significance of Chao and Chang in the history of modern historiography is well summed up by E.G. Pulleyblank in his part of the Introduction to *Historians of China and Japan*: in the former "we find a man who could see beyond the isolated details and make the kind of inductive generalizations about trends of social and institutional history that modern historians seek to establish." On the other hand, the latter propounded "general ideas about the nature and meaning of history which for the first time tried to break out of the traditional mould and approached a conception more like our modern one." (p. 7)

But even as late as the eighteenth century, when Chinese historiography came closer to its counterpart in the West as shown in the cases of Chao I and Chang Hsüeh-ch'eng, there is still no evidence that Chinese historians ever conceived of history as a process of linear progress toward some definite end. In other words, no Hegel, Marx, Spengler or Toynbee can be found in the Chinese tradition. It is true that Liu Tsung-yüan, Wang Fu-chih and Chang Hsüeh-ch'eng all developed the idea that the *Tao* evolved in history. However, a closer scrutiny shows that none of them conceived of the *Tao* in terms of Hegel's *Geist*, which uses "history" to realize its own end. On the contrary, the *Tao* really does nothing and its evolution depends entirely on the work of Man, especially the sages. For all of them still believed in the fundamental truth first discovered by Confucius that "It is Man who is capable of broadening the *Tao*. It is not the *Tao* that is capable of broadening Man." (*Analects* XV.29)

As shown above, Chinese historians were not wholly unaware of the operation of "impersonal forces" in history. They also recognized the existence of "historical trends" or "patterns of change" in the past. However, when they ventured generalizations, these generalizations are invariably limited in time and confined to a particular aspect. It never occurred to them that it was their business to establish "universal historical laws" or theorize about the entire process of human history. Deeply influenced by the cosmology of the *I ching* (*Book of Changes*), it was one of their "absolute presuppositions" that the historical process will never be complete. Every educated person in traditional China knew that the last hexagram in the *I ching* is called "Before Completion" (*wei-chi*): "Things cannot exhaust themselves. Hence there follows, at the end, the hexagram of 'Before Completion'."[48] The idea of "end of history" in both its senses was simply inconceivable to the mind of the traditional Chinese historian. In this connection, Wang Fu-chih whose historical ideas are primarily based on the cosmology of the *I ching* may be called back to the witness stand. As succinctly summed up by Ian McMorran,

> one can only appreciate how a trend in *shih* (condition) works by a thorough analysis of the various factors which constitute it … . Such a trend, however, is not necessarily irreversible; only change itself is inevitable. With the constant evolution of the universe, conditions are constantly changing, too, but the manner of their change is neither predetermined nor absolutely inevitable. Man must do what he can to influence it.[49]

Needless to say, what Wang thinks about the universe applies with equal validity to history. The central importance of human agency in Chinese historical thought leaves little room for a thoroughgoing determinism of any kind.

The lack of an impulse to speculate on the whole process of history on the part of Chinese historians makes it rather difficult for us to assert with any degree of definiteness whether Chinese historical thought is linear or cyclical. There is a general tendency among Western scholars to put China on the cyclical side largely because of the great popularity of the idea of "dynastic cycle," which, as far as I can see, is a highly misleading term. Even in the realm of political history, there has been an unmistakable trend among Confucian scholars since the Sung dynasty to make the claim that their own dynasty surpassed the previous ones in certain aspects. Yang Lien-sheng has proposed to characterize this mentality as "dynastic competition," which implies "progress" in a limited sense. With regard to material life and social customs, the T'ang institutional historian Tu Yu (735-812) stated in no uncertain terms that the Chinese had progressed from barbarism in high antiquity to a highly civilized way of life in his own day.[50] In philosophy, Huang Tsung-hsi (1610-1695) also said that the Ming was by far superior to earlier dynasties.[51] Very often we find the same historians holding a cyclical view on one occasion and the idea of linear development on another, Ssu-ma Ch'ien included. However, in the Chinese case, progress does not necessarily imply irreversibility. Nor does process of evolution presuppose "universal laws" or specific "end." In this context I would like to suggest that the difficulties in applying the distinction between "progress" and "cycle" to Chinese historical thought may extend just as well to all the long-established Western dichotomies such as "the universal versus the particular," "objectivity versus moral judgment," "explanation versus interpretation," or "history versus chronicle."

From Hegel to modern Sinologists, Chinese historiography as a whole has been consistently described, when compared with that of the West, as being mainly concerned with "facts" and lacking "opinion or reasoning" (Hegel) or "the kind of abstract thinking required for reaching a synthesis."[52] I choose not to respond directly to this kind of judgment here because it would take a great deal more of "reasoning" or "abstract thinking" than I can possibly afford in the present context. But I must say it does have some basis in fact and cannot be lightly brushed aside as another Western "prejudice."

To bring my reflections to a close, I wish to relate this allegedly negative feature of Chinese historiography to some other points raised in Burke's paper, such as the West's preoccupation with epistemology and causal explanation. Yüeh-lin Chin (1896-1984), a noted Chinese philosopher thoroughly trained in Western philosophy and logic, made a rough comparison between Chinese and Western philosophy. In his view, "One of the features characteristic of Chinese philosophy is the underdevelopment of what might be called logico-epistemological consciousness." As a result, there was also a lack of systematic development of science. Moreover, the emphasis in Chinese philosophy on "the unity of Heaven and Man" ("Heaven" here perhaps means more "nature" than "the supernatural") also prevented the Chinese from developing a Baconian attitude toward the natural world.[53] I believe Chin's characterization of Chinese philosophy applies to Chinese historiography *mutatis mutandis*. As Burke points out, the early origin of "cause" in Greek historical writing indicates that "the Western ideal of a historiography modeled on the natural sciences is an old one." For simplicity I would take both epistemology and causal explanation as ultimately rooted in what is usually referred to as "theoretical reason" in Western culture. Thus the so-called lack of reasoning or lack of abstract thinking, quoted above, can be understood as resulting from the underdevelopment of "theoretical or speculative reason" in the Chinese tradition. I emphasize the word "underdevelopment" advisedly. For underdevelopment is not the same as total absence. If we look at Chinese philosophy, especially Neo-Confucian philosophy, instead of Chinese historiography, we can also find a great deal of abstract reasoning even though it still pales before its Western counterpart. According to my own reading, traditional Chinese historians were equally concerned with why a particular event of some historical significance happened as it did. Ssu-ma Ch'ien's inclusion of Chia I's essay, "The Faults of Ch'in," at the end of the "Basic Annals of the First Emperor of Ch'in" is but one example showing that the Grand Historian was looking for the "causes" of the fall of the Ch'in Empire.

However, by and large, no systematic attempt was made to theorize about "ultimate causes" or search for "general laws" in history as such. In contrast to Western theorists of history, nor was the Chinese historian disposed to develop a systematic theory out of an important historical observation due perhaps to his rather underdeveloped "theoretical reason." For example, the importance of economic basis to moral consciousness and social order had long been emphasized by Chinese historians as clearly shown in Pan Ku's "Treatise on Food and Money" in the *Han Shu*.[54] But a theoretical development along the lines of *The German Ideology* by Marx and Engels was not even dreamed of. Perhaps there is some truth in Karl Mannheim's suggestion: "In Germany there has always existed a tendency to go to extremes in pushing logical arguments to their ultimate conclusions."[55] As far as I can see, this seems to be a general feature characteristic of Western thought not unrelated to its fully-developed "theoretical reason." But the development of "theoretical reason" in historiography has its own high cost as well. It tends not only to proliferate one theory after another, but also, at times, to be pushed by its own inner logic to attempt to create a grand system of this or that kind with pretension to universal validity. Chinese historians in the twentieth century have been primarily captives of Western grand theories. The time has indeed come for them to be liberated from this century-long captivity. There can be no question that "theoretical reason" deserves to be developed in Chinese historiography, not to try another grand theory, but to reach meaningful synthesis—in whatever manageable research topics—without doing injustice to the nature of the source material, which necessarily varies from case to case. The noted Russian historian Aaron I. Gurevich, very recently freed from the strait-jacket of what he calls "historiosophy" (which is, of course, of Western origin) has this message to offer:

> It seems to me that all these considerations imply the necessity of elaborating an epistemology specific to history. In contrast to historiosophy, which is now discredited, the specific epistemology of history suggested here need not create a single universally-applicable framework. Instead of a single system applied from without to the infinitely varied materials of history, we suggest an ad hoc hermeneutical method that will develop within the process of research itself. This method should be based both on the particular historical sources being studied and the analytic methods being used.[56]

With this wise counsel my reflections rest.

Notes:

1. E.H. Carr, *What Is History?*, New York, 1962, 145-6.
2. This view has been expressed in many Chinese journal articles. It can also be found in a General Preface to the *Kuo-hsüeh ta-shih ts'ung-shu* ('The Great Masters of National Learning' Series). See, for example, Kuo Ch'i-yung and Wang Hsüeh-ch'ün, *Ch'ien Mu p'ing-chuan*, Nan-ch'ang, 1995, esp. Chang Tai-nien, 'General Preface', 1-4.
3. Herbert Butterfield, *The Origins of History*, New York, 1981, 13.
4. Charles S. Gardner, *Chinese Traditional Historiography*, Cambridge, Mass., 1961, 3.
5. Hu Shih, 'The Scientific Spirit and Method in Chinese Philosophy', in *The Chinese Mind, Essentials of Chinese Philosophy and Culture*, ed. Charles A. Moore, Honolulu, 1967, 130-1.
6. D.W.Y. Kwok, *Scientism in Chinese Thought 1900-1950*, New Haven, 1965, 28-29; Charlotte Furth, *Ting Wen-chiang, Science and China's New Culture*, Cambridge, 1970, 13-14.
7. Arthur F. Wright, 'On the Uses of Generalization in the Study of Chinese History', in *Generalization in the Writing of History*, ed. Louis Gottschalk, Chicago, 1963, 47.

8. Peter Novick, *That Noble Dream. The "Objectivity Question" and the American Historical Profession*, Cambridge, Mass., 1988, 589.

9. Ibid., 628.

10. Ying-shih Yü, 'Changing Concepts of National History in Twentieth-Century China', in *Conceptions of National History. Proceedings of Nobel Symposium 78*, eds Erik Lönnroth, Karl Molin, Ragnar Björk, Berlin and New York, 1994, 157-9.

11. Teng Ssu-yü, 'Ssu-ma Ch'ien and Herodotus: A Comparative Study', (in Chinese) in *Bulletin of the Institute of History and Philology, Taipei Academia Sinica*, No.28, (December 1956), 445-63.

12. Arnaldo Momigliano, *The Classical Foundations of Modern Historiography*, Berkeley, 1990, 42.

13. Fung Yu-lan, *A History of Chinese Philosophy*, tr. by Derk Bodde, vol. II, Princeton, 1953, 81.

14. Ku Chieh-kang, *Shih-lin tsa-shih* [*Notes on Chinese History*], Peking, 1963, 226-233.

15. Arnaldo Momigliano, 'Tradition and the Classical Historian', in *Essays in Ancient and Modern Historiography*, Middletown, 1982, 163.

16. Momigliano, *Classical Foundations*, (see note 12), p.30.

17. Ssu-ma Ch'ien, *Shih Chi* [*Records of the Grand Historian*], vol. II, Peking, 1973, 509.

18. Ch'ien Chung-shu, *Kuan-chui p'ien* [*Notes on Books*], Peking, 1979, Vol.I, 252.

19. Burton Watson, *Ssu-ma Ch'ien, Grand Historian of China*, New York, 1958, 66.

20. Charles William Fornara, *The Nature of History in Ancient Greece and Rome*, Berkeley, 1983, 47.

21. Ying-shih Yü, 'Some Preliminary Observations on the Rise of Ch'ing Confucian Intellectualism', *Tsing Hua Journal of Chinese Studies*, n.s.10 (1975), 105-46; Donald R. Kelley, *Foundations of Modern Historical Scholarship, Language, Law and History in the French Renaissance*, New York, 1970.

22. Hu Shih, 'The Responsibility and Methodology of Evidential Investigation', (in Chinese) included in *Hu Shih-chih hsien-sheng nien-p'u ch'ang-pien ch'u-kao* [*A Chronological Biography of Hu Shih*], ed. Hu Sung-p'ing, Taipei, 1984, vol.V, 1933-42.

23. Paul Demieville, 'Chang Hsüeh-ch'eng and his Historiography', in W.G. *Historians of China and Japan*, eds G. Beasley and E.G. Pulleyblank, London, 1961, 184-5; David S. Nivison, *The Life and Thought of Chang Hsüeh-ch'eng (1738-1801)*, Stanford, 1966, 291-3; Yü Ying-shih, 'Chang Hsëh-ch'eng and Collingwood. A Comparative Study of Their Historical Ideas', (in Chinese) in *Lun Tai Chen yü Chang Hsüeh-ch'eng* [*On Tai Chen and Chang Hsüeh-ch'eng*], Hong Kong, 1976, 197-242.

24. Butterfield, *Origins*, (see note 3), 140.

25. Kwang-chih Chang, *Shang Civilization*, New Haven, 1980, 34.

26. James Legge, *The Ch'un Ts'ew with the Tso Chuen. The Chinese Classics*, Hong Kong, 1960, vol.V, 290-1.

27. Watson, *Ssu-ma Ch'ien*, (see note 19), 70-1.

28. Momigliano, *Classical Foundations*, (see note 12), 20.

29. Nivison, *Chang Hsüeh-ch'eng*, (see note 23), 101-4.

30. Fung Yu-lan, *Chinese Philosophy*, (see note 13), vol. I, 32.

31. In chapter 85 of the *Romance*, a poem explicitly says that the novelist follows the rules of praise and blame as laid down by the Neo-Confucian philosopher Chu Hsi (1130-1200). For a detailed study of the novel, see C.T. Hsia, *The Classic Chinese Novel*, New York, 1968, ch. II: "The Romance of the Three Kingdoms"; Andrew Plaks, *The Four Masterworks of the Ming Novel*, Princeton, 1987, ch. 5 "*San-kuo chih yen-i*: Limitations of Valor."

32. Watson, *Ssu-ma Ch'ien*, (see note 19), 30.

33. Ssu-ma Ch'ien, *Tzu-chih t'ung-chien* [*Comprehensive Mirror for Aid in Government*], Peking, 1956, vol.V, 1934-5.

34. Liu Tseng-fu and Liu Ting-sheng, eds *Liu I-cheng shih-hsüeh lun-wen chi* [*Liu I-cheng's Essays in Historiography*], Shanghai, 1991, 4 ('Preface').

35. Michael Walzer, *Interpretation and Social Criticism*, Cambridge, Mass., 1987, 61.

36. Lien-sheng Yang, 'The Organization of Chinese Official Historiography: Principles and Methods of the Standard Histories from T'ang through the Ming Dynasty', in *Historians of China*

and Japan, 50. For an authoritative account of the so-called court historian in T'ang China, see Denis Twitchett, *The Writing of Official History under the T'ang*, Cambridge, Mass., 1992.

37. Watson, *Ssu-ma Ch'ien*, (see note 19), 61.
38. Ibid., 144-50.
39. Lien-sheng Yang, 'Toward a Study of Dynastic Configurations in Chinese History', in *Studies in Chinese Institutional History*, Cambridge, 1961, 12f.
40. Fornara, *Nature of History*, (see note 20), 78.
41. E.G. Pulleyblank, 'Chinese Historical Criticism: Liu Chih-chi and Ssu-ma Kuang', in *Historians of China and Japan*, (see note 23), 163.
42. Jo-shui Chen, *Liu Tsung-yuan and Intellectual Change in T'ang China 773-819*, Cambridge, 1992, 96. It should be noted, however, that before Liu several writers in the mid-eighth century had already proposed to see history as a long-term impersonal process with patterns and trends. See David McMullen, 'Historical and Literary Theory in the Mid-Eighth Century', in *Perspectives on the T'ang*, eds Arthur F. Wright and Denis Twitchett, New Haven, 1973, 321-6.
43. Ian McMorran, 'Wang Fu-chih and the Neo-Confucian Tradition', in *The Unfolding of Neo-Confucianism*, ed. Wm. Theodore de Bary, New York, 1975, 455-7; On-cho Ng, 'A Tension in Ch'ing Thought: Historicism in Seventeenth- and Eighteenth-Century Chinese Thought', *Journal of the History of Ideas*, 54 (1993), 568.
44. Nivison, *Chang Hsüeh-ch'eng*, (see note 23), 145.
45. Chang Hsüeh-ch'eng, *Wen-shih t'ung-i* [*General Principles of Literature and History*], Peking, 1956, 34-40.
46. Ch'en Chih-ch'ao, ed., *Ch'en Yüan lai-wang shu-hsin chi* [*Correspondences of Ch'en Yüan*], Shanghai, 1990, 686.
47. Liang Ch'i-ch'ao, *Intellectual Trends in the Ch'ing Period*, tr. Immanuel C.Y. Hsü, Cambridge, 1959, 70.
48. Richard Wilhelm, *The I ching or Book of Changes*, tr. Cary F. Baynes, Princeton, 1977, 714.
49. McMorran, 'Wang Fu-chih', (see note 43), 457.
50. Yang Lien-sheng, 'Ch'ao-tai chien pi-sai' [Dynastic Competitions] in *Yang Lien-sheng lun-wen chi* [*A Collection of Essays by Yang Lien-sheng*], Peking,1992, 126-38. The remark of Tu Yu is quoted on p.133.
51. Huang Tsung-hsi, *The Records of Ming Scholars*, ed. Julia Ching, Honolulu, 1987, 46.
52. G.W. F. Hegel, *Lectures on the Philosophy of History*, New York, 1956, 135; Etienne Balazs, 'History as a Guide to Bureaucratic Practice', in *Chinese Civilization and Bureaucracy*, New Haven, 1964, 129.
53. Yüeh-lin Chin, 'Chinese Philosophy', *Social Science in China*, no. 1 (1981), 83-93.
54. Nancy Lee Swann, *Food and Money in Ancient China: The Earliest Economic History of China to A.D. 25*, Princeton, 1950, 114-5; 132-4.
55. Karl Mannheim, 'Conservative Thought',," in *Essays on Sociology and Social Psychology*, London, 1953, 79.
56. Aaron I. Gurevich, 'The Double Responsibility of the Historian', in *The Social Responsibility of the Historian* ed. Francois Bedarida, Providence, 1994, 80-1.

Must History Follow Rational Patterns of Interpretation?

Critical Questions from a Chinese Perspective

THOMAS H.C. LEE

I am writing from the viewpoint of a Chinese historian with an educated interest in Western historical thinking. My comments will thus be based on my knowledge of China's sense of the past. I would like to raise three issues, which may clarify Mr. Burke's points, in order that my central argument could be placed in a proper perspective.

The first pertains to Mr. Burke's thesis 1.2., in which he uses the concept of "equilibrium" in connection with the cyclical view of history. Mr. Burke does not readily say that the idea of "equilibrium" is the same as the cyclical view of history, but a clearer distinction may be necessary. An equilibrium should more appropriately mean a state of ceaseless interaction among many constituent elements in search of balance. This word may be more appropriate for describing a state of historical existence than historical process. Specifically, I would think that the conception of equilibrium is the acknowledgement of the existence of competing but somewhat uneasily co-existing notions, or *Weltanschauungen*, in any given time, with not one single notion or factor standing out more prominently than others. Placed in the context of historical thinking, then, to say that history is a process of changing equilibriums does not necessarily mean that there is a regularity in cyclical pattern. The endless repetition of different notions, perspectives or systems following a predictable pattern or regularity is a cyclical view of history, but what if the process of changing equilibrium does not follow any pattern or regularity? The cyclical view of history is thus constructed on the assumption that change followed a certain regularity or pattern, even if it was repetitious. As such it is more than just changing equilibriums. To me, there is no real attempt in the Western tradition to understand history as changing equilibriums.

Notes for this section can be found on page 177.

The second issue has to do with epistemological acumen in historical knowledge. Of all the distinct characteristics of Western historical thought, it is the attempt "to understand" that appears to me to stand out most distinctly. It would seem to me that the Western tradition is above all concerned with explicating the nature, rather than the meaning, of human experiences. While attempts to describe the process (such as linear-over-cyclical, or identifying agents of historical change, etc.) vary, almost all of them center on finding the reason (causes) or pattern (based on rational study or investigation) of historical change. I would even say that the need for "literary artifact" as a foundation for historical knowledge came from the concern for "explanation": literary emplotment will enable historians to better articulate (or categorize) the genuine human experience. In short, I believe that the overall concern of Western historical tradition should best be characterized as concern with the nature of historical experiences. Mr. Burke indeed does not consider moral or ethical judgement that traditionally informed the Judeo-Christian belief to be a characteristic of the Western tradition.

The third issue is the Western preoccupation with rationally, or even logically, describing the regularity or pattern in history.[1] I believe that this concern in general leads to a teleological approach. Although Mr. Burke does not use the word "teleological" in his theses, the predominance of linear concept of time in the West implies it. Even cyclic view of history could also suggest orderly succession of changes, and implies predictability, if not salvation. In short, the preoccupation with pattern or regularity in historical process, without a doubt, is the most important deep-structural assumption in the Western tradition. The development of hermeneutical approach in the twentieth century, however, may present a meaningful challenge to this. It is perhaps more useful to view historical process from a microcosmic standpoint, by explaining changes as hermeneutical cycles, than to offer macrocosmic interpretations of patterns or "directions." In short, if we allow in more hermeneutical dimension in the thinking on history, we may be better able to describe historical change from an interestingly new perspective.

I think the Chinese tradition is primarily concerned with equilibrium, meaning and hermeneutical cycle. Whereas Western historians are more concerned with describing the nature and process of historical change, Chinese historians are more concerned with the equilibrium of random factors, which constitute the endless process of historical changes (be the process cyclical or linear). The preoccupation with equilibrium by Chinese historians may complement Western historians' fixation with regularity or pattern. Historical reflection is to determine not so much the causal relations between preceding and succeeding historical events, but to describe why (and scarcely how) equilibrium broke down in favor of a dominant factor; and how this factor then creates the context within which new factors reappropriate themselves into a new equilibrium.

Take ideas as an example: Chinese historians accept that contending ideas coexist at the same time. Ideally, these ideas should exist in harmonious balance. It is therefore as important to understand why and how the equilibrium of ideas broke down as to decide which idea is more rational (read moral) and more corresponding to natural and human "law" or "order." A teleology or regularity-oriented historical thinking is more concerned with the search for truth, or at least how one idea competes better than the other. For a Chinese thinker, such a concern is not as important as why a complex of ideas could not be maintained with their equitable balance, much less harmony. There is thus less concern with what truth is than with how the equilibrium could be restored. In other words, it is always the Chinese position that ideas coexist at all times, and it is of foremost importance that they are restored to their original state of harmony (equilibrium). No one single idea is perfect if it does not interact harmoniously with other ideas. In this way, the history of ideas can be viewed as a prolonged state of the loss of the primeval equilibrium; it is a history of desperation, and lacking in salvation. It is a common Chinese view that the history of ideas is a series of random aggregates of ideas. There is little concern over whether one could speak of direction or pattern in them.

The history of ideas viewed as a series of random aggregates of disparate and uncoordinated ideas should suggest to us history as a process of irregularity. It is really not right therefore to characterize the Chinese view of time as cyclical in the sense Polybius or St. Augustine used it. Rather, a Chinese historian would say that history is like the Brownian Movement in physics.

The hermeneutical approach to some extent speaks to the Chinese historical mind. If every period of time, according to the Chinese view, is a collection of discordant elements in imbalance, and that historical change shows little or no pattern, then the best way to explain changes would be hermeneutical cycle.[2] I will not enter into a systematic discussion here except by saying that, first, interpretation of long-term historical changes was never a strength in Chinese historical studies, and, second, causal relations were employed in a microscopic or microcosmic manner. It is to live out the meaning in history that has preoccupied Chinese historians.

As mentioned above, while Western historical philosophy did not lack emphasis on finding the meaning of history, it seems to me that such attempts were believed to be feasible only if we first know the nature of changes. But the Chinese tradition sees little use for such a belief. Chinese historians are not particularly concerned with knowing the nature of history: since Confucius and before, the moral order of universe has been self-evident, and all that is needed is to restore that original order. The preoccupation has always been with how moral lessons could be derived from examining the relationship between failure of moral rectitude, and the breakdown or dislocation of equilibrium. In short, the central concern of the Chinese tradition is to project human moral experiences to historical changes. It is the overriding concern with moral significance of history—assuming that an individual's personal history resonates with historical changes, making them understandable to the posterity—which makes up the most important feature of Chinese historical thinking. It does not presume that predictability is essential to the discovery of the hidden messages.

The strength of Western tradition, in a very general sense, lies in its stress on knowledge; it presumes a uniformity of experiences past and present, and a regularity in historical process. The notion is at least as old as Xenophanes. However, without abandoning the assumption of uniformity in human nature, one could still argue that the aggregate of the multifarious elements at work in any given time of history, does not necessarily act according to any regularity or pattern, much less direction. The historical process is a series of endless minute changes, which are constantly at work, randomly, in search of equilibrium. It would seem that a hermeneutical cycle best approximates this kind of search. However, Chinese historians are not interested in describing the "process" per se of any "hermeneutical circle"; they are, rather, interested in using the data bank for moral lessons. They do so without being bothered by the question of the nature of history. The nature of history is already evident, above all, in the necessity of moral life in human experiences. The meaning of history is to use such self-evident moral knowledge to bear upon the process of changes, and to hope for the ultimate restoration of the original equilibrium or harmony.

My questions thus become:

1. Is it necessary for us first to understand the nature of history before we can know its meaning?
2. Could history be understood as a series of disparate elements (factors) without direction or pattern? If so, where and when does salvation come in?
3. If we conceive of history as aggregates of interacting factors without an overall pattern or regularity, does this necessarily mean that we cannot understand it rationally? Does this mean that the subject matter is beyond comprehension? And does this mean that there is then no salvation?

We are here asking a question central to the hermeneutical tradition, but this is a question extremely important to our search for meaning in humankind's historical experiences.

Notes

1. I am using "rational" in a very general sense to mean that history could be understood "rationally" because its structure or process is subject to rational understanding, even if its very nature could prove to be irrational. To a Chinese historian, such a preoccupation has little meaning.

2. Occasional attempts to discern regularity—be it linear, spiral or cyclic—existed, but they were not in the mainstream.

Some Reflections on
Early Indian Historical Thinking

ROMILA THAPAR

One would like to believe that we have arrived at a point where there can be a comparative study of the "historical culture" of any part of the world, or of what might be easier, everyone's perceptions of the past. However, it is more often than not that a sense of history is denied to all but those that conform to a particular kind of history. A historical culture therefore would need more careful definition, if history is perceived from the point of view of an Enlightenment project. But the Enlightenment sense of history is, in itself, historically specific as has been demonstrated in recent theoretical writings on understanding the past. Conceding that it is the basis of what we have regarded as the discipline of history (and the presence of historical writing in other cultures has been measured by this), nevertheless it should be possible to comment on other representations of the past—not only in terms of whether they conform to history as we understand it, but also in terms of how they reflect upon their past and provide a function for a historical consciousness. My response therefore, will be largely in the nature of explaining how I perceive historical consciousness in early India, since the general view is that it was absent. Because of this denial, any discussion of its presence has to be prefaced with descriptions of the texts in which it may be located.

The texts which I shall be referring to vary in time and form.[1] The chronology of these texts falls in the time bracket of approximately A.D. 400 to 1200. This allows for a certain distance from the past and the events being narrated. I would like to include four categories of texts: the *Puranas*, Buddhist monastic chronicles, historical biographies and finally chronicles relating the history of a dynasty or a region. These are all texts that are associated with what has been called the *itihasa-purana* tradition, which is now translated as the "historical tradition" although it should not be understood as history in the modern sense. *Itihasa* literally means "thus it was," and *purana* is that which is

---

Notes for this section can be found on page 186.

regarded as ancient. The term *itihasa* is not applied as a label to the four categories listed above, nevertheless there is an association with them.

The *Puranas* were religious sectarian texts, each either dedicated to a Hindu deity or to an aspect of Hindu belief and practice.[2] Some of the early texts, such as the *Vishnu Purana*, has as one of its five constitutive parts, a section that narrates genealogies. These begin with the first ruler, Manu, who, as we know from the *Matsya Purana*, survives the great Flood and is ancestor to a large number of descent groups through his progeny. The most respected of these are the Solar line and the Lunar line and there are significant differences between them. These lineages are said to have splitt off and settled in various directions. Their eventual destruction takes place through a major war, which is described in the epic, the *Mahabharata*. Similar to the Flood, this is a second time-marker. The narrative about these early *rajas* is drawn from the epic and the oral traditions, which have generally been dismissed as unproven historically. If for the moment we set aside the attempts to determine the historicity of these successions, there is much that can be derived from the patterning of the genealogies in relation to political authority and social forms.[3] These are as legitimate a concern of history as are political events. Subsequent to World War I, the pattern to the narration of dynasties changes radically, with lists of rulers, regnal years and some indications of origins, all described in the future tense. Many of these dynasties are attested to in other sources such as inscriptions. These sections of the *Puranas* have been significant to the piecing together of early India chronology. That they were included in a text that pertained to the cosmology, mythology, rituals and worship of Vishnu, was in part to give the data sanctity, but perhaps more as an insurance that the data would be preserved and handed down.

Buddhist monastic chronicles have survived from Sri Lanka and also date to about the middle of the first millennium A.D.[4] The *Dipavamsa* chronicles the history of the island but is less reliable than the *Mahavamsa* which is the history of the powerful monastery, the *Mahavihara* in Sri Lanka. The narrative of events speaks of the people of the island—some indigenous and some migrants—the political authority of small kingdoms, with the coming of Buddhism from India as the turning point. From this point on, the text narrates the interface of state power and the authority of the *sangha* or Buddhist Order, a narrative that also draws in the history of Indian dynasties apart from the politics of Sri Lanka of that time. Chronologies are based on a fixed point in time, the *mahaparinirvana*, or the date of the death of the Buddha in the later fifth century B.C.[5] The narrative describes the vicissitudes of the monastery and its eventual emergence as a powerful institution. The historicity of the Buddha, the centrality of the date, the need to be clear about sectarian breakaways and to keep records of the acquisition of property, all contributed to a sharper sense of maintaining monastic records. Nevertheless it was probably the changing relations between monastery and court that also motivated a more precise history. The monastic chronicles are in a sense also substitute epics, where the hero is the *Mahavihara* monastery, which is the foundational Buddhist institution of the *sangha*, or Buddhist Order, in Sri Lanka.

The second two of the four categories are founded on the literature of the courts, which were powerful centers of politics and culture during the first millennium A.D., and even later. The emergence of well-established kingdoms and the consciousness of the state as a distinct entity resulted in the past being seen in fresh forms, no longer embedded in religious texts (although not divorced from religion), and having traveled a distance from the obsessive genealogies of earlier times. These biographies were not meticulously detailed accounts of the activities of the person, but rather intended to convey a flavor of the times and the court over which the king presided.[6] This was generally done by taking up one set of events which was crucial to the reign of the king. This could be the acquisition of a city and area regarded as foundational to any claim to suzerainty, such as the acquisition of Kannauj by Harshavardhana described in Banabhatta's *Harsacarita*; or the quelling of a rebellion that had threatened the authority of the king, as in Sandhyakaranandin's *Ramacarita*. Since the biography was essentially literature in the court tradition, there was a considerable overlap in style and form between the biography and the prose fantasy, as is evident from a comparison between the two works of the much respected seventh-century biographer, Banabhatta—the *Harsacarita* and the *Kadambari*. In such texts, the tempering of history by a literary genre has to be conceded.

The fourth main category is that of chronicles other than those pertaining to religious institutions. These are chronicles either of dynasties or of kingdoms as regions. The generic name is *vamshavali*, or "the path of succession." Such chronicles follow a pattern. They begin with demarcating the area where the activities began; and if there are myths associated with the area, these are related. Thus many chronicles of Himalayan kingdoms begin with narrating the mythology of the existence of a lake in the valley that was drained through some supernatural feat. The earliest section attempts to link the region with the heroes and clan-chiefs referred to in the genealogies of the *Puranas*.[7] This is a form of incorporation through both the history, as well as the geography of origins. Subsequent to this, the beginning of the kingdoms are described, and gradually the narrative takes on the character of chronicling persons and events. The latter can be compared with the inscriptions issued by various kings, which have been regarded as more authentic sources by modern historians. The inscriptions corroborate and supply additional data, but on occasion they also contradict the statements of the chronicle. Such contradictions, even if occasional, can also occur in other chronicles from the neighborhood. Conquests and claims to social origins are the issues contested.

Chronicles in a more summary form are frequent in the inscriptions issued by dynasties, and such accounts increase in the period after the seventh and eighth centuries A.D. Sometimes the history of the dynasty, for example the Chandellas of Bundelkhand in central India, can be reconstructed from the inscriptions issued by the rulers and by others associated with the court.[8] Many of the more important inscriptions—such as those issued at the dedication of a temple—carry a concise account of the origins and previous rulers of the dynasty, and major accomplishments of dynasty rulers.[9] These are necessarily the official version of events, as would be expected from court proclamations, and require that modern historians relate them to other versions that may be available, such as epic poems and the folk tradition. Such inscriptions may not be labeled as "history" but their intention as historical compositions is evident.

To return to the question of historical culture, one way of proceeding would be to inquire as to why some societies, cultures, civilizations have been denied history in the nineteenth century when there was a premium on the historical foundations of knowledge. Perhaps the most striking example of this is the dismissal of Indian civilization as being ahistorical. The search for histories of India by Orientalist scholars in the late eighteenth and early nineteenth centuries had a negative result, the only exception being the *Rajatarangini* of Kalhana, a twelfth-century history of Kashmir.[10] This was recognized as history for three main reasons: the introduction sets out the details of the sources consulted by the author, together with an assessment of the reliability of each category; the narrative is presented in chronological order with a sequential rendering of events; and there is an evident change from the more mythological to the more realistic as the contemporary period approaches, and this presentation is subject to some degree of causal explanation. This was in keeping with the Enlightenment sense of historical consciousness and therefore the *Rajatarangini* was readily accepted as history. There was clearly a consciousness that history is not just a matter of a text indicating a perception of the past, but also of an awareness of how such a perception was created. This implies that there is a context within which the data is presented and of which the modern reader should be aware. Also that there is more than a single source, and a comparative study of many sources might result in a fuller explanation of past events. And finally, there is the question of what is accepted as causal explanation.

Since only a single text conformed to what was then believed to be the definition of history, it was argued that Orientalist scholarship would have to "rediscover," the Indian past and subject it to a presentation determined by the European canons of historical writing. This of course eminently suited colonial policy, which in the nineteenth century was concerned with restructuring India as a colonial economy. The providing of a fresh narrative of the past could be useful to this purpose, particularly if it could also provide an identity from what were viewed as the scattered fragments of the past. Yet interestingly there are many other texts in addition to the *Rajatarangini*, with ingredients of historical consciousness, but these elements are more embedded and therefore difficult to recognize easily. These are texts that are intended as encapsulations of historical consciousness when their context is examined. They are set out as a chronological, sequential narrative and they carry notions of causation, which—not being too different from those of medieval Europe—carry the imprint of the accepted social ethics. But obviously they would not be recognizable to those looking for Enlightenment-formulated histories.

European post-Enlightenment history, it has been said, is characterized by a sense of time and space and the idea of progress. Its history is associated with linear time and a clearly defined geography, both of which differ in the Indian case. India and the classical world had a cosmology based on cyclic time, and Indian cyclic time supposedly precluded history. This has been one of the constant mythologies about Indian time.[11] The cosmology of the *Puranas* speaks of four cycles—the Satya., Treta, Dvapara and Kali—which go into the making of the grand cycle, the *mahayuga*. The structure of these cycles is mathematical with a decline in length that conforms to arithmetical progression. The total length of the grand cycle is 4,320,000 years. What is significant, however, is that within the last of the four cycles, namely the current Kali age, there are various mechanisms of linear timereckoning and at least two relate entirely to historical consciousness. In the genealogical chapter of the *Visnu Purana*, which sets out in genealogical patterns the heroes and kings who ruled from the beginning of time to about the mid-first millennium A.D., the chronology is according to generations, and later it changes to dynasties—each with its own king-list and details of regnal years. This is a text of some importance in the reconstruction of the chronology of early India. Apart from this, there is also the awareness of eras; and in the inscriptions of the period after the mid-first millennium A.D. (which inscriptions are in effect the annals of early Indian history), the pinning of the text to an era is frequent. There is, therefore, in works pertaining to the early Indian perceptions of the past, an interfacing of many forms of time, cyclic and linear. The multiplicity of forms raises the question of the function of each, and the degree to which each confirms or contests a particular historical consciousness. Where cosmological time is seen in recurring cycles, there possibly the otherness of the past is reduced.

Cycles of time are not devoid of notions of progress, because at the end of the cycle there is the coming of a fresh cycle. Since the utopian golden age is placed at the start of the cycle, the coming of a new cycle brings the return of the utopia. However this is not the focus of the eschatology as is, for instance, the Day of Judgement in the Christian and Islamic traditions of linear time. Cyclic return denies a specific goal and the time span of the *mahayuga* is too large for there to be a specific goal. But the activities of the individual reach out to the greater glory of man and (later) of the kingdom, and the characteristics of a well-established state are aspired to.

Each of the four ages has a component of *dharma* or virtue, which decreases from the first to the last. In one text it is described as a bull standing on four legs in the first age, but reduced to one leg in the fourth age, symbolizing the decline of the moral and social order.[12] The decline of *dharma* in the fourth age when it reaches its nadir, moves towards an upswing. In at least two of the eschatologies prevalent in historical texts, there is not even a waiting for the return of the new cycle. In the northern Buddhist tradition, the coming of the last of the Buddhas, Maitreya, heralds the return of utopian conditions and suggests elements of millenarianism as it is dated to a specific time. Similarly, Hinduism based on the *Puranas*, also predicts the coming of Kalkin, the tenth incarnation of Vishnu. This again results in a restoration of *dharma* and marks the end of a *mahayuga*.

The decline in *dharma* is expressed in historical terms as the change from the initial period of the heroes—descended from the most honored *ksatriya* lineages—to the emergence of kingdoms ruled by dynasties among whom there are families that originate as upstarts, servile administrators, and low-status foreigners (probably a reference to the Hellenistic Greeks). The change is indicated in the switch from patterns of descent listed in a seamless continuity, to dynastic identities separated by dynastic names and regnal years. This is a record of change where one generation does stand on the shoulders of another but the change is irreversible. Nor is there mention of a repetition of events in succeeding cycles, as is assumed by those who argue that cyclical time denies the uniqueness of historical events. There is a loss at one level where the heroes disappear, but there is also the coming of the greater power with kingship extending to large kingdoms. It is these dynastic rulers who formed the prototype for the historical biographies of the late first millennium A.D.

The spatial dimension as projected in geography carries the element of a contradiction. Cosmological geography is not clearly defined and is possibly deliberately vague as such geographies frequently are. The vision of the universe, dominated by concentric circles eventually focuses on an area that suggests the subcontinent, but not in precise geographical terms. Names such as Jambudvipa, Bharatavarsha and Aryavarta are more in the nature of cultural markers than precise geographical locations, as is evident from the manner in which they are described. This is a contrast to the regional chronicles such as the *Rajataranigini*, or the *vamshavalis* of Chamba and various other places, in which the geographical context to the evolution of a kingdom is indicated in some precise detail. In the chronicle of Chamba such detail makes it possible to observe changes in the form of the kingdom by the locations mentioned and the associations with these locations. Therefore, generalizations about the awareness of space in forms of historical consciousness in early India, would relate to the specificity of the text.

This specificity is most apparent in the historical biographies. Their beginnings may be traced to a sense of using the authority of the past to legitimize the present. This appears to have had its origins in epigraphic sources. An impressively large pillar at Allahabad becomes a kind of palimpsest of history in stone.[13] Originally carrying the inscriptions of the Mauryan king Ashoka of the third century B.C. and portraying his concern for social ethics and the well-being of the Buddhist Order; it also has a lengthy eulogy of a Gupta king of the fourth century A.D., listing his various conquests and alliances; and finally has a seventeenth-century inscription of the Mughal king Jahangir, setting out his ancestry. Each of these statements projects a distinctively different view of the authors, yet the latter two are evidently seeking the legitimacy of the past by placing their statements on this pillar. Statements such as these differ from biographies as they are partially autobiographical, carry the imprint of authority and are essentially political statements.

By way of an aside, it may be said that there was a widespread use of the past to legitimize the present. This may not exactly be the articulation of history, but it again points to the awareness of a historical consciousness. Two quite different examples of this can be quoted. Spurious charters of land grants are known in medieval India in which an earlier grant was forged in an attempt to derive a legal benefit.[14] The performance of sacrificial rituals sometimes required deliberately archaic technologies to emphasize the links with the past, although this is not made evident in the ritual.[15]

Historical biographies or *caritas* were, for the most part, biographies of contemporary rulers. What makes them texts incorporating historical consciousness is that they do have a history of the dynasty prior to the history of the person, and that the author has to provide his credentials by a chapter—at the start or the end—which is autobiographical but includes a history of his family. There is a continuity from the past into the present. Events described in the biography are seen as unique to the person and the time. References to the *karma*, the accumulated merit of the individual, were sometimes introduced into the discussion of the actions of the person. Hindu and Buddhist texts do not speak of the unreality of a person, for even if, on occasion, the world as we see it is described as an illusion, man is never an illusion. Events are not openly debated, but the debate can be implicit in the writing of a biography. For example, one of the themes that seems to recur implicitly is the need to justify the usurping of the throne by a younger brother. The legality of the usurpation requires a reordering of events and personalities, and may even draw on the intervention of a deity. The biographies are written in a highly stylized, courtly form so that the political question is hidden in the rhetoric.

This raises the question of the degree to which a text claiming to narrate the past should have seived the data and made the appropriate selection. Kalhana's statement in the *Rajatarangini* was what impressed Orientalist scholars: he lists the sources that he has used, and his priorities in choosing them and assessing their reliability. This is of course not done with the precision of the modern social sciences, but in a general way in broad descriptive sweeps. The assessment does not emerge out of a legal system of weighing evidence, but out of an attempt of narrating the past as truthfully as possible—without too much concern for the magical and the supernatural—and with a conscious concern for impartiality.

A few decades ago such statements would have been necessary for categorizing a text as historical, but now with the extensive discussions on the writing of culture by anthropologist—and more extensive discussions among deconstructionists and postmodernists on the implicit seiving and selecting processes inherent in any text—the question seems to have moved to the domain of the context rather than of the text alone. Objectivity, which was claimed by virtually every reading of a source, is now more realistically, rarely claimed and is aspired to within the limitations of the text and its interpretation. The emphasis on the presentation being detached is a late development in European writing. Earlier texts would have valued a close attachment to purpose and function, and detachment would have been at a discount.

Without necessarily subscribing to postmodernist analyses, critical theory has some methodological validity when applied to the reading of ancient texts. Sources for the data were often-floating oral traditions, as was the case with the genealogies and descent lists that were ultimately fashioned and incorporated into the *Puranas* in the early centuries A.D. The selection was severely conditioned by the purpose and function of the text, and therefore the ideological perspective of the author does become of primary importance in assessing the text, as does the general background of the period when it was being written. History from this perspective was viewed as a series of genealogical constructions and changes in these patterns at specific points were significant. The "reading" of the genealogies today becomes a matter of considerable expertise, but doubtless in the period when they were composed the rhetoric was familiar, and the levels of meaning clear. Selectivity does not have to be demonstrated and explained, but lies in the ideological and other perspectives of the text. Enlightenment history would find this unacceptable, but to insist that only texts with a conscious discussion of sources and selection can be counted as history would be to unnecessarily limit the number of histories available from the ancient world.

The discipline of history as we know it today has grown substantially out of the requirements of the Enlightenment view of the past. This introduced a major change both in perceiving the past through a process of sieving and selecting, and in recognizing the function of the past in the present. The agency of human action also changed from institution, such as kingship, monasteries, and clans, to the state. These processes were known to the pre-Enlightenment "historians" but were experienced and practiced in an implicit manner. That implicity was made explicit by the emphases that emerged from Enlightenment thought. Prior to this the constituents of history were not identical in varying cultures, even if a dialogue between them had been possible. The concern with a rational causality was new. The increasing secularization of the state meant that narratives that incorporated deities or the supernatural began to be doubted.

It is therefore necessary that we compare like with like. We cannot find an Enlightenment view of history from early Indian writing. Post-Enlightenment analyses of history have opened up the possibilities of other ways of arriving at both historical consciousness and history; as indeed they also extended the

dimensions of what comes under the purview of history. This in itself has
resulted in changed ways of defining history. If quantitative history requires
records that are only available in industrialized societies, then the study of oral
traditions can only be effective through an empathy with non-capitalist societies.
A comparison between the two methods is of considerable value. In the case of
early India, we have a respectable narrative of history based on the discipline as
established in the last two centuries. An analysis of the way in which the past was
viewed by earlier authors claiming to narrate the *"itihasa"* (whether or not it
conformed to Enlightenment methods) would in itself add considerably to our
understanding of the perceptions that early Indian society had of its past.

Notes

1. C.H. Philips ed., *Historians of India, Pakistan and Ceylon*, London, 1961; A.K. Warder, *An Intro-duction to Indian Historiography*, Bombay, 1971; R. Thapar, 'Society and Historical Conscious-ness', in *Situating Indian History* eds S. Bhattacharya and R. Thapar, New Delhi, 1986.
2. F.E. Pargiter, *Ancient Indian Historical Tradition*, London, 1922; *The Purana Text of the Dynasties of the Kali Age*, London, 1913.
3. R. Thapar, 'Genealogical Patterns as Perceptions of the Past', *Studies in History* n.s. 7.1. (1991), 1-36.
4. L.S. Pereira, 'The Pali Chronicle of Ceylon', in *Historians* ed. C.H. Philips, (see note 1) 29-43.
5. Recently some scholars have favored an advancing of the date to even 368 B.C. See H. Bechert ed., *The Dating of the Historical Buddha*, Göttingen, 1991. But this is a separate issue. The point is that these chronicles locate their chronologies to a fixed date.
6. V.S. Pathak, *Ancient Historians of India*, Bombay, 1966.
7. J. Ph. Vogel, *Antiquities of Chamba State*, Calcutta, 1911, ASI, vol. XXXV.
8. N.S. Bose, *History of the Candellas of Jejakabhukti*, Calcutta, 1956; S.K. Mitra, *The Early Rulers of Khajuraho*, Calcutta, 1958.
9. E.g. the inscription of Dhanga, a Chandella king of Khajuraho, *Epigraphia Indica* vol. 1 1892, 122ff.
10. M.A. Stein, *Kalhana's Rajatarangini. A Chronicle of the Kings of Kashmir*, London, 1900.
11. R. Thapar, *Time as a Metaphor of History. Early India*, New Delhi, 1996.
12. *Manu* I, 81-2.
13. Allahabad Pillar Inscription. A. Cunningham, *Corpus Inscriptionum Indicarum*, vol. 1, 'Inscrip-tions of Asoka', Varanasi, 1961 (reprint) 37ff, E. Hultzsch, CII, vol. 1, *Inscriptions of Asoka*, New Delhi, 1991 (reprint), xix, 155ff.
14. D.C. Sirca, *Indian Epigraphy*, Varanasi, 1965, 435ff.
15. R. Thapar, 'The Archaeological Background to the Agnicayana Ritual', in *Agni. The Vedic Rit-ual of the Fire Altar*, , ed. F. Staal, vol. II, Berkeley, 1983, 19-26.

III: Afterword

Reply

PETER BURKE

I should like to begin this response by thanking everyone who has taken the trouble to comment on my original paper, offering counterexamples, making distinctions, providing references and (not least) exposing my assumptions. A special word of thanks to the scholars whose native language is neither English nor German for making their comments in one of these languages.

I am sure that the critics will understand why I have not replied to them individually, and also why I have concentrated on the comments that engaged most directly with the paper. In order to sum up both the debate and the volume, I shall discuss four general issues and then respond to the comments on my ten theses one by one. The four general issues are (1) the problem of viewpoint, (2) the appropriateness of the initial question, (3) the structure of historiographical revolutions, and (4) the need for more or sharper distinctions.

1

I was not surprised to be told that my theses reflect a Western point of view, that (as Hayden White puts it), they offer a Western perspective on a world perspective, and that (as François Hartog suggests), they are also distinctively European, perhaps also British or even English. The theses doubtless reflect my gender, social class and generation as well. All the same, I would have welcomed more concrete details concerning these "Occidentalisms." On one occasion where details were offered (by Aziz Al-Azmeh), I have to say that I did not recognize myself as a "vitalist" or a Hegelian. Like many Western intellectuals (especially British intellectuals), I consider the analogy between cultures and organisms to be a dangerous one and tried hard not to present "the West" as "homogeneous in time" or "coherent in space." Indeed, like Al-Azmeh and François Hartog, I insisted that the West is a "historical construct"—which is not to say that it has always been seen as such. As a recent collection of essays suggests, some views of the West may be characterized as an "Occidentalism" parallel to Said's Orientalism.[1]

For this reason, I welcomed the comments that distinguished between various Wests, noting, as Godfrey Muriuki does, the "intellectual conflict inherent in the Western historical tradition," or developing my remarks about the ancient world as Mediterranean rather than Western. It might also be useful to emphasize the differences between the European Wests and what might be called the "Far Wests," the "Neo-Europes" or "Europoid" cultures which developed in the Americas after 1492 and later in Australia. Or again, like Georg Iggers, one might distinguish different periods in Western culture, identifying my theses or at least the majority of them with "modernity." This was a problem too important to omit, but I remain somewhat uncomfortable with the concept of modernity, essentially because Western Europeans have been talking about the "modern" or the "moderns" more or less continuously from the twelfth century onwards, while giving this term a number of different meanings. Like an overfilled suitcase, this concept is splitting apart. As Iggers admits, some of the features I attributed to Western historiography go back to the Greeks, others to the Middle Ages and the Renaissance, yet others to the Enlightenment. All the same, they do combine to make a "modern" package, a point that has become visible in our own "postmodern" age. Even if postmodernism is a Western invention, the movement offers us an opportunity to reevaluate non-Western traditions, as Romila Thapar suggests in the conclusion to her comment.

2

Linked to the first point is the suggestion that even to ask what is distinctive about Western historiography is a Western question, or even (as Tarif Khalidi suggests) the wrong question. To this suggestion my response would be "Yes and no." Yes, in the sense that members of a particular group are especially interested in what makes them distinctive. Looking back on Max Weber's famous studies of China, India and the Middle East, they now look less like an Olympian comparative history than an attempt to define what is Western by contrasting European traditions (feudalism, capitalism, bureaucracy, the Protestant ethic, a certain style of music, and so on) with those of other cultures. Particularly dangerous is the contrast between some feature that is present in Western culture and absent in others, leading to a concern with China's "failure" to develop modern science, or Africa's "failure" to develop feudalism.[2] In the historiographical field, this kind of contrast diminishes the value of one of the few explicitly comparative studies, Donald Brown's book on the "social origins of historical consciousness."[3]

However, I also want to contest the dismissal of the fundamental question addressed by my paper as a Eurocentric one, on the grounds that the process of comparison is reversible. Instead of asking why Africa failed to develop knights, we can ask why Europe failed to develop mandarins, admitting along the way that in certain places and periods a group rather like a mandarinate did come into existence, as in the case of professors in German universities.[4]

3

Khalidi also suggested that the "right" question to have asked was one about the "structure of historiographical revolutions," while Al-Azmeh and Frank Ankersmit give this question a political answer. I would agree with all of them that this is a fascinating question, and that in certain important cases the political answer is an extremely plausible one. Khalidi himself has discussed the relation between the emergence of Islamic historiography and the "painful birth of the early empire."[5] Ankersmit cites the cases of the French invasion of Italy in 1494, the English Civil War of the 1640s, and the French Revolution as "traumatic" events to which the new histories of Guicciardini, Hyde and Ranke were responses, while Sadik Al-Azm discusses the case of Napoleon's occupation of Egypt in 1798. In this last case, one might argue that the crucial factor was cultural as well as political, a violent encounter with the West parallel to the later experiences of China and Japan in the nineteenth century. (I am not sure why Al-Azm attributed the phrase "benign encounter" to me. My point was and is simply that there are some positive consequences to encounters of this kind.) In the cases of 1494, 1649 and 1789 I can only agree with what was said. As in the case of political thought, historical writing seems to be stimulated by violent conflict.

Other examples of historiographical revolution are less clear-cut, however. I was not altogether convinced by Ulrich Raulff's recent and ingenious attempt to link Marc Bloch's historiographical innovations to his experiences in World War I, since Bloch had already been thinking along new lines before the war broke out.[6] In the case of World War II, it might be argued that the traumatic experience of the Germans delayed rather than encouraged a historiographical revolution, making them unwilling to move away from the history of events. The war may have been an important catalyst for Braudel's thought, but he was already traveling in the direction of the *longue durée*.[7]

On the other side, it is possible to find important historiographical paradigm shifts that have relatively little to do with politics. This is not the place to offer the necessary evidence, but I am convinced that the rise of social history in the eighteenth century in France, Britain, Italy and Germany has to be explained by social change, including changes in the reading public (including its feminization). A quiet revolution and a long revolution, but nevertheless a profound change in the practice of history.

4

A fourth point that occurred in a number of commentaries was the need for distinctions, not only between "Wests" (discussed above) but between non-Wests, between periods, and between concepts and forms of "history." This point I wholeheartedly accept. From a cultural as well as a geographical point of view, what used to be called the "Near East" is indeed closer to Europe than is the Far East. For example, the Greek heritage is visible in Muslim as well as in Christian historical writing.

In the case of concepts and forms of history, I agree with Thomas Lee that it is useful to keep the notions of cycle and equilibrium distinct. I would argue, though, that the interest in political and economic equilibriums—rather than the cultural equilibrium that he stresses—has been traditional in Western historiography since 1500 or so, while some medieval writers assumed the existence of a kind of moral equilibrium, which might be disturbed but would ultimately be restored. I also agree with Hartog that we should try to distinguish "history," *Geschichte, shih, târîkh, hikayat* and so on. In similar fashion, when we discuss concepts such as "facts" or "causes" across cultures, we ought to comment on the indigenous equivalents for these concepts (if indeed they are true equivalents). Since most of us know only a few languages, a solution to this problem might be to compile a historical dictionary of terms used in different cultures to describe the past and the literary genres employed to speak and write about it.

The most difficult question seems to be that of periodization. My story of divergence between the West and other cultures, followed by convergence, does not command assent, but the critics do not agree with one another. Leaving aside points about the Middle Ages and the Renaissance, let me focus on the big issue: today's "global community" of historians (without which, incidentally, this volume and the conference that led to it would not have been possible). Is it, as White suggests, "a matter of non-Western scholars adopting Western historiographical practices"? Yes, in the sense that the dominant model is largely Western. No, in the sense that contributions to the model have been made from outside the West (Muriuki offers oral history as an example), and also that parallel practices developed in some places independently. As a specialist in the field wrote recently, Arab historians needed the West not to offer them something quite new but "to remind them of certain pre-modern principles of historiography, primarily demythologization and documentation."[8]

In any case, cultural models are never adopted without modification. To take an example from within the non-monolithic "West," Ranke's style of history may have been received with enthusiasm in the English-speaking world, but as Iggers has shown, it was understood in terms of the prevailing culture of empiricism.[9] It would be fascinating to read similar studies of the reception of Ranke or of other Western historians in Russia, Egypt, China and India. Among other things, such studies might illuminate the importance of the differences between "history," *shih, tårîkh* et cetera mentioned above.

At this point it may be useful to return to the ten theses and to the criticisms made of them, more exactly to nine of the theses, since number eight (on quantitative history) did not elicit counterexamples. To conclude, I will discuss Mamadou Diawara's suggestion that an eleventh thesis be added.

1.

The stress on development or progress, in other words the "linear" view of the past. Both Al-Azmeh and Muriuki reminded me of the relevance of Zoroaster here. I am not sure whether to interpret Zoroastrianism as a counterexample or as yet another illustration (along with the Bible, Aristotle et cetera) of the importance of the Middle Eastern heritage in the constitution of the "West"; but in either case the point is taken.[10] Romila Thapar made the point that in traditional Indian cosmology, organized as it is around the idea of cycles, "there are various mechanisms of linear time-reckoning and at least two relate entirely to historical consciousness." As the original paper suggested, both cyclical and linear views of time can be found in most cultures. However, the emphasis on one rather than the other and the forms each view takes allow us to distinguish between cultures and also between periods in the history of a given culture.

Some critics took me to task for suggesting the superiority of the linear model over the cyclical. Actually, I made no such suggestion. My own view is that we need both models, each compensating for the defects of the other. Like Al-Azmeh and Khalidi, I find the idea of a historical "spiral" illuminating. I wish someone would write its history. The first reference to spirals I know in the Western tradition comes from the seventeenth century, when Sir Thomas Browne attacked it. "The lives, not only of men, but of Commonwealths," he wrote, "and of the whole world, run not upon a helix that still enlargeth, but on a circle."[11]

2.

A "concern with historical perspective" or the "sense of anachronism," or even (as Johan Galtung puts it) a sense of property, "my period." Muriuki quotes counter-examples from Africa, notably from Kenya, the generations or "age-sets" constructed by initiation and, in his words, "associated with the major historical events that were considered to be peculiar to their time." This is extremely interesting, but not quite what I meant by a sense of anachronism. In the Western Middle Ages too, history was divided into periods according to important events, but a sense of anachronism was lacking. That is, people were not aware of changes in customs or styles of clothes, building and so on, as the images of, say, Augustus or Moses dressed as medieval kings or knights demonstrate. From the Renaissance onwards, this sense of anachronism has been unusually acute in the West, although it can be found elsewhere, for instance in the ninth-century Arab rediscovery of the epoch before Muhammad.[12]

3.

"Individuality," in the sense of an awareness of, or an interest in the specific, in what makes one person, or group, or culture different from others. I did not and do not want to deny Galtung's point about a Western interest in generalization, but this interest is, I think, shared by other cultures, whereas the intensity of Western concern with the specific is specifically Western.

Al-Azmeh suggests that this point is "a diluted reassertion" of the old Eurocentric assumption that only Western culture considers human beings as individuals. I did not say—and do not think—this. To subvert this assumption it is perhaps sufficient to refer (as I did) to the traditions of portraiture and biography outside the West, particularly strong in China.[13] My point was that the interest in, or perhaps obsession with, individuality was and perhaps still is unusually strong in Western culture. In a Christian culture, unlike a Hindu or Buddhist one, this interest is uninhibited by views of the self-consciousness of the individual as essentially illusory. Whether the world of Islam should be placed on the Western or the Eastern side of this divide I do not know.

4.

Collective agency (an imprecise category, as Galtung is right to observe) is given unusual stress in Western historiography. Muriuki suggests that the extended family or clan is important in African historiography. It may be wise to retreat to the more limited alternative proposition offered in the original paper, to the effect that "certain collective agents," notably assemblies and voluntary associations, have been given unusually important roles in Western historiography as indeed in Western politics.

5.

"Western historiography is distinctive in its preoccupation with epistemology, with the problem of historical knowledge." I prefer not to accept White's suggestion that I speak of "methodological" or "conceptual" issues because my intention was and is to emphasize the preoccupation with the problem of knowing the past—whether it is discussed at a general level by the historical "Pyrrhonists" or at a more practical and local level by "source criticism." I should probably have limited my point to the general level. I was not surprised to learn from Al-Azm that Muslim scholars were also interested in practical criticism: the same point could be made about Chinese scholars and doubtless about other parts of the world as well. However, if there was a major debate among traditional Muslim scholars about the possibility of knowing the past, I should be glad of details about it.[14] My thanks to Khalidi for engaging with the questions I posed concerning the relation between law and historical epistemology in the world of Islam. It may also be worth remarking that the rise of early modern science in Western Europe has been linked to the "European legal revolution" of the Middle Ages, the revival of Roman law and so of the emphasis on general principles, analogous to the "laws" of nature.[15]

6.

"Attempts at historical explanation are universal, but the couching of these explanations in terms of "causes" is a distinctively Western characteristic." This is one of the points in the discussion where the problem of communication across languages is particularly acute. It was extremely interesting to learn of the debate in which Al-Ghazali and Averroes were involved, but it would be helpful—even for readers without Arabic like myself—to know what their key concepts were. In English, the language of "cause" has a scientific or mechanical ring to it, which helps explain why it was found so attractive at the beginning of this century, when historians dreamed of making their subject a science; and why it has often been rejected since. Is this the case in Arabic? And what about the language of medicine? Was the Hippocratic as well as the Aristotelian tradition of relevance to Averroes? A similar point might be made as a response to Lee's comment that understanding is an especially distinct feature of Western historical thought. If he means the self-conscious idea of understanding formulated in reaction to the tradition of causal explanation (*Verstehen* versus *Erklärung*), I think he is probably right. But to pursue the matter further it is probably necessary to make a comparative study of the vocabulary of explanation and understanding in Chinese, Arabic and other languages. Lee's point about the Western preoccupation with the logic or the rationality of history (as opposed to the irrationality or "folly" of historical agents), deserves to be investigated in similar fashion.

7.

"Western historians have long prided themselves on their so-called objectivity." Masayuki Sato offers some important East Asian counterexamples to this generalization, or more exactly to the first part of it, traditional "impartiality" rather than modern "objectivity."

8.

"The literary forms of Western historiography are distinctive as its content." White wants me to say something more explicit about rhetoric, while Khalidi would like me to keep away from tropes. Relevant to both points is a longstanding Western debate—whether or not uniquely Western I am, unfortunately, unable to say—a debate which I think that White himself might have addressed more specifically in his own work, since it concerns the dangers of "the association of ... historical writing with rhetoric." Western historians have often defined their enterprise as antirhetorical, and sometimes by contrast to specific literary forms, from the tragedy to the newspaper and the novel, dismissing colleagues and rivals as "mere" tragedians, journalists or writers of romance.

I am not saying that these historians learned nothing from the genres against which they defined their own enterprise. It might indeed be argued that the antirhetorical attitude is itself a form of rhetoric, a way of persuading readers of the reliability of the story of the past which follows. Once again, however, distinctions might be useful. Some historical writers are more rhetorical than others, more hostility to rhetoric has been displayed in some periods than others. For example, there was a reaction against rhetorical history in early seventeenth-century Europe, when a group of historians including Paolo Sarpi, Jacques-Auguste de Thou, Emmanuel van Meteren and William Camden chose to exclude invented speeches from their work and to insert documents instead. As for culturally specific plots, Masayuki Sato has kindly responded to my question about the "nobility of failure" in Japan.

9.

"Western historians have characteristic views of space no less than of time." It was interesting to see that only one critic, Galtung, chose to comment on this topic, and he comes from one of the few European countries in which, like the neo-Europes, population density is low, making space more palpable in the Norwegian present as in its past.

10.

Diawara's suggestion that I add an eleventh thesis about the "scriptocentrism" of Western history might be considered under this heading. I am sorry that this topic did not occur to me at the time of the original paper, doubtless evidence of my own scriptocentrism. Two comments on this. The first is that this topic divides up the world differently from other theses, since in this case we find the Europeans and the Chinese in the same camp—the camp of written texts and more especially of official documents—while other cultures, from Mali to Peru, placed a greater emphasis on orality and on memory—sometimes aided by mnemonics, such as drums or the knotted cords or *qipu* used by Peruvian historians before the Spanish conquest.

The second point is that this feature of Western historiography has its own history, becoming more pronounced from the thirteenth century onwards, still more so from the seventeenth century, and most of all from the nineteenth century. For it was in the nineteenth century that the extraordinary term "prehistory" was invented, together with the division of labor between "history" based on written documents, "archaeology" based on other material remains, and "folklore" based on oral tradition. The positive attitude to oral tradition in the European study of folklore (*Volkskunde*, *Folkliv* for example) deserves to be emphasized, as well as the negative attitude of the professional historians. There is a link, which someone should trace, between the tradition of the European folklorists and the European oral history movement of the 1960s. The earlier history of attitudes to oral tradition also deserves to be written. I can think of only two relevant studies, both limited to England. Daniel Woolf has commented on the decline in the attention given to oral sources in English historical writing between the early sixteenth-century antiquary John Leland—for whom the "common voice," as he called it, deserved to be taken seriously—and seventeenth-century scholars such as John Selden and William Dugdale, who treated oral sources as second-class evidence.[16] This change in the practice of historians was a delayed response to a slower, more profound and more general shift in attitudes to evidence, especially in courts of law: the shift "from memory to written record," from trusting witnesses to trusting writing. This shift has been dated, in the case of England, to the period 1066-1307.[17] Today, on the other hand, we see a shift in the opposite direction, exemplified not only by the oral history movement but by the rise of interest in medieval archaeology, industrial archaeology, and more generally in material culture both as a part of history and a source for history.

This conclusion closes the volume but not the debate. The reactions published here suggest that at least some of the theses advanced here might be tested and refined by further comparative—and co-operative—research.

Notes

1. James Carrier, ed., *Occidentalism*, Oxford, 1995.
2. Joseph Needham, 'Poverties and Triumphs of the Chinese Scientific Tradition', in *Scientific Change*, ed. Alistair C. Crombie, London, 1963, 117-49; Jack Goody, 'Economy and Feudalism in Africa', *Economic History Review* 22 (1969), 393-405.
3. Donald E. Brown, *Hierarchy, History and Human Nature. The Social Origins of Historical Consciousness*, Tucson, 1988.
4. Fritz K. Ringer, *The Decline of the German Mandarins*, Cambridge, Mass., 1969.
5. Tarif Khalidi, *Arabic Historical Thought in the Classical Period*, Cambridge, 1994, 14, 232.
6. Ulrich Raulff, *Ein Historiker im 20. Jahrhundert. Marc Bloch*, Frankfurt, 1995.
7. Pierre Daix, *Braudel*, Paris, 1995, 148ff.
8. Khalidi, *Arabic Thought* (see note 5), 234.
9. Georg G. Iggers, 'The Image of Ranke in American and German Historical Thought', *History and Theory* 2 (1962), 17-40.
10. Cf. Tarif Khalidi, 'The Concept of Progress in Classical Islam', *Journal of Near East Studies* 40 (1981).
11. Thomas Browne, *Religio Medici* (1642), London, 1906, 21.
12. Khalidi, *Arabic Thought* (see note 5), 87; cf. 97, 187.
13. Pei-Yi Wu, *The Confucian's Progress: Autobiographical Writings in Traditional China*, Princeton, 1990; Richard Vinograd, *Boundaries of the Self. Chinese Portraits 1600-1900*, Cambridge, 1992.

14. The references in Khalidi, *Arabic Thought* 131, 163 (see note 5) interesting as they are, do not suggest the same degree of preoccupation with the topic that we find in the European controversy over historical 'Pyrrhonism'.

15. Toby E. Huff, *The Rise of Early Modern Science. Islam, China and the West*, Cambridge Mass., 1993, ch. 4.

16. Daniel R. Woolf, 'The Common Voice. History, Folklore and Oral Tradition in Early Modern England', *Past and Present* 120 (1988), 26-52.

17. Michael T. Clanchy, *From Memory to Written Record. England 1066-1307*, London, 1979.

Notes on Contributors

Editor

Jörn Rüsen, Professor Dr., born in 1938, studied History, Philosophy, Literary Studies and Pedagogy at the University of Cologne. 1974-1989 Professor of Modern History at the University of Bochum. 1989-1977 Professor of History and Historical Theory at the University of Bielefeld. 1994-1997 Director of the Center for Interdisciplinary Research (ZiF) at the University of Bielefeld. Since April 1997 President of the Institute for Advanced Study in the Humanities (*Kulturwissenschaftliches Institut [KWI] im Wissenschaftszentrum Nordrhein-Westfalen*) in Essen. His publications include: *Begriffene Geschichte*, 1969; *Historische Vernunft*, 1983; *Rekonstruktion der Vergangenheit*, 1986; *Zeit und Sinn*, 1990; *Konfigurationen des Historismus*, 1993; *Studies in Metahistory*, 1993; *Historische Orientierung*, 1994; *Historisches Lernen*, 1996.

Assistant editor

Christian Geulen, born in 1969, studied at the University of Bielefeld and the Johns Hopkins University, Baltimore. Ph.D. candidate in History at the University of Bielefeld. Since 1998 research assistant at the Institute for Advanced Study in the Humanities (*Kulturwissenschaftliches Institut [KWI] im Wissenschaftszentrum Nordrhein-Westfalen*) in Essen.

Contributors

Peter Burke, Professor Dr., born in 1937, studied at Oxford University and taught at University of Sussex 1962-1979. Since 1979 Professor of Cultural History at the University of Cambridge and Fellow of the Emmanuel College and the British Academy; member of the Academia Europea. His publications include: *A Social History of Knowledge*, 2000; *Varieties of Cultural History*, 1997; *The European Renaissance: Centers and Peripheries*, 1998.

Sadik J. Al-Azm, Professor Dr., born in 1934 in Damascus, studied at Yale University and taught at Yale, at the Hunter College, New York, at the American University of Beirut, at Princeton University and at the University of Oldenburg. Fellow of the *Wissenschaftskolleg zu Berlin* and the Woodrow Wilson International Center of Scholars in Washington, D.C. Since 1977 Professor at the University of Damascus. His publications include: *Unbehagen in der Moderne: Aufklärung im Islam*, 1993; *Kant's Theory of Time*, 1967.

Aziz Al Azmeh, Professor Dr., born in 1947 in Damascus. 1985-1996 Professor of Islamic Studies at the University of Exeter, Fellow of the *Wissenschaftskolleg zu Berlin*. His publications include: *Ibn Khaldun*, 1996; *Reconstituting Islam*, 1996; *Islams and Modernities*, 1993.

Frank R. Ankersmit, Professor Dr., born in 1945, studied Physics, Mathematics, History and Philosophy in Leiden and Groningen. Professor of Intellectual History and Historical Theory at the University of Groningen. His publications include: *Exploraties*, 3 vol., 1996-7; *Aesthetic Politics: Political Philosophy beyond Fact and Value*, 1996; *History and Tropology: The Rise and Fall of a Metaphor*, 1994.

Mamadou Diawara, born in 1954, studied African History and Social Anthropology at the École des Hautes Etudes en Sciences Sociales (EHESS) and at the Sorbonne in Paris. Permanent member of the Institut des Science Humaines (ISH) in Bamako, Mali. 1994-1995 Fellow at the *Wissenschaftskolleg zu Berlin*; 1996-1997 Professor at Yale University, 1997-1999 at the University of Bayreuth. His publications include: *Le graine de la parole*, 1990.

Johan Galtung, Professor Dr., born in 1930, studied mathematics and sociology at the University of Oslo. Professor of Peace Studies at the Universities of Witten-Herdecke, Granada, Ritsumeikan and Tromsö. His publications include: *Macrohistory and Macrohistorians: Perspectives on Individual Social and Civilizational Change*, 1997; *Peace by Peaceful Means: Peace and Conflict, Development and Civilization*, 1996; *Eurotopia: Die Zukunft eines Kontinents*, 1993.

François Hartog, Professor Dr., born in 1946, Directeur d'ètudes à l'Ecole des Hautes Etudes en Sciences Sociales for ancient and modern historiography. His publications include: *Mémoire d'Ulysse: Récits sur la frontière en Grèce ancienne*, 1996; *Le miroire d'Hérodote: Essai sur la répresentation de l'autre*, 1991; *Le XIX siècle et l'histoire: le case Fustel de Coulanges*, 1988.

Georg G. Iggers, Professor Dr., born 1926 in Hamburg, Professor of History at the State University of New York, Buffalo. Visiting professor at the Technical University Darmstadt and at the University of Leipzig. Winner of the Alexander v. Humboldt Research Award in 1995. His publications include: *Historiography in the Twentieth Century: From Scientific Objectivity to the Postmodern Challenge*, 1997; ed. *Ein anderer historischer Blick: Beispiele ostdeutscher Sozialgeschichte*, 1991; *Social History of Politics: Critical Perspectives in West German Historical Writing since 1945*, 1985.

Tarif Khalidi, Professor Dr., born 1938 in Jerusalem, studied History at Oxford University and Islamic Studies at the University of Chicago. Professor of History at the American University of Beirut and at Cambridge University. His publications include: *Arabic Historical Thought in the Classical Period*, 1994; *Classical Arab Islam*, 1984; *Islamic Historiography: The Histories of Mas'udi*, 1975.

Thomas H.C. Lee, Dr. born in 1945, studied at Yale University and taught at the Chinese University of Hong Kong. Currently member of the History Department at the City College, New York. His publications include: *Education in Traditional China: A History*, 2000.

Klaus E. Müller, Professor Dr., born in 1935, studied Music, Theater Studies, Philosophy, Ethnology, Turkology and Islamic Studies at the University of Munich. Since 1971 Professor of Ethnology at the University of Frankfurt am Main. His publications include: *Der Krüppel: Ethnologia passionis humanae*, 1996; *Das magische Universum der Identität: Elementarformen sozialen Verhaltens*, 1987; *Die bessere und die schlechtere Hälfte: Ethnologie des Geschlechterkonflikts*, 1984; *Geschichte der antiken Ethnographie und ethnologischen Theoriebildung: Von den Anfängen bis auf die byzantinischen Historiographien* 2 vol., 1972.

Godfrey Muriuki, Professor Dr., born 1946 in Kenya, studied History at the Makerere College in Uganda. Honorary Fellow of the Historical Association of Great Britain. Visiting Professor at Stanford University and at Truman University, Missouri. His publications include: *United States Educational Influence on Kenya*, 1995; *People round Mount Kenya*, 1978; *A History of the Kikuyu: 1500-1900*, 1975.

Masayuki Sato, Professor Dr., born 1946 in Japan, studied Economy, Philosophy and History at Keio University and at Cambridge University. Visiting Professor at the University of Illinois, Urbana-Champaign. Professor of Social Studies at Yamanashi University. His publications include: Comparative Ideas of Chronology, in *History and Theory* (1991); Historiographical Encounters: The Idea of Chronology in East Asia, in *East Asian Sciences: Tradition and Beyond*, 1995; The Chinese and Western Traditions in Turn of the Century Japan, in *Storia della Storiografia*, 1992.

Romila Thapar, Professor Dr., born 1931 in India, Professor of History at Jawaharl Nehru University in New Delhi. In 1983 President of the Indian History Congress, and in 1986 Honorary Fellow at the Lady Margaret Hall in Oxford. Her publications include: *From Lineage to State*, 1984; *Ancient Indian Social History: Some Interpretations*, 1978; *Asoka and the Decline of the Mauryas*, 1973.

Hayden White, Professor Dr., born in 1928; Professor of the History of Ideas at the University of California and of Comparative Literature at Stanford University. His publications include: *Figural Realism: Studies in the Mimesis Effect*, 1999; *The Names of History: On the Poetics of Knowledge*, 1994; *Metahistory: The Historical Imagination in Nineteenth Century Europe*, 1975.

Ying-Shih, Yü, Professor Dr., born in 1930, studied at the New Asia College in Hong Kong and at Harvard and Yale Universities. He was Director of the New Asia College and Co-Director of the Chinese University in Hong Kong. Currently Professor at the East Asian Department of Princeton University. His publications include: *Li-shih jen-wu yü wen hua wei-chi* (Historical Figures and The Crisis of Culture), 1995; *Wen-hua p'ing-lun yü Chung-kuo cg'ing-huai* (Cultural Criticism and Chinese Sentiments), 1988; ed. *Early Chinese History in the People's Republic of China*, 1981; *Trade and Expansion in Han China*, 1967.

Index